Offender Reentry

Offender Reentry

Beyond Crime & Punishment

Elaine Gunnison
Jacqueline B. Helfgott

LYNNE
RIENNER
PUBLISHERS

BOULDER
LONDON

Published in the United States of America in 2013 by
Lynne Rienner Publishers, Inc.
1800 30th Street, Boulder, Colorado 80301
www.rienner.com

and in the United Kingdom by
Lynne Rienner Publishers, Inc.
3 Henrietta Street, Covent Garden, London WC2E 8LU

Library of Congress Cataloging-in-Publication Data
Gunnison, Elaine.
  Offender reentry : beyond crime and punishment / Elaine Gunnison and
Jacqueline B. Helfgott.
    p. cm.
  Includes bibliographical references and index.
  ISBN 978-1-58826-912-6 (hc : alk. paper)
    1. Prisoners—Deinstitutionalization—United States. 2. Ex-convicts—Services for—
United States. 3. Criminals—Rehabilitation—United States. 4. Criminal Justice,
Administration of—United States. I. Helfgott, Jacqueline B. II. Title.
  HV9304.G8 2013
  365'.6630973—dc23
                                     2013012998

British Cataloguing in Publication Data
A Cataloguing in Publication record for this book
is available from the British Library.

For all the wonderful boys in my life: Daniel, Zachary, and Evan
For my parents: Walter and Jane
—E. G.

For my daughter, Zalia, who fills my world with hope
—J. B. H.

Contents

Acknowledgments

THIS RESEARCH WOULD NOT HAVE BEEN POSSIBLE WITHOUT THE support of many individuals. We first owe our gratitude to the ex-offenders who were willing to share their stories with us about their struggles and successes, many of whom took off work without pay to contribute, and all of whom have an extraordinary amount of resilience, hope, and determination to succeed and to make meaningful contributions to society. These individuals are members of our community, and we hope that even though we use the term *ex-offender* in this book to refer to them, our readers recognize that having committed a crime and spending time in prison does not define who a person is or determine who a person can be in the future. Second, we are very fortunate that we were able to interview community corrections officers about successful reentry. We appreciate these individuals taking time out of their busy schedules to speak with us about reentry and give us their candid view of the struggles they face in the difficult work they do every day. They too have an extraordinary amount of resilience, hope, and determination, and they care—more than they are given credit for—about helping ex-offenders to succeed.

Additionally, we would like to thank the Dean's Office of the College of Arts and Sciences at Seattle University for awarding us a scholarship that allowed us to hire two graduate students to assist with this research. We are so very thankful to Teneshia Thurman, who assisted us with transcribing our interviews, and to Cecilie Wilhelm, who has been our research assistant from the beginning. Cecilie has been a tremendous asset to us, from scheduling and transcribing interviews to editing our manuscript and assisting in other ways, throughout this project. Further, we would like to thank the Seattle University Criminal Justice Department Advisory Board and representatives from local criminal justice, social service, and nonprofit agencies for assisting with referrals for interview participants. Not least, thank you to our Criminal Justice Department colleagues and staff who have been so supportive throughout this project: Matthew Hickman, Stephen Rice, Peter Collins, Jennifer Sumner, William Parkin, Kate Reynolds, and Devin MacKrell.

We also would like to acknowledge Lynne Rienner Publishers for providing us with an opportunity to write this book. Thank you, Andrew Berzanskis, our acquisitions editor, for your support and guidance throughout this process. You have truly been a pleasure to work with. A very warm thank you to Lillia Gajewski, our copyeditor, who did a fabulous job at editing our book so meticulously. Another big thanks to Senior Editor Lesli Brooks Athanasoulis for her editing efforts and to Karen Maye for her work in promoting our book. Also, thanks to the anonymous reviewers who provided substantive recommendations for improving our book.

Finally, we would like to thank our family, friends, and loved ones who championed us along the way. Elaine is thankful to her husband, Daniel, who provided both emotional support and encouragement for yet another one of her projects. Thanks, Daniel, for giving up some of our "us" time and wrangling the boys so Elaine could get her work done. You rock! Elaine is also thankful to her lovely boys, Zachary and Evan. They both are sweet, smart, loving, beautiful boys, and Elaine feels so lucky to be their mom. As she wrote this book, she spent many days with the boys on bike rides, walks, or just driving them to their activities and spent her evenings working on the computer. It was a perfect arrangement. Elaine must also thank her miniature dachshund, Snaps, who slept next to her almost the entire time when she worked on this book. Snaps is a faithful companion. Elaine would also like to thank her many friends from graduate school and beyond for cheering her on; and her parents, Walter and Jane, for all their support. Jackie would like to thank her daughter, Zalia, who makes her proud, and inspires her every day. Jackie would also like to thank her family—her mom, Esther; brothers, Ian and Scott; and other family members—and friends who have been incredibly supportive throughout this project.

We hope the ideas in this book and the stories shared by the ex-offenders and community corrections officers help make the world a little better place.

—E. G. and J. B. H.

Offender
Reentry

1

Understanding Offender Reentry

THE STEREOTYPE OF OFFENDER REENTRY MIGHT LOOK SOME-
thing like the classic Coen brothers movie *Raising Arizona*. In the 1987
movie H. I. McDunnough, played by Nicolas Cage, is seen repeatedly
entering and returning to prison and having his mug shot taken again
and again. It appears that H. I. is a serial recidivist. Movie scenes like
this provide a powerful example to the audience that offender reentry is
not a successful endeavor and that prison serves merely as a pit stop in
the revolving door of justice. In 2011, just under 7 million offenders
were serving under some form of correctional supervision (i.e., prison,
jail, probation, and parole). Of that total, approximately 1.2 million offenders were serving sentences in prison. Every day in the United States
1,600 adults (700,000 annually) leave federal and state prisons and return to society (Glaze and Parks, 2012). Thus, each day offenders are
attempting to successfully reintegrate back into their communities.
However, successful reentry is an evasive goal for many. P. A. Langan
and D. J. Levin (2002), in a 1994 study of recidivism rates tracked
300,000 prisoners in fifteen states. They reported that 67.5 percent of
offenders were rearrested within three years. Clearly, as the Hollywood
images have portrayed, prison may serve as a revolving door for many
offenders.

While successful reentry is an issue for prisoners, it is also a concern for those serving probation or parole sentences. In 2011, 4.8 million offenders were currently serving such sentences and represent the
majority (70 percent) of those being supervised in state and federal correctional systems (Maruschak and Parks, 2012). The Bureau of Justice
Statistics conducted several studies on offenders during the 1980s and
reported that recidivism rates, defined as rearrest within three years, to
be 43 percent for felony probationers and 62 percent for parolees (Beck

and Shipley, 1989; Langan and Cuniff, 1992). Correctional administrators walk a tightrope as they try to balance community safety and foster offender reentry success while facing cutbacks to their budgets. The cuts to the budgets of departments of corrections are a national problem (Scott-Hayward, 2009). In fact, the cuts have been so severe the Vera Institute of Justice labeled the problem as a "fiscal crisis in corrections" (Scott-Hayward, 2009, p. 1).

The public may tolerate approximately 5 million offenders serving sentences in the community, but if these offenders commit crimes, the community becomes outraged. In 2002, Elizabeth Smart was abducted from her bedroom in the middle of the night in Salt Lake City, Utah, and her case drew national media attention and scrutiny. The police focused their attention on Richard Ricci, a parolee, who had been hired as a handyman by the Smart family (Henetz, 2003). A media circus enveloped Ricci as he seemed to "fit" the profile. To the media and the public, Ricci was another example of a parolee who could not reintegrate successfully into society following his prison sentence and harmed an innocent community member. However, Ricci refused to confess to the crime, maintained his innocence, and ultimately died from a brain hemorrhage in jail a few weeks later. Ultimately, Smart was found nine months later alive in the custody of Brian Mitchell and Wanda Barzee (his wife)—her kidnappers.

Beyond protecting the public, correctional administrators are expected to ensure that those offenders returning to their communities will successfully reintegrate and assimilate back into society. However, offenders face many barriers. Research on offender reentry over the past thirty years has demonstrated that offenders' ability to reintegrate successfully is hindered by numerous obstacles such as difficulty in obtaining employment, acquiring housing, and being admitted to higher education (Allender, 2004; Cowan and Fionda, 1994; Delgado, 2012; Harlow, 2003; Harris and Keller, 2005; Hunt, Bowers, and Miller, 1973; Nagin and Waldfogel, 1998; Paylor, 1995; Rodriguez and Brown, 2003; Starr, 2002; Whelan, 1973) along with serious social and medical problems (Petersilia, 2003). Newly released offenders encounter stigmatization (Bahn and Davis, 1991; Funk, 2004; Steffensmeier and Kramer, 1980; Tewksbury, 2005), lose social standing in their communities (Chiricos, Jackson, and Waldo, 1972), and are in need of social support (Cullen, 1994; La Vigne, Visher, and Castro, 2004; Lurigio, 1996) and substance abuse and mental health treatment (Petersilia, 2003). Thus, correctional administrators struggle to protect the public while at the same time promoting offender reentry success in the face of what seem like insurmountable obstacles with limited resources.

All too often, offender reentry is viewed as an afterthought by politicians and the public. The focus of the criminal justice system has been centered on punishment over the last several decades, specifically tough penalties for offenders due to the "get tough on crime" philosophy. This attention gap has left many ex-offenders struggling to successfully reintegrate back into society. The term *ex-offender,* as used in this text, is defined as an offender who has received and has completed any form of correctional punishment including a prison sentence, probation, parole, or any range of intermediate sanction (e.g., home confinement, work release, halfway house).[1]

Whereas the public may have not paid much attention to the struggles ex-offenders face during reentry (i.e., the process of reintegrating back into society following a punishment), researchers have not ignored this group, examining and identifying their needs and challenges. However, much of the focus on ex-offender reentry has revolved around *failure* rather than *success.* That is, an overwhelming amount of discussion surrounding offender reentry has mostly centered on examining recidivism rates as offenders reintegrate back into the community. Such discussions of offender reentry have been void of the identification of what factors could contribute to successful reentry and what makes for successful reentry. Also missing from the literature on offender reentry are the voices of ex-offenders—their own success stories about how they beat the odds—and perspectives of practitioners regarding the necessary ingredients to foster successful reentry for ex-offenders.

In this book, we seek to fill this gap by providing an overview of research on offender reentry and the inclusion of original research. In the rest of this chapter, we address historical and contemporary perspectives on offender reentry. In Chapter 2, we provide factors and profiles of successful transition and reintegration. The identification of the needs and challenges of ex-offenders during reentry to create opportunities for successful transitions is presented in Chapter 3. Chapters 4 and 5 explain how success may differ for ex-offenders in regard to race, ethnicity, gender, and social class. Chapters 6 and 7 provide original data with the inclusion of qualitative findings from interviews with twenty-one ex-offenders and nineteen community corrections officers (CCOs) in the state of Washington in 2012. In these interviews, ex-offenders and practitioners were asked to identify factors that foster successful reentry, to provide examples of successful reentry narratives, and to offer their opinions as to what needs to be done to increase reentry success. Ex-offenders were asked to provide their own accounts of their success and to explain, in their own words, what contributed to their success, and CCOs were asked to recall success stories of former clients that they had supervised.

In conclusion, Chapter 8 outlines current policies that have the potential to enhance offender reentry and new policy ideas are presented.

Before getting to those viewpoints later in the book, we will define what is meant by the term *reentry* and to provide a detailed history of the policies and practices that have had an impact on offender reentry in the United States.

What Is Offender Reentry?

The term *reentry* may conjure up images of parolees from mainstream Hollywood movies who have attempted to "make it" outside the prison walls. In the 1994 film, *The Shawshank Redemption,* the main character Andy (played by Tim Robbins) was sentenced to a forty-year prison sentence for the murder of his wife, but later escapes from prison. One of his friends in the movie, Red (played by Morgan Freeman) is released on parole. Upon Andy's escape, he exposes the corruption taking place at the prison where he was incarcerated. Both Andy and Red are able to slip into a comfortable postprison existence. On the other hand, in the 1999 thriller, *Double Jeopardy,* the main character Libby (played by Ashley Judd), who was falsely convicted of killing her husband, who was actually alive, struggles upon receiving parole and commits numerous parole infractions and new crimes in a quest to find where her husband is hiding and uncover her lost son's whereabouts. In the 2006 film *Sherrybaby,* Maggie Gyllenhaal plays ex-offender Sherry Swanson, who struggles with postprison issues, including addiction and being reintroduced to her daughter. The film similarly shows the difficulties faced when ex-offenders return to society. With pop cultural images of offender reentry such as these, it is no wonder why most in society do not have a clear understanding of the real-world experience of reentry or a clear understanding of who the offenders are that are attempting to reintegrate back into society.

Reentry is most commonly referred to as the transition of offenders from state and federal prisons to community supervision (e.g., parole) (Hughes and Wilson, 2004). This definition suggests that the only individuals who are attempting to reintegrate back into society are those who have served their full prison term sentence or those released early from prison via parole. However, reentry occurs for many types of offenders besides those on parole. J. Travis notes,

> reentry is a nearly universal experience for criminal defendants, not just returning prisoners. . . . Everyone who is arrested, charged with a crime, and then released from custody moves from a state of imprisonment to a state of liberty. Everyone who is released on bail, placed on probation

after a period of pretrial detention, sentenced to weekend jail, or released to a drug treatment facility experienced a form of reentry. (2001, p. 26)

Thus, offenders can also be sentenced to probation, and probationers make up another group that is attempting to reintegrate back into society after the commission of a crime (Travis, 2001). After all, probationers have to abide by conditions of their probation sentence, which can include obtaining legal employment, obtaining educational or vocational training, and participating in substance abuse treatment. Yet other examples of offenders attempting to reenter society would include those who had gone through work release programs, halfway houses, and day-reporting centers.

Work release programs can be described as community-based treatment correctional programs where offenders reside, after serving most of their prison sentences, to assist them in reintegrating back into society (Elmer and Cohen, 1978). These programs allow certain offenders to serve the remainder of their sentences in the community under close supervision (Turner and Petersilia, 1996). Offenders can also be directly sentenced to a work release program in lieu of serving a jail sentence first. At the work release program, offenders participate in programming, search for employment, and begin to reestablish family connections. The offender is required to abide by the work release program rules (e.g., curfew and drug/alcohol testing) while participating in the program. These programs help facilitate the successful transition of offenders into their communities. For example, offenders receive referrals for services (e.g., clothing, education, licensing) and are required to seek employment (Turner and Petersilia, 1996).

Similar to those in work release facilities, offenders serve some, or all, of their sentence in a community-based residential treatment program known as a halfway house. By being directly sentenced to a halfway house, offenders are diverted from serving time in the local jail. Utilizing this type of sentence, judges can alleviate the overcrowding in local jails by ordering offenders to participate in a program that may assist them in transitioning into their communities (Latessa and Smith, 2011). Much of the programming found in a halfway house may not be found in jails due to budgetary restrictions and the diverse populations that jails serve. The time served in the halfway house can be anywhere from one month to several months, and residents are required to obtain legal employment, find housing, and participate in programs (e.g., Alcholics Anonymous). Additionally, halfway houses may be used as a bridge between prison and reintegration. The use of halfway houses for prisoners prior to release assists in alleviating overcrowding conditions at the prison as well as fostering successful transition for the offender from prison to the community. Thus, some offenders are not directly released on parole and sent into the community, but rather these offenders are released to a halfway house for a range of time that can be as long as eighteen months. After demonstrating the ability to abide by curfew and find adequate housing and legal employment, these offenders are then released in their communities.

Another example of offenders attempting to reintegrate into society outside the scope of parole are those offenders serving in day-reporting centers. Typically, offenders serving these sentences include persons over the age of eighteen; persons charged with a crime who are incarcerated or facing incarceration; pretrial detainees, sentenced offenders, and postsentence violators; and misdemeanants and felons (Latessa and Smith, 2011). The offenders are supervised by a probation officer and are required to report to the center on a daily basis. At the day-reporting centers, the offender will also be required to participate in programming such as mental health counseling, education programs, social skills training, and substance abuse treatment. Participants in day-reporting center programs are monitored for drug and alcohol use. Since pretrial detainees can be included as participants in day-reporting center programs, the time served in these programs for offenders can range from less than one week for offenders who have not gone to trial to as much as one year for those offenders who have been formally sentenced to a day-reporting center as punishment.

In sum, a wide range of offenders are attempting to reenter society. Some of these offenders serve long sentences postrelease, while others serve short sentences. The term *offender reentry* as used in this book refers to the postrelease experience of any offender who completed any sentence in the correctional system (i.e., prison, probation, parole, or any form of intermediate sanction) and is transitioning back into the community. Given the wide range of offenders reintegrating back into society and the various resources that may be available to assist these offenders, offenders face an uphill battle in the bid to successfully reenter their communities. To better understand offender reentry in the present day, we need to examine how reentry was viewed in the past and the policies that have an impact on the ability of offenders to successfully reintegrate back into their communities after serving a short- or long-term correctional sentence.

Historical Underpinnings

To understand the evolution of the offender reentry movement in the United States, one must examine the influence of early writings of criminologists. Early criminologists viewed criminality as being due to biology or atavistic traits. One of the most influential early theorists was Cesare Lombroso who in 1876 published *L'Homme Criminel* (The Criminal Man). In this book, Lombroso presents results of his research whereby he examined the physical characteristics of male Italian prisoners and compared them to male Italian soldiers. He claimed that criminals are born as criminals and appear distinctly different from noncriminals as they have various atavistic traits such as twisted noses, broad shoulders, excessive moles, long arms, or an extra finger or toe.

While these claims seem laughable by current research standards, interestingly discussion still resonates in today's culture around the appearance of offenders. Much of the dialogue regarding the appearance of offenders can be viewed in some of the most notorious or current captivating cases in the criminal justice system. For instance, many in society are flabbergasted that men, defined as handsome by many in the media, such as Ted Bundy (infamous Northwest serial killer) and Scott Peterson (husband living in the suburbs of California who killed his wife and unborn child) could commit homicide. Additionally, the media presented the 2011 Florida trial coverage of Casey Anthony as a pretty yet wild (as depicted by images of her partying that were posted on her Facebook page) mother who is a pathological liar and may have killed her daughter (Hightower, 2011). In yet another example, Amanda Knox, a University of Washington student who was studying abroad in Italy was convicted in 2009 of killing her roommate. Throughout her Italian trial and subsequent appeals, Amanda was referred to as "Foxy Knoxy" by the press in the United States and Europe (her murder conviction was overturned in 2011) (Johnson, 2009). The past and current discussion regarding the physical appearance of the aforementioned criminal defendants in the media and by the public provides a more recent example of Lombroso's proposition that offenders are somehow supposed to look different (i.e., perhaps unattractive) from nonoffenders. Lombroso's claims that criminals are born, not made, influenced the focus of the nascent correctional system in the United States during the 1800s. That is, as the thinking of the times went, if offenders are plagued by biological deficits, the main focus of corrections should be on punishment, specifically incarceration, rather than rehabilitation. Thus, reentry of offenders into the community after serving their sentences was not a concern of correctional administrators or encouraged by the public.

With the inception of the Walnut Street Jail in 1790 in Philadelphia and subsequent jails and prisons that opened in the late 1700s and early 1800s in the United States, the primary goal of their use was punishment with rehabilitation being a secondary goal. After all, if as Lombroso proposed, individuals were biologically determined to commit crime, efforts to reform them were futile. However, as more jails and prisons opened, the idea that offenders may need assistance, as opposed to just incarceration, and support upon release was on the minds of some. John Augustus, considered the Father of Probation, as he coined the term *probation* and developed the first probation program in 1841 in Boston, was one of the first reformers to push for rehabilitation for offenders (Latessa and Smith, 2011). Augustus believed that one of the objects of the law was to reform criminals (Dressler, 1962). He recognized that incarcerated offenders had needs (e.g., alcohol addiction) that were not being addressed in the jails. Using his own money, he bailed out first-time offenders (e.g., those who had committed petty crimes or displayed public intoxication) from jail and persuaded the court to release the offenders to his custody. While the offenders were in Augustus's care, they were rehabilitated and obtained legal employment. He then would return them to court and demonstrate that they were now reformed. At the time, he was considered by many to be a fanatic or just a fool. Unfortunately, Augustus was ahead of the times as the chief concern of the public and correctional administrators was not on rehabilitation of the offender but rather on punishment of the offender.

The ideological shift of the focus in offender corrections from strictly punishment to rehabilitation originated from the 1870 National Prison Association meeting in Cincinnati, Ohio (Latessa and Smith, 2011). At this historic meeting, reformers laid out seven principles of corrections including one with a focus on reforming or rehabilitating the offenders. Throughout the late 1800s and early 1900s, progressive reformers began lobbying for the importance of rehabilitation and urging its implementation within the correctional system (Cullen and Gilbert, 1982). During this period, the time was ripe for rehabilitation to be considered a viable focus of corrections by both correctional administrators and the public. With growing social awareness by the public following the Civil War, massive prison overcrowding, and the shifting view on offending behavior by criminologists, the time was "right" for a change in corrections (Latessa and Smith, 2011). For instance, criminologists were moving away from solely biological explanations of criminality and began proposing that the environmental factors (e.g., neighborhood, peers) and strains played a role in the onset and shaping of criminality (see Agnew, 1992; Merton, 1938; Shaw and McKay, 1938; Sutherland, 1947b). From the 1940s through the 1970s, discourse on the nature of the location of criminal behavior in biology, personality, and environment occurred in criminology. There was a movement away from the location of criminal behavior in biological and personality factors, and a movement toward utilitarian, free will models of criminal behavior and toward treatment approaches and criminal justice responses that reflected that view (Andrews and Bonta, 2010). As a result of the National Prison Association meeting and new criminological perspectives on offending, sentencing practices shifted from determinate (fixed sentences) to indeterminate (range in a sentence from a minimum to a maximum), thereby fostering the implementation of probation and parole programs across the United States. The shift in correctional philosophies and changes in sentencing practices enabled probation and parole programs to focus their energies in assisting offenders.

With the renewed focus on rehabilitation and the use of indeterminate sentencing, preparing offenders for release from prison to parole was a chief concern of correctional administrators during the first half of the 1900s. Thus, educational and vocational programs, substance abuse counseling, and mental health programs were all integral parts of the prison experience. By the mid-1900s, all states were utilizing indeterminate sentencing practices and parole boards to make the decisions about when to release offenders (Clear and Cole, 1997). If offenders demonstrated that they had participated in correctional programming, had gained insight into the root causes of their criminal behavior, and had "changed," then offenders were granted early, yet supervised, release on parole. In fact, parole became an integral part of the correctional systems, and its use peaked in the 1970s. In 1977, the Bureau of Justice Statistics reported that during that year, 72 percent of all offenders being released from prison were being released on parole. However, the focus on rehabilitation of offenders and promoting successful offender reentry abruptly changed in the late 1970s and early 1980s.

Changes in societal climate of the 1980s and 1990s brought a "get tough" approach with a focus on mandatory sentencing such as "three-strikes" legislation and "civil commitment" for sexual predators. In civil commitment sentences, offenders are confined to a special commitment center once they have served their prison sentences. The offenders remain at the special commitment center until they have demonstrated they can be safely reintegrated back into society, which for some sex offenders might be never. This time also saw the introduction of the actuarial prediction to make decisions at all stages of the criminal justice process from pretrial to sentencing to release (Harcourt, 2006). This late-modern shift from the social welfare era to a culture of control was marked by mass imprisonment, actuarial justice, a focus on surveillance, and crime prevention through environmental design strategies. Predictive policing on one hand, and the maintenance of the notion of the superpredator "other" who can be controlled through the use of actuarial tools, environmental and situational crime prevention strategies, and technological advances on the other supplanted the social welfare model of rehabilitation, indeterminate sentencing, and reintegration of the 1960s and 1970s (Garland, 1990, 2001a, 2001b). This dramatic shift in attitudes and practices directed toward crime and its response has led to mass imprisonment, which some have argued has increased rather than decreased crime (Harcourt, 2006). This movement within criminal justice has disenfranchised poor minority males, broken up families, weakened the social-control capacity of parents, eroded economic strength, soured attitudes toward society, and distorted politics in impoverished neighborhoods, a trend that can only be rectified through sentencing reforms and philosophical realignment (Clear, 2007).

The abrupt departure from rehabilitation can also be partly attributed to research conducted by R. Martinson (1974). In 1974, Martinson, who reviewed 231 studies of prison rehabilitation programs, declared that nothing works in regards to rehabilitation and that offender treatment was essentially ineffective. This research shook the foundation of correctional administrators and the public. If rehabilitation was as futile as Martinson claimed, then perhaps it should not be the focus anymore. The abandonment of rehabilitation became the platform for many conservatives who were already disillusioned with the use of rehabilitation. These same conservatives viewed the use of rehabilitation to be indicative of being soft on crime, which was at odds with their "get tough on crime" philosophy.

Criminologists, who had long since abandoned the idea that offenders were biologically determined to commit crime as Lombroso had claimed, but who had previously brought in the role of environment (see Sutherland, 1947b) and its relationship to crime rate and discussed that failure to commit crime was due to social bonds (see Hirschi, 1969) were now proposing that offenders decided to commit crime. That is, offenders made a rational decision within the situational and environmental context of routine activities and increased temptation and decreased controls (Felson, 2002, 2006) to commit a crime after weighing the costs and benefits of doing so. According to D. B. Cornish and R. V. Clarke (1986), decisions to engage in crime by offenders are based on the offender's expected effort and reward compared to the likelihood, or certainty, of punishment, along with its severity, as well as other costs of crime (e.g, losing friends). R. Seiter and K. Kadela explain that inmates were no longer viewed as sick and needing assistance in the form of rehabilitation programs, "but as making a conscious decision to commit crime" (2003, p. 363). Research was emerging to support the claim that ex-offenders were making a rational decision to get out of crime just as their decision to enter crime was also rational (Cusson and

Pinsonneault, 1986; Mischowitz, 1994; Shover, 1996). When reflecting on the character H. I. from the movie *Raising Arizona,* many in society would view his failures to keep himself out of prison as due to his choices. After all, many believe that all ex-offenders need to succeed is to "just make a different choice," and they can alter their life-course trajectory of committing crimes. Even CCOs can hold the perspective that criminal behavior revolves around choice. In a survey of 132 state and federal CCOs in Seattle, E. Gunnison and J. B. Helfgott (2011) found that CCOs in their sample felt that offenders make decisions to reoffend, or violate, believing that offender success is primarily due to rational choice.

The idea that criminals make rational decisions to commit crime resonated with the media and the public in the 1980s and continues today, regardless of one's social or celebrity status. In 2001, actress Winona Ryder was arrested for stealing designer clothes from a Sak's Fifth Avenue store in Los Angeles. She was convicted a year later despite her celebrity status (Deutsch, 2002). A few years later, in 2004, Martha Stewart was convicted of obstruction of justice after she lied to investigators about a stock sale (McClam, 2004). A firestorm of media publicity surrounded Stewart regarding her crime, and the public demanded that Stewart, like Ryder, be punished regardless of her social position or celebrity status. The media and public deemed other recent celebrity cases, those of heiress/socialite Paris Hilton (drug conviction) and actress Lindsay Lohan (DUI, theft), to have deliberately decided to commit crimes, and thus should be punished despite their social status (McCartney, 2011; Silva, 2010). Apart from the social or celebrity status of an offender, where the public attributes their criminal behavior to rational choice, there are crimes that members of the "general public" commit that are also deemed as rational, such as gang banging, homicide, and prostitution. Members of the public and even researchers might view prostitution as a rational crime (Calhoun and Weaver, 1996). After all, a prostitute can set his or her own price for specific sexual encounters and also decide where the location of the act will occur. This line of thinking holds this act to be very rational to some and perhaps the sole reason for why a prostitute is engaged in the sex trade.

In 1979, Martinson recanted his earlier proclamation that nothing works in regard to rehabilitation and noted that some studies demonstrate that rehabilitation can be effective. However, the damage had already been done. The pendulum in corrections had already swung, and corrections entered the crime control era in the late 1970s and early 1980s. The crime control model dictated that the focus of corrections be back on punishment, particularly harsh punishments, and just desserts

(Hollin, 2000). Infamous cases, such as the case of Willie Horton in Massachusetts, were splattered on the news and further solidified support for the crime control model. Massachusetts governor Michael Dukakis allowed first-degree murderers such as Willie Horton to be released for the weekend as part of a rehabilitation program known as the prison furlough program. However, when Willie Horton was released in 1986 for his rehabilitative furlough, he did not return but rather he physically and sexually assaulted a young couple (Anderson, 1995). Following this case, outrage by the public and politicians resulted in the closing of the furlough program in 1988. A similar series of cases in Washington State during this time solidified the public's distrust of the rehabilitation system: convicted rapist Charles Campbell was released on furlough after serving his sentence and went to the home of his rape victim to murder her, her eight-year-old daughter, and a neighbor who was visiting; Westley Dodd, after a history of arrests and periods of short-term confinement, went on to rape and murder three little boys; and Earl Shriner, after a twenty-four-year history of sexual assaults against children, was released from prison to rape, sexually mutilate, and murder a seven-year-old boy. These devastating failures of the correctional system fueled legislative changes in Washington State that led to major shifts in sentencing policy and attitudes toward offenders, demonstrated in the introduction of "two-strikes" and "three-strikes" legislation and civil commitment of sexually violent predators. At the same time, "determinate-plus" sentencing was also introduced for sex offenders. Under determinate-plus sentencing, offenders mandatorily serve a minimum sentence in the state of Washington and then the Indeterminate Sentencing Review Board evaluates whether they might be released back into the community or continue serving time (Helfgott, 2008; Helfgott and Strah, 2013).

Between the 1970s and the 1990s, both state and federal governments began to shift their funding from rehabilitation and funnel it instead to crime prevention (e.g., policing of hot spots, enhanced surveillance) and other forms of deterrent punishments, known as intermediate sanctions, sentences that are alternatives to probation such as house arrest (Seiter and Kadela, 2003). With prisons becoming overcrowded during this time, correctional administrators needed cost-effective alternatives to traditional incarceration that ensured public safety and were considered to be tough by both politicians and the public (Latessa and Smith, 2011). Because intermediate sanctions attempted to fill these lofty goals, the implementation and use of these sanctions exploded during this time period. Intermediate sanctions have been defined as "a punishment option that is considered on a continuum to fall between traditional probation and traditional incarceration" (US Department of Justice, 1990, p. 3). E. J. Latessa and P. Smith (2011) state that intermediate sanctions allowed the punishment to be individually tailored to the offender, and the offender is still held accountable for his or her behavior. A wide range of punishments fall under the intermediate sanctions umbrella including day fines, intensive supervision probation, day-reporting centers, shock incarceration, house arrest, electronic monitoring, and boot camps (Latessa and Smith, 2011). These punishments were designed to enhance the surveillance and control of offenders in society, not to foster successful reentry. Occasionally, discussions in the mainstream media occur as to whether these punishments are suitable for anyone, especially celebrities who often find themselves on the receiving end of one of these sentences. For instance, in 2011, Lindsay Lohan was sentenced to house arrest after a parole violation (McCartney, 2011). Discussion in the media during this time period revolved around whether her punishment was too soft and not in line with the crime control model.

Beyond the change in sentencing options beginning in the 1970s, sentencing practices shifted from indeterminate to determinate due to prolific prison overcrowding, disillusionment with rehabilitation, sentencing disparity, and disparity in parole (Seiter and Kadela, 2003). Prior to the passage of sentencing guidelines, judges had the ability to impose any sentence they deemed acceptable for a convicted offender as long as it fell within statutory guidelines. I. Weinstein explains, "In the mid-1980s, federal criminal sentencing was characterized by almost completely individualized and unreviewable judicial decision-making" (2003, p. 89). Since federal judges could impose any sentence they wanted to, sentencing disparity occurred for many offenders, particularly minority offenders (Bahn, 1977). The passage of the Sentencing Reform Act of 1984 and the Anti-Drug Abuse Act of 1986 established sentencing guidelines for judges and mandatory minimum sentences for offenders convicted of a crime (Weinstein, 2003). With sentencing guidelines now in place, judges would be forced to sentence offenders based on their prior record and current offense, with a mandatory minimum, in an attempt to remove biases based on skin color. Before the establishment of federal sentencing guidelines, some states had already implemented their own guidelines and many more states adopted their own guidelines following the federal legislation. J. S. Albanese explains, "Between 1976 and 1982, forty-three states passed mandatory sentencing laws for certain crimes and nine states adopted determinate sentencing systems" (1984, p. 270). The newly established guidelines by no means assisted offenders in successful reentry in any way shape or form. Rather these guidelines aimed to make sentences and release from prison equitable and fair for all offenders.

With the departure from indeterminate sentencing and concerns about disparity in the parole system, many states began to abolish parole. Maine was the first state to do so in 1976 with six other states following suit by 1979 (Krajick, 1983). The federal system soon followed. The Comprehensive Crime Control Act of 1984 established the use of determinate sentencing in the federal system and the phasing out of the use of parole for federal offenders (Hoffman, 2011). Currently, fifteen states have abolished parole (Seiter and Kadela, 2003). Washington, for example, abolished parole in 1984. The Board of Prison Terms and Paroles, as it was then known, was disbanded and replaced with the Indeterminate Sentence Review Board (ISRB) in 1986. The ISRB makes parole decisions for felony offenders who committed crimes before July 1, 1984, and were sentenced to prison terms (ISRB, 2008). Additionally, the ISRB makes decisions regarding release for sex offenders, under the determinate-plus sentencing policy enacted in 2001 (ISRB, 2008). In 2011, an estimated 6,956 offenders were on parole in Washington State, in stark comparison to the state of California, which had the highest number of parolees in 2011 at approximately 105,000 (Maruschak and Parks, 2012).

The abolishment or limitation on the use of parole has had a profound impact on the number of offenders that are granted parole. In twenty years, the granting of parole dropped from 72 percent of releases in 1977 to just 28 percent in 1997 (Bureau of Justice Statistics, 1977, 1997). Approximately 853,000 offenders were on parole in 2011 across the United States (Maruschak and Parks, 2012). In those states that kept parole, new state statutes defined which offenders, depending on the crime they committed, could even be eligible for parole (Seiter and Kadela, 2003). For instance, many states require that offenders, no matter their crime, serve a significant portion of their sentence before they are eligible for parole, a requirement due in part to truth-in-sentencing laws that were passed in the 1980s.

Truth-in-sentencing laws usually require that violent offenders serve a greater percentage of their sentences, typically 85 percent or more, in order to be considered for parole (Travis, 2001). Violent offenders are those convicted of Part 1 violent crimes of the Uniform Crime Reports and include murder and nonnegligent manslaughter, forcible rape, robbery, and aggravated assault (Shepherd, 2002). The federal government encouraged states to adopt truth-in-sentencing laws and provided them with financial incentives for the implementation of these laws with the implementation of the Violent Offender Incarceration and Truth in Sentencing Incentive Grants program as part of the Violent Crime Control and Law Enforcement Act of 1994 (Seiter and Kadela, 2003; Shepherd, 2002; Turner et al., 2006; Weinstein and Wimmer, 2010). J. B. Weinstein and C. Wimmer (2010) report that in 1994, states' use of parole sharply declined when the federal government earmarked $10 billion for new state prisons to those states that implemented these laws. Some states expanded the definition of which offenders would be required to serve the majority of their sentences. For example, in Mississippi, the truth-in-sentencing laws, adopted in 1995, require that all offenders (not just violent or sex offender) serve 85 percent of their sentences (Wood and Dunaway, 2003).

Prior to the Violent Crime Control and Law Enforcement Act of 1994, only five states had truth-in-sentencing laws (Shepherd, 2002). The impact of the pressure on states by the federal government incentives was enormous, and by 1999, thirty states had changed their laws to align with the truth-in-sentencing philosophy (Weinstein and Wimmer, 2010). As explained by Weinstein and Wimmer, "because these truth in sentencing laws—so-called transparency requirements—were not accompanied by any statutory reduction in authorized sentences, they resulted in a sudden, dramatic increase in length of time served for a broad variety of offenses" (2010, pp. 1–13). Besides discouraging parole or eliminating it altogether, truth-in-sentencing laws reduced the amount of credits an offender could receive for good behavior while incarcerated and discouraged many offenders from participating in programming while incarcerated (Seiter and Kadela, 2003). Whether or not offenders behaved well in prison and participated in programming did not matter now as the incentive of parole no longer existed. The adoption of truth-in-sentencing laws across the nation contributed to the explosion in the use of incarceration during the 1980s and 1990s (Kadela and Seiter, 2003). Subsequent evaluations of the impact of truth-in-sentencing laws have been mixed (Shepherd, 2002; Turner et al., 2006). Results from research conducted by S. Turner and coauthors (2006) cast doubt on the effectiveness of truth-in-sentencing laws in being a direct cause of actual time served. The researchers found that "the percentage of sentence served by released violent offenders has increased since 1993 for both truth-in-sentencing and non-truth-in-sentencing states" (Turner et al., 2006, p. 364). However, J. Shepherd (2002), utilizing county-level data, found that truth-in-sentencing laws deterred violent offenders and increased the portion of prison sentences actually served.

While more research is needed on the actual impact of these laws on offenders, these laws clearly inhibited successful offender reentry. With offenders required to serve more time in prison, their ability to

successfully reintegrate into society postrelease is stifled. These offenders have an even more difficult time making an earnest attempt to transition into a law-abiding citizen upon release as their lengthy incarceration sentences make it more challenging for them to find employment
and reestablish family connections.

The absence of parole has had unintended consequences such as
prison overcrowding, the loss of the incentive for inmates to participate
in rehabilitation programs in prisons, the costs of caring for a growing
geriatric inmate population, and the absence of parole board experts to
guide offenders in formulating a release plan for reentering their communities (Latessa and Smith, 2011; Seiter and Kadela, 2003). Additionally, the reduced use of or absence of parole has left a gaping hole in the
support structure for offenders (Travis, 2001). Many offenders are serving their time in prison and being released back into their communities
with no supervision or support. While some offenders may feel a disconnect, or social distance, between themselves and CCOs (Helfgott,
1997), and social distance between correctional personnel and offenders
can be viewed as a day-to-day psychological survival strategy for correctional staff enabling them to do their job in a difficult context that
requires sharp personal boundaries (Swanson, 2009), the lack of a prosocial advocate in the form of a CCO may stifle successful reentry. The
CCO plays a vital role in assisting parolees in obtaining needed services
(e.g., substance abuse treatment, employment and housing referrals) and
holding the offenders accountable for their behavior, such as the failure
to actively look for employment. In fact, the CCOs may be the only
prosocial people in the lives of the offenders and the only people to
whom the offenders must answer for their behavior. Without prosocial
contact, offenders are left to their own devices and will likely reestablish connections with antisocial friends. These antisocial associates will
likely continue the cultural transmission of ideals that are deviant or
criminal or both (Shaw and McKay, 1972; Sutherland, 1947b).

Those states that still offer parole for offenders have had difficulties
in facilitating successful offender reentry. With shrinking budgets for
corrections operations, many parole agencies are underfunded (Scott-
Hayward, 2019; Travis, 2001). The underfunding of parole agencies has
resulted in increased caseloads for CCOs. In 2006, the national average
caseload for CCOs with parolees was 38; however, some CCOs in individual states had caseloads as high as 100 (Bonczar, 2008). Since CCOs
have larger caseloads, supervision and surveillance of the offenders
becomes their first concern with successful reentry for the offenders
becoming a secondary goal. Seiter and Kadela explain that "for most of
the 1990s, community supervision (probation and parole) underwent a

transition from helping and counseling offenders to one of risk management and surveillance" (2003, p. 366). CCOs are expected to ensure public safety although this goal can all too often be compromised.

A relatively recent example of the failure of parole can be witnessed in the Jaycee Dugard case. In 1991, eleven-year-old Jaycee Dugard was abducted from outside her home in California. Her abduction was witnessed by her stepfather. Despite a national manhunt, Jaycee could not be located, and her case remained unsolved for over eighteen years. In 2009, her whereabouts were finally uncovered when she showed up at a parole agency with her kidnapper, Phillip Garrido. Phillip Garrido, a sex offender on parole at the time he abducted Jaycee, hid Jaycee in a tent for over eighteen years in his backyard with the help of his wife, Nancy. He also repeatedly raped Jaycee, which resulted in pregnancies, and she gave birth to two daughters (Leff, 2011). When Jaycee's identity was finally uncovered, the community erupted in outrage. Citizens wondered whether the parole officer was doing his job since he was required to inspect Garrido's residence when he visited. Jaycee Dugard, her mother, and her daughters sued the state for negligence, and they were awarded a settlement of $20 million (La Ganga and Goldmacher, 2010). Philip Garrido and his wife pled guilty to kidnapping and rape in 2011 and were sentenced to 431 years and 36 years to life, respectively (Leff, 2011).

With approximately 600,000 offenders returning to their communities each year and the fact that 95 percent of state prisoners will eventually leave prison, discussion has returned to offender reentry (Hughes and Wilson, 2004; Petersilia, 2003). The failure rates for those on supervision (probation and parole) are high—50 percent or greater (Hughes and Wilson, 2004; Langan and Levin, 2002). L. Winterfield and colleagues explain that "the high recidivism rates of released prisoners, along with a fuller understanding of their need for services, have prompted policymakers to realize that the lack of access to and the largely fragmented nature of existing programs and service delivery networks need to be addressed" (2006, p. 4). While a shift back to a pure rehabilitation model for corrections is not under way, the recognition that rehabilitation plays a role in successful reentry has been noted by policymakers. However, with cuts to state correctional budgets and the fiscal difficulties states are experiencing, more programming, in-prison or postrelease, will not be added to assist offenders in successfully reintegrating back into society (Scott-Hayward, 2009; Winterfield et al., 2006).

In 2003, the federal government instituted the Serious and Violent Offender Reentry Initiative (SVORI) and provided sixty-nine agencies funding, specifically $100 million, to implement or enhance reentry programming for both juvenile and adult prisoners (Winterfield et al., 2006). As explained by P. K. Lattimore and her colleagues,

> the goals of the initiative are to improve quality of life and self-sufficiency through employment, housing, family and community involvement; improve health by addressing substance use (sobriety and relapse prevention) and physical and mental health; reduce criminality through supervision and by monitoring noncompliance, reoffending, rearrest, reconviction, and reincarceration; [and] achieve system change through multi-agency collaboration and case management strategies. (2004, p. 2)

P. K. Lattimore and C. Visher further explain, "The complexity of the disadvantages confronting prisoners after release means that individual offenders often require more than a single program or intervention" (2009, p. 5). Initial findings regarding housing support for high-risk offenders appear to support Lattimore and Visher's (2009) assertion. In a meta-analytic review of twelve research studies that had examined housing assistance for mentally ill individuals and ex-offenders, M. Miller and I. Ngugi (2009) found that housing assistance provided for serious violent offenders in tandem with other services (e.g., substance abuse treatment) resulted in a 12 percent reduction in recidivism for this group.

Specifically, the SVORI programs connect correctional agencies with many government, community, and faith-based organizations to provide needed services or resources to those transitioning back into their communities (Winterfield et al., 2006). Often, many agencies attempt to assist offenders in their communities. If these agencies do not communicate with one another, then they may be providing offenders with overlapping services, thereby wasting both agencies' precious resources. Additionally, if the agencies are not aware of one another, then each agency would not be able to refer an offender to another for services. In the city of Seattle, many agencies attempt to assist offenders in their transition: AAHAA (Alcoholics and Addicts Helping Alcoholics and Addicts) Sober Living, Saint Vincent de Paul (assists the homeless and low-income individuals with meals and clothing), Interaction Transition (a private nonprofit agency in Seattle, Washington, dedicated to assisting ex-offenders in the reentry process), United Way, Dress for Success (business attire for low-income women including offenders), Northwest Treatment Centers (mental health treatment), the Salvation Army, work release facilities (e.g., Helen B. Ratcliff and Madison Inn), Catholic Community Services, and many more.

The literature is mixed on the success of SVORI programs. On one hand, researchers have found that SVORI programs have assisted offenders in the areas of employment, housing, and substance use abstention (Bouffard and Bergerson, 2007; Lattimore, 2008; Lattimore and Visher, 2009; Winterfield et al., 2006). For instance, J. A. Bouffard and L. Bergerson (2007), in an investigation of a SVORI program in the Midwest, found that SVORI participants were less likely to test positive for drug use while on parole and had lower postparole rearrest rates compared to non-SVORI participants. Lattimore and Visher (2009), in a multisite evaluation of SVORI programs (twelve adult and four juvenile) consisting of approximately 2,400 participants, report that SVORI program participants did receive an increase in the number of services and programs and were more likely to have reentry plans. Additionally, SVORI program participants had lower substance use rates when compared to non-SVORI participants. Overall, the researchers report, "The results suggest modest improvements in outcomes for the adult SVORI participants and few differences between the juvenile SVORI and non-SVORI participants" (Lattimore and Visher, 2009, p. vi). However, research regarding the success of SVORI programs has reported on several problems plaguing them including service delivery (i.e., quality), staffing issues (insufficient staff or staff resistance), and communication problems (Lattimore et al., 2005). The failure in service delivery is not surprising given that many treatment programs are plagued by the lack of a theoretical foundation or a solid plan for later methodological inquiries into their effectiveness (Lattimore and Visher, 2009). M. Henderson and D. Hanley explain,

> Given the massive number of federal dollars available for the development of reentry programs, many agencies hasten developing and obtaining funding for reentry programming without first considering how the program fits within the larger criminal justice system in their jurisdiction and without coordinating with community-based organizations. The end result is a reentry initiative that lacks program integrity and ultimately fails to reduce barriers offenders face when returning to the community. (2006, p. 64)

Clearly, more research is needed to determine the overall merits of these programs in fostering successful offender reentry in the future.

Recognition that offenders released from prison need support in reentry continues. In 2008, the Second Chance Act was passed. This federal legislation was designed to assist offenders in making a successful transition from prison to their communities and to reduce recidivism rates (Bureau of Justice Assistance, 2011). The Second Chance Act provides "federal grants to government agencies and community and faith-based organizations to provide employment assistance, substance abuse treatment, housing, family programming, mentoring, victims support, and other services that can help reduce offending and violations of probation and parole" (Carothers, 2010, p. 5–13). For 2010, $100 million and for 2011, $50 million were earmarked for Second Chance Act programs (Reentry Policy Council, 2011). Funding was funneled to, among other entities, reentry courts, reentry substance abuse treatment programs, family-based treatment programs, mentoring programs, technology career training, reentry research, mental health treatment, and education programs in prisons (Reentry Policy Council, 2011). Following the passing of this legislation, many states began implementing their own reentry initiatives, including Washington State. In Washington, the Department of Corrections is dedicated to fostering successful reentry for offenders (either released from prison on supervision or not) through the Reentry Initiative. As part of the Reentry Initiative, the Washington State Department of Corrections invests in intervention programs and services that help offenders, thereby improving public safety. "Even as budget resources become scarcer, DOC [Department of Corrections] still considers evidence-based re-entry programs to be a high priority and will continue to invest in basic and vocational education, life skills, additional community justice centers, expanded chemical dependency and mental health treatment, and family centered programming" (Washington State Department of Corrections, 2011, p. 14).

In sum, the definition and understanding of offender reentry has often been overshadowed by the preoccupation with offender reentry postrelease and horrific stories of offenders reintroduced into the community after a period of incarceration who go on to commit atrocious crimes and present an extreme threat to public safety. Additionally, the historical shift from the social welfare focus on rehabilitative support for ex-offenders to the late-modern focus on surveillance, control, actuarial prediction, and maintenance of the "us versus them" stance toward offenders' reentry has been fraught with policies that served to stymie any institutional supports that could benefit individuals who are released from prison with the sincere and wholehearted intention to engage in a prosocial lifestyle and to succeed as a law-abiding and productive citizen upon release. Today, although research, discourse, and programs are directed toward offender reentry, still very little discussion or research can be found on the successes of those offenders who managed to reintegrate into their communities despite all the odds stacked against them. This emphasis on success, rather than failure, in the reentry process will be the focus of the following chapters. We will present profiles of those reintegrating; the needs and challenges offenders face; gender, race, and social class issues; the voices of offenders who have succeeded; and the voices of practitioners regarding their perspectives on what is needed. We will follow with a discussion of policy recommendations to further assist in successful offender reentry.

Note

1. We use the term *ex-offender* for the purpose of clarity and because it is the most commonly used term in the scholarly literature and the criminal justice system. However, for many individuals who have been convicted, incarcerated, and released, the term *ex-offender* brings with it a pejorative tone implying "once an offender, always offender." Terms such as *ex-convict, ex-inmate, ex-felon,* or *former prisoner* also carry stigma and are equally problematic for some individuals for different reasons. Thus, whereas we use the current terminology, *ex-offender,* in this book, we hope that this research, and a more hopeful look at the successes rather than failures of ex-offenders, will inspire and support current and future ongoing dialogue about potential shifts in academic, public, and private terminology that carry less of a stigma and a more hopeful mind-set of success rather than failure.

2

Profiles of Transition and Reintegration

IN THE UNITED STATES 1,600 ADULTS (600,000 ANNUALLY) LEAVE federal and state prisons each day and return to society (Petersilia, 2003). However, this estimate just scratches the surface of the sheer number of offenders who are undergoing reentry. Many other types of offenders are attempting to reintegrate into society who are not being released from prison but from other forms of sanctions such as jail, day-reporting centers, or halfway houses. For instance, Lindsay Lohan, a young actress, is probably not the image of a reintegrating ex-offender that may come to most people's mind. However, Lindsay Lohan is indeed undergoing reentry into society after a conviction for driving under the influence and probation violations (McCartney, 2011). The media has tracked Lohan's downward spiral and struggles, yet no reporters ever uttered the term *reentry* when discussing her current plights. Everyday citizens are encountering ex-offenders who are attempting to rejoin the community without even knowing it. These ex-offenders are driving on freeways, shopping in the supermarket, and drinking coffee at the next table over at Starbucks. We cannot know how many or which strangers in our midst, sitting next to us in a movie theater, standing behind us in a bank line, purchasing the latest technical gadget at the Microsoft Store, cutting the tree down in our front lawn in a landscape design crew, or working with us on a project might be ex-offenders currently reintegrating back into society.

Ex-offenders are everywhere—on every block, in every store, in every classroom. Often unknown to the average citizen beyond the utter complexity of offender reentry are the actual numbers of those reintegrating (i.e., totality of all offenders under community corrections sentence) and the profiles of offenders reentering their communities (e.g., race, gender, and social class). In this chapter, we will break down Hollywood images and stereotypes and provide an accurate profile of those who are reentering society. Discussion and statistics will be provided as to the number of those serving community corrections sentences, the number of those reintegrating back into society, and the type of sentences (e.g., parole, day reporting, work release) that offenders served prior to their reentry. Additionally, we will briefly highlight the gender, race, and social composition of those reintegrating back into their communities. Finally, we will attempt to paint a portrait of what successful reentry looks like utilizing the voices of ex-offenders, and we will discuss what factors, according to ex-offenders, are critical to their success in the challenging reintegration process.

Background Statistics

As mentioned earlier, over 600,000 offenders are released from state and federal prisons each year (Petersilia, 2003) with one in every thirty-four people in the United States under some form of correctional supervision (Glaze and Parks, 2012). Utilizing only these statistics, however, would provide an inaccurate estimate of the volume of offenders who are reentering society postpunishment. When examining the statistics for probationers and parolees, we discover staggering numbers. In 2011, 4.8 million offenders were currently serving probation and parole sentences and represented the majority (70 percent) of those being supervised in state and federal correctional systems (Maruschak and Parks, 2012). Specifically, approximately 3.9 million were offenders on probation, and approximately 850,000 offenders were on parole (Maruschak and Parks, 2012). With approximately 735,000 offenders serving jail sentences, more offenders are reintegrating into society each day (Minton, 2012). T. D. Minton discusses the high turnover in the jail population and states, "Local jails admitted an estimated 11.6 million persons during the 12-month period ending June 30, 2012. The number of persons admitted in 2012 was about 16 times the size of the average daily population (735,983) at mid-year 2012 (2012, p. 4). Clearly with almost 12 million individuals being admitted to jails in 2011, additional offenders are reentering society that are often not considered in discussions of offender reentry.

In sum, approximately 18 million offenders are reentering society. However, this large figure is misleading and obscured by countless other offenders who are sentenced to punishments that are outside the range of jail, probation, and parole. For instance, many offenders are sentenced to boot camps. Boot camps are short-term punishments (i.e., lasting 90 to 120 days) that are typically utilized for first-time offenders and are similar to basic training in the military (Latessa and Smith, 2011). At the state level, an estimated 21,000 adult offenders went through boot camp programs in the year 2000 (Camp and Camp, 2000). In addition, in 2000, approximately 40,000 adult offenders were serving work release sentences, and 8,700 were participating in day-reporting center programs (Camp and Camp, 2000). Thus, when one adds these numbers into the bigger picture of reentry, the number of offenders reintegrating back into society pre- and postpunishment is clearly well over 18 million. Yet this astronomical figure is rarely if ever factored into media reports on or public perceptions of offender reentry. Rather, the focus of such reports and perceptions is usually on the failures of those reentering rather than the success stories of those who have reentered society. With such a staggering figure, developing a clear picture of those reentering in regard to gender, race, and social class is difficult. The following sections contain short snapshots to develop useful and accurate profiles of ex-offenders.

Gender

The images many people have in their minds of ex-offenders reentering society are often influenced by fictional media depictions or news stories (Bennett, 2006). For those who do not personally know someone who has reentered the community after a period of incarceration, media depictions of ex-offenders may paint an unrealistic picture of these individuals.

Who are these 18 million ex-offenders reentering our communities? Most of the individuals reentering society are male. Of the approximately 3.9 million offenders on probation in 2011, 75 percent were male (Maruschak and Parks, 2012). When examining the gender of the approximately 850,000 offenders who were on parole in 2011, we find similar percentages to probation. Specifically, 89 percent of parolees in 2011 were male, with females accounting for less than 100,000 state and federal parolees of the 850,000 parolees nationwide (Maruschak and Parks, 2012). A similar picture emerges upon inspection of the approximately 744,000 offenders serving jail sentences in 2012. Minton (2012) reports that males represented the majority of those serving jail sentences in 2012 at approximately 87 percent and females accounted for approximately 13 percent of the national total. Upon closer inspection of the total national jail population in 2012, females represented approximately 98,000 of those sentenced (Minton, 2013). We must note once again that the gender of the almost 12 million offenders admitted to jail in 2011 is not nationally reported. However, given that females represent a smaller percentage of those committing crimes each year, one can expect that males will continue to represent a significantly larger portion of the jail admissions (Belknap, 2007).

Beyond differences in representation, other similarities and differences have emerged regarding the reentry profiles of male and female ex-offenders. Both male and female ex-offenders experience similar obstacles in terms of finding adequate housing, obtaining employment, obtaining substance abuse and mental health treatment, or even being admitted to higher education (Allender, 2004; Cowan and Fionda, 1994; Harlow, 2003; Harris and Keller, 2005; Hunt, Bowers, and Miller, 1973; Nagin and Waldfogel, 1998; Paylor, 1995; Petersilia, 2003; Rodriguez and Brown, 2003; Starr, 2002; Whelan, 1973). While some similarities can be seen in the struggles all ex-offenders face toward successful reentry, sex differences in the reentry process present special challenges that may differentially shape the reentry pathway for male and female ex-offenders. In terms of the nature of offending, males are more likely to commit violent crimes while females are more likely to commit property crimes (Belknap, 2007; Chesney-Lind and Pasko, 2004); thus, males are more likely to face having to overcome a previous history of violent criminal activity. Males will likely find that their violent criminal histories make housing and employment options even more unavailable to them. This, in and of itself, creates a unique challenge for this group. Making a transition from a life of pervasive violent criminal involvement (e.g., gang activity) to a crime-free existence postrelease is difficult. This type of transformation takes significant time, which is often not afforded in short-term community corrections sentences, as well as the support of family and other professionals (e.g., mental health workers). Therefore, the needs of males reentering society are often distinct from the needs of females reentering society as a result of the nature of their crimes.

In addition to type of offense, males and females find other subtle differences that distinguish their reentry experience. For instance, sexual abuse figures prominently within the life histories of female offenders. Research has indicated that women in prison have a higher level of sexual victimization than the general population (Belknap, 2007; Siegel and Williams, 2003). In fact, research indicates that the level of victimization may be two to three times higher for female offenders when compared to male offenders (Harlow, 1999). Research has consistently supported prior sexual abuse as a moderate to strong predictor of female offending (Belknap, 2007; Siegel and Williams, 2003). Sexual abuse in women has been related to running away (Belknap, Holsinger, and

Dunn, 1997), instigation of a criminal career (Chesney-Lind, 1989), prostitution (Simons and Whitbeck, 1991), drug use (Kilpatrick et al., 2000), and aggression (Baskin and Sommers, 1998). The extant literature clearly suggests that prior sexual abuse and physical abuse are catalysts for the onset of offending patterns as well as the persistence in offending patterns for females (Belknap, 2007; Chesney-Lind and Pasko, 2004; Gunnison and McCartan, 2005). Thus, female offender reentry may be complicated by prior abuse histories that are still a significant issue for the ex-offenders in the present time. Clearly, the continuation of mental health treatment and support is needed for this group in regard to their past abuse histories.

Another area of gender difference in reentry revolves around the issue of parenthood. J. Belknap reports that "approximately four out of five women and three out of five men entering prison are parents" (2007, p. 201). L. E. Glaze and L. M. Maruschak (2008), in their analysis of the minor children of state and federal prisoners, found that the majority of the mothers in state and federal prisons reported residing with their children prior to their incarceration. Additionally, researchers have reported that female offenders were more likely than males to have custody of their children prior to incarceration (Berry and Eigenberg, 2003; Koban, 1983; Mumola, 2000). Thus, females reentering society are struggling with many of the same issues that males are, such as finding housing and adequate employment, but also have the additional hardship of caring for their children or gaining back custody of their children. Some female ex-offenders who have substance abuse problems run a significant risk of losing custody of their children (Grella and Greenwell, 2006). As S. Covington states, "for many women, the only source of hope and motivation they have while involved in the criminal justice system and while in transition back to the community is the connection with their children" (2002, p. 7). With the loss of custody of their children, female offenders suffer from intense psychological pain, and this despair has been linked to their commission of various drug- and alcohol-related crimes (Ferraro and Moe, 2003). C. Coll and colleagues state,

> Many women that fall [back] into prison have the problem that their children have been taken away. When they go out to the street, they don't have anything, they have nothing inside. Because they say "I don't have my children, what will I do? I'll go back to the drug again. I will go back to prostitution again. And I'll go back to prison again. Why fight? Why fight if I have nothing?" (1998, p. 266)

Thus, the loss of custody of their children or the reestablishment of a parental bond with their children is a source of strain for female offenders.

Both the issues of prior sexual abuse and parenthood for female offenders will be further discussed in Chapter 4.

Race

Ignoring the role of race in the criminal justice system is difficult. From arrest to sentencing, racial disparity and discrimination have plagued minorities in the United States—particularly African Americans (Walker, Spohn, and DeLone, 2007). With 18 million offenders reentering society, that figure needs further dissection to obtain an accurate picture of where race fits in. In the case of race of probationers in 2010, Caucasians represented the highest number at both the federal and state level at approximately 1.5 million (Glaze and Bonczar, 2011). L. E. Glaze and T. P. Bonczar (2011) further report the following approximate numbers for federal and state probationers: 813,000 African American; 351,000 Hispanic/Latino; 27,000 American Indian/Alaska Native; 21,000 Asian; and 6,800 Native Hawaiian/other Pacific Islander. When examining the race of the approximately 840,000 offenders who were on parole in 2010, one finds similar proportions to those on probation. Specifically, Caucasians represented the highest number at both the federal and state level at approximately 343,000 (Glaze and Bonczar, 2011). Glaze and Bonczar (2011) further report the following approximate numbers for federal and state parolees: 319,000 African American; 147,000 Hispanic/Latino; 8,500 American Indian/Alaska Native; 6,000 Asian; and 1,300 Native Hawaiian/other Pacific Islander. A similar picture emerges upon inspection of the approximately 735,000 offenders serving jail sentences in 2011. Minton (2013) reports that Caucasians represented the majority of those serving jail sentences in 2012 at approximately 341,000, and that African Americans represented approximately 274,000 of those sentenced while Hispanics represented about 112,000 of those sentenced. Also, almost 12 million jail admissions took place from mid-2011 to mid-2012, and the race of those admitted is not reported in national jail statistics.

Social Class

As with race, one cannot ignore the role of social class when examining the criminal justice system. Evidence suggests that social class can be either an insulator against or another contributing factor to contact with the criminal justice system, in the form of arrest or sentencing (M. Anderson,

2008; D'Alessio and Stolzenberg, 1993; Thornberry, 1973). M. Anderson states, "Arrest statistics show a strong correlation between social class and crime, with the poor more likely than others to be arrested" (2008, p. 198). While national statistics do not report on the socioeconomic status of convicted offenders, discussions of social class as it relates to those serving various community corrections sentences (i.e., probation and parole) have appeared in the empirical literature (Caldwell, 1951; England, 1955; Landis, Mercer, and Wolff, 1969). For instance, R. England (1955) examined 500 male and female federal offenders who had successfully completed probation and examined recidivism rates for these offenders six years later. One factor related to failure, defined as convictions for both misdemeanor and felony offenses, was socioeconomic background. Specifically, England found that those from lower socioeconomic, or economically disadvantaged, backgrounds have a higher rate of failure. Additionally, J. R. Landis, J. D. Mercer, and C. E. Wolff (1969), in their study of 791 adult probationers in California, found that those probationers from lower socioeconomic backgrounds were more likely to fail (i.e., violate their probation or commit a new crime). P. Gendreau, T. Little, and C. Goggin (1996) report, in their meta-analysis of the predictors of adult recidivism, that socioeconomic status is one predictor although it is not a robust predictor.

Clearly, socioeconomic status plays some role in the success of offenders reintegrating into society. While the above-mentioned explanations regarding gender, race, and social class and their relationship to reentry were discussed separately, it is important to note the intersectionality of these factors. That is, for many offenders, these factors coincide, making successful reentry even more complicated. The following sections will provide a portrait of offenders who have successfully reintegrated using a combined quantitative and qualitative approach.

Offender Reentry Success

The pathway to reentry success is fraught with bumps and obstacles. Ex-offenders are limited in their housing, employment, and educational choices. Many have a limited income to sustain themselves while they get back on their feet. Ex-offenders with sex crime convictions find successfully maneuvering in their reentry process even more difficult. Overwhelmingly, the empirical literature on offender reentry recounts the failure of offenders during reintegration and the struggles they face. As T. K. Kenemore and I. Roldan assert, "there is a paucity of knowledge about the subjective experience of ex-offenders entering our communities" (2006, p. 7). Similarly, the media coverage and exposés on offender reintegration focus on the failure of offenders and the havoc these offenders wreak on the community. For instance, in the 2010 Pulitzer Prize–winning book entitled *The Other Side of Mercy: A Killer's Journey Across the American Divide,* Ken Armstrong and Jonathan Martin (*Seattle Times* journalists) provide a detailed account of a paroled offender from Arkansas named Maurice Clemmons who made his way to Washington State in 2004. After arriving in Washington, Clemmons committed a series of crimes culminating in the tragic killing of four Lakewood city police officers in 2009 at a coffee shop. With the attention to ex-offenders overwhelmingly focused on failures, researchers have a difficult task unraveling the factors that can promote offender reentry success and constructing a realistic profile of what a successfully reintegrated ex-offender looks like.

The transition from incarceration to the community is the first step toward possible successful reentry, but it is a traumatic leap for many. In their qualitative study of the experiences of ex-offenders, Kenemore and Roldan (2006) report on some of the initial feelings ex-offenders had upon release. For example, ex-offenders stated,

- "I was afraid to get on the 'El' [elevated train] and the bus myself. I was afraid of people. It took me awhile."
- "Cause when I first came out it was like I was shell-shocked. It was like I was in another foreign country."
- "When I got out of jail I had a hard time going in a store or a restaurant being—being around people that were, what they say, in society so to speak. I didn't feel like I fit in" (p. 14).

N. McCall writes about his experiences being paroled: "For a long time, everything felt alien, like one of those movies where a person is frozen in a block of ice, and when it thaws he discovers he's in the same place but in a different time. It seemed I was moving about at a different pace than the rest of the world; like for three years, the world had been speeding ahead while I'd stood still" (1994, p. 228). Thus, for some ex-offenders, fear and a sense of discomfort were two of the initial feelings they experienced during reentry. Further, Kenemore and Roldan (2006) report on the experiences of the ex-offenders at release and their apprehension about reintegrating.

- "Like when I was leaving, the guard, I don't think he meant anything by it. He said, 'See you later.'"

- "They [the prison guards] said, 'Here, go to Safer Foundation and here's $50.00, and we'll see ya next time you come back,' basically."
- "All you think of is going home, you know. Then when that time comes, there's no home to come to. The door is closed in your face. You don't know where to turn" (p. 14).

K. Hanrahan, J. J. Gibbs, and S. E. Zimmerman (2005), who examined young adult paroled offenders, report on the fear and uneasiness of reentry for those in their sample. One ex-offender stated, "I felt like I was on top of the world. Later on, after I came down, I was scared. I was scared about what I missed. Or, you know, what am I going to do . . . not to come back?" (p. 259). Another male in their sample reported,

> In here, you ain't got nothing but time to fantasize, and you fantasize a lot about what you want, you know, and you thinks it's going to be this easy. I hear a lot of talk about, "We don't go here and do this," or "I'm going to go here and start this business," and they don't realize it's hard to do that. You got to be dedicated to what you want in order to make it out there. And to apply yourself. It's just a lot of fantasy. A lot of nonrealistic thinking. You know what I'm saying? (p. 259)

Although the journey to successful reentry or "staying straight" was fraught with initial difficulties at the moment of release, many of the ex-offenders attribute incarceration for their successful transformation:

- "I don't look back on [prison] as a bad time in my life. I look back on that as the stepping stone. I look back on that as the catalyst."
- "And I did feel that in a lot of ways, internally, I had sort of re-created myself while I was there."
- "Yes, the desire was within me. It was a burning, intensive fire that said, 'This is not your place. You are definitely in the wrong place.' I always knew that I wanted to overcome that" (Kenemore and Roldan, 2006, p. 14).

Marriage

For some ex-offenders marriage can be a turning point that fosters successful reentry (McCall, 1994; Sampson and Laub, 1993). In their age-graded theory of crime, which suggests that persistence tapers off as offenders grow older, R. J. Sampson and J. H. Laub (1993) describe how the development of social capital through social institutions such as marriage can foster desistance from crime. However, Sampson and Laub caution that the act of marriage alone does not foster desistance but rather the marriage must be of quality and have reciprocity. Subsequent researchers have found that quality bonds in marriage are indeed important in promoting desistance from criminality (Maume, Ousey, and Beaver, 2005; Petras, Nieuwbeerta, and Piquero, 2010; Tripodi, 2010). J. Horney, D. W. Osgood, and I. H. Marshall (1995), who examined 658 newly released males from prison, found that those who lived with their wives were less likely to reoffend. However, those males who lived with their girlfriends doubled the odds that they would recidivate. Additionally, M. Warr (1998) found that those who were married spent less time in antisocial peer associations. Research has emerged on the role of marriage as it relates to offender reentry success (Landis, Mercer, and Wolff, 1969; McCarthy and Langworthy, 1987; Morgan, 1991; Olson, Alderden, and Lurigio, 2003). For instance, Landis, Mercer, and Wolff (1969), in their study of 791 male probationers in California, found that those who were successful were more likely to be married. K. Morgan (1991), who examined 266 felony probationers in Tennessee, found that those probationers who were unmarried were more likely to fail (i.e., violating their probation, abscond, or commit a new offense) on probation. However, S. J. Bahr and colleagues (2005), who examined reentry for fifty-one male and female parolees did not find that marriage was associated with either fostering or inhibiting successful reentry. Further, D. E. Olson, M. Alderden, and A. J. Lurigio, in their examination of approximately 3,400 male and female probationers in Illinois, found that "being married appears to 'protect/insulate' men against probation failure, but seems to increase the risk of probation failure for women" (2003, p. 49). Olson, Alderden, and Lurigio's findings are intriguing as they would suggest that marriage fosters successful reentry for males but not females.

Research by A. M. Leverentz (2006b) sheds some additional light on Olson, Alderden, and Lurigio's (2003) findings. Leverentz (2006b) interviewed forty-nine female ex-offenders and their partners in an effort to explore the role of romantic relationships on the reentry experiences for this group. In her study, she found that these women have relationships with other ex-offenders or recovering drug users. Clearly, these associations and partnerships could stymie successful reentry. Many females in Leverentz's (2006b) sample were victims of physical and emotional abuse. This finding regarding abuse experienced by female offenders has been discussed by several researchers (see Belknap, 2007; Chesney-Lind and Pasko, 2004), and, again, these horrific experiences can thwart successful reentry. As Leverentz explains, "several of the women described these relationships as 'kill or be killed'" (2006b, p. 471). While Bahr and colleagues (2005) did not find marriage to be associated one way or the other with reentry success for males or females in their sample in their quantitative analyses, ex-offenders had their own opinions. One female named Marie in their sample reported, "My downfall was my husband" (p. 256). Despite Bahr and colleagues' conclusions, based on other researchers' findings, the case for female ex-offenders may be that they are less likely than male ex-offenders to be married to prosocial partners. Additionally, the impact of marriage may differ for females of different races. G. D. Hill and E. M. Crawford (1990) found that marriage had an impact on decreasing future criminal acts for African American women but not Caucasian women. Further research is needed to firmly gauge the impact of marriage on reentry for both male and female ex-offenders as well as for ex-offenders of various races and ethnicities.

Employment

Another factor related to ex-offenders' successful reintegration into society after incarceration or serving a community corrections sentence is the acquisition of gainful employment (Brown and Bloom, 2009; Caldwell, 1951; Kusuda, 1976; Landis, Mercer, and Wolff, 1969; Morgan, 1991; Renner, 1978; Tripodi, 2010; Uggen and Staff, 2001). In an analysis of 403 federal probationers, M. Caldwell (1951) found that one factor related to postprobation success was the obtainment of full employment. Landis, Mercer, and Wolff (1969) add that, in their research, unsuccessful postprobation reentry was attributed to unstable employment. However, finding legal employment opportunities was extremely difficult during reentry for both males and females and across geographical locations (Garland, Wodahl, and Mayfield, 2011; Hanrahan, Gibbs, and Zimmerman, 2005; Richie, 2001). Hanrahan, Gibbs, and Zimmerman describe one ex-offender's struggles:

> You're walking down the street, looking for a job, and you just got turned down three times because they wanted a fax, and you didn't send them a fax with a resume. You don't even know what a resume is, and you're walking down the street and some guy comes to you and says, "Hey, I remember you; yeah, yeah, yeah. How you doing? Yeah man, you look down and out. . . . Look like you can use some money. Here. Here's $50. Go buy yourself something to eat or something." "Oh, thanks man." "Matter of fact, you need to make some

money?" "Yeah." "Well, I'll tell you what. See me later." You know, that's how it starts. And I've seen it. I've seen it in the halfway house. (2005, p. 258)

The deficiencies in training ex-offenders how to find employment is yet another barrier to success during reintegration. B. E. Richie (2001) reports on one female ex-offender's struggles in regard to employment: "I am 35 years old and have never had a legit [legitimate] job. No one taught me how to do an application, how to get dressed and show up, how to get someone to hire me. Now that I have this X on my back [a criminal record], I'll never find someone to pay me. Not for a legit job anyways" (p. 377). N. La Vigne (2010) states that women reentering society after prison experience more difficulties than men in meeting their financial needs and are twice as likely as their male counterparts to earn income illegally. Further, La Vigne adds that even when female ex-offenders do acquire legal employment, they still struggle more than males with their finances, earning on average $1.50 less per hour than male ex-offenders who obtained legal employment. The finding that female ex-offenders earn less than male ex-offenders is not surprising as it mirrors the national trend that females earn less than males (Rothenberg, 2010).

For ex-offenders who found a job, keeping the job was a concern (Garland, Wodahl, and Mayfield, 2011). In a qualitative investigation of forty-three male offenders, B. Garland, E. J. Wodahl, and J. Mayfield (2011) state that ex-offenders expressed fear about losing their jobs and that they often felt stuck or trapped in their current jobs. One participant reported, "If I leave my job to look for a better one, my parole officer will violate me" [charge me with a violation] (p. 98). Additionally, Garland, Wodahl, and Mayfield state that employment can provide ex-offenders with a daily structure, thereby alleviating stress and boredom. This theme—that a daily routine provided by employment can foster reentry success—has been found by other researchers. In a study of ex-offender reentry in Houston, D. Brazzell and N. G. La Vigne state, "according to respondents, obtaining a job is critical not only because it provides income and self-sufficiency, but also because a daily routine can help individuals avoid negative influences and stay focused on reentry success" (2009, p. 2). Further, the economy may play a role in ex-offender reentry success. When the overall economy in the United States is weak, as it has been over the last few years due to the recession, successful prisoner reentry can be inhibited as ex-offenders face additional obstacles in obtaining not only a job but a job with decent pay (Hannon and DeFina, 2010). If ex-offenders can obtain quality and stable employment, that experience can serve as a turning point (Sampson and Laub, 1993; Uggen and Staff, 2001). Thus, gaining legal employment that pays well is a pathway for reentry success for many ex-offenders.

Substance Use

Drug and alcohol use is both a contributor to the onset of criminality for both males and females as well as a factor contributing to future criminality (Belknap, 2007; Olson, Alderden, and Lurigio, 2003). However, breaking the cycle from past addictions is also related to offender reentry success for both genders in all types of communities (i.e., rural or urban) (Frease, 1964; Kusuda, 1976; Renner, 1978; Wiederanders, 1983; Wodahl, 2006). For some offenders, the opportunity to break away from past addictions may sometimes occur in prison, yet many offenders do not seize the chance to engage in substance abuse programming while incarcerated. B. E. Richie reports on one woman's struggles to get clean and sober while incarcerated:

> Inside, there were some treatment groups, but they only met every once in a while. I'd try to get there, but sometimes the officers forgot to call me out of my housing area. Or I'd get there and the group would be canceled for some reason. Other times, we'd just be there talking, but not getting very deep. It was good to get a distraction, but I wouldn't say I worked on my issues. I'm an addict and have been for eight years. I really need help, but didn't get it in jail. So, when I came out, I went right back [to drug abuse]. Nothing changed. And even though I stopped using while I was locked up, that was just because I couldn't use there. I wish I could have used my time [in jail] better cause there certainly isn't any programs in the streets. Now I'm back where I started. Running the streets, chasing that drug until I get locked up again. (2001, p. 372)

Other researchers have suggested that the increased use of imprisonment coupled with a lack of adequate substance abuse treatment programs and lack of incentives for offenders to participate in such programs has contributed to ex-offenders' reentering society with continued drug and alcohol issues (Petersilia, 2001a). Further, Richie adds, "Advocates and service providers agree that substance abuse treatment is one of the most significant needs for women returning to their communities from jails and prisons" (2001, p. 372). In another study of female ex-offenders in Washington, DC, La Vigne (2011) reports that they needed a lot of assistance with their drug addictions upon reentry, more so than male ex-offenders.

Ex-offenders have reported on their cessation of drug use in the reentry process. When Bahr and colleagues queried paroled ex-offenders about the temptation to use drugs, one subject reported, "Now, I've only been out today, but I'd say the desire is gone. I've completed two years of substance abuse, graduated from the program, I think the desire's gone" (2005, p. 258). Another participant in their study reported, "Honestly, there is no need for that because I love life. There is a lot of life in life if you just, you know. It's bad. Drugs are bad. They take it all out of you. They take away your life" (p. 258). I. Sommers, D. R. Baskin, and F. Fagan (1994) examined the cases of thirty female former street offenders and discovered that some women made a conscious decision to stop their involvement in crime and cease their drug use, whereas others sought formal treatment to assist them in their recovery. One subject reported,

> After I decided to change, I went to a party with my friend. And people was around me and they was drinkin' and stuff, and I didn't want to drink. I don't have the urge of drinking. If anything, it would be smokin' crack. And when I left the party, I felt like I was missing something—like something was missing. And it was the fact that I wasn't gettin' high. But I know the consequences of it. If I take a drink, I'm gonna smoke crack. If I, uh, sniff some blow, I'm gonna smoke crack. I might do some things like rob a store or something stupid and go to jail. So I don't want to put myself in that position. (1994, p. 142)

N. J. Tiburcio (2008), who conducted a qualitative interview of one female ex-offender who was a heroin and cocaine user but had desisted drug use for eleven years, states that ex-offenders can maintain long-term abstinence from drugs if they develop coping strategies and are given support (e.g., positive peer support, exercise, meditation, motivational tools, and skills enhancement). Whatever the exact cause for the change in substance abuse patterns during reentry, offenders who are successful in reintegration are clearly also able to break from their past addictions.

Mental Health

Another aspect to successful reentry is access to mental health treatment. However, often offenders are reluctant to seek out treatment because they fear being labeled as weak or they feel the therapist cannot help them. Kenemore and Roldan state that one offender reported, "I would have never experienced interviewing or being interviewed by a therapist or any kind of therapist . . . because it appeared to me that [if] you had mental problems upstairs that you had to go see a psychiatrist or need therapy in any way" (2006, p. 16). Some offenders perceive social distance between themselves and their therapists, which further inhibits successful treatment. For instance, one offender recalled, "I've gone to the counselors where they just went to school for that [a degree in substance abuse counseling] and never drank, never smoke, never did this, never did that. And they're just sitting there trying to tell me something they learned out [of] a book" (pp. 16–17). In Kenemore and Roldan's study of male ex-offenders, the ex-offenders reported that treatment would be more likely to be effective if the therapist talked "straight" to them or challenged the ex-offenders on their behavior. Not uncommonly, however, ex-offenders reported reintegrating into the community without mental health support. One ex-offender stated, "No matter what programs or services are out there when you get out of prison, the main thing is to have someone to talk to and rely on as you sort out the changes" (p. 18). Another subject in Kenemore and Roldan's study reported, "Most people wanna be well. Most people realize that something is wrong for them to be there [prison]. Most people realize that what they did is wrong. But most of them don't come out and get affiliated with any sort of therapy or any sort of organization that is gonna refer them to therapy. So they just come out and do the best they can" (pp. 17–18).

This theme that male ex-offenders are often returning to their communities with unresolved mental health issues has also been found for female ex-offenders as well (Richie, 2001). Given the higher incidences of prior abuse (sexual and physical) for female offenders, female ex-offenders are suffering from many mental health problems including, but not limited to, depression, behavioral disorders, and posttraumatic stress disorder (Richie, 2001). One female ex-offender in Richie's study reported, "I have had mood problems all of my life. I hear voices at times, and I black out without knowing where I have been. Sometimes I feel so badly, I want to die. Yes, I've tried to kill myself and I am not ashamed to show you these cuts on my arms. It's the voices that tell me to do it. I know it would make my family feel really sad, but it is the only way I can think to solve my problems" (2001, p. 374). Another female offender detained in jail reported,

> I was seriously tripping (having a flashback) when I got arrested. The officer put his hands on me, and I went right back to the last time I was raped. And I fought like hell. I wasn't ever going to let a man touch me like that again. So I kicked him and tried to grab his gun and

> if I'd gotten it, I would have shot him. I know I would have. Ever since I've been here, I can't trust anyone. If someone moves towards me too fast, I'll just go off. And then I have nightmares all night long. I spend most of my time alone or in the bing [solitary confinement] because I just can't get along with people anymore. (Richie, 2001, p. 375)

As reported by N. La Vigne (2010), female ex-offenders struggle with mental health problems, with depression being one of the most prevalent mental health issues afflicting this group.

Aging Out

Numerous researchers focusing on the age-crime curve have noted that criminal involvement declines with age (Farrington, 1986; Gottfredson and Hirschi, 1990; Hare, McPherson, and Forth, 1988; Hirschi and Gottfredson, 1983). Involvement in crime for most individuals regardless of sex, race, or social class peaks in the adolescent years, typically between the ages of fifteen and seventeen, and declines in the early twenties and gradually more so thereafter (Blumstein et al., 1986; Elliott, 1994; West and Farrington, 1977). Eventually, around the age of forty, most individuals desist from future criminal activity. Thus, many offenders have a natural tendency to age out of crime. Perhaps as individuals age, they come to recognize that continued involvement in crime is no longer exciting or that the costs (e.g., formal punishments or informal social control punishments) of committing a crime outweigh the gain. For instance, in a qualitative study of persistent thieves, N. Shover (1996) explains that age can have an impact on a person's decisionmaking process. As one ages, he or she may be more self-reflective and engage in more positive rational decisionmaking about whether to continue in or desist from involvement in criminality. The age-crime decline may also be explained in part by neurobiological changes that are a natural part of the aging process. For example, R. E. Collins (2004) found that serotonin, a neurotransmitter that is found to be negatively associated with criminal behavior (e.g., lower serotonin levels are associated with increased potential for antisocial and criminal behavior), increases with age and that this increase may have a moderating effect on impulsive, aggressive, and violent behavior during middle age.

Some research has attributed successful reintegration to ex-offenders' aging out of crime. For example, A. L. Solomon, C. Gouvis, and M. Waul (2001), in a study of fourteen males and female ex-prisoners in Washington, DC, reported that one factor that was related to successful reentry was aging out. Several ex-offenders in their study contributed their successful reentry to getting older and recognizing that they were now ready to change. One subject reported, "When I came out of jail I was 33 years old, never had worked before, had no skills, no education and I tend [*sic*] to want to blame everybody. So I had to look at myself" (p. 7). Another subject in their study reported, "Allow other people to help you. . . . I'm 44 years old and I just started listening to somebody else" (p. 7). In an examination of five men in Ireland who had desisted from crime for a decade, B. Marsh (2009) identifies age as one factor related to desistance and, as a result, a contributor to successful reentry. One man in the sample reported, "The older I got I saw my life was going absolutely nowhere and I actually wanted it to be going somewhere, I had achieved nothing. That desire arrived as I got older, I wanted to be a man, I wanted to hold my own" (p. 29). In a study of female ex-offenders who successfully reintegrated, J. E. Cobbina reports that a subject claimed, "I'm getting too old for that. I don't want to be handcuffed again. And I'm just tired. I'm tired. I don't like to be told what to do all the time" (2009, p. 160). Perhaps as individuals mature, they reexamine their environment and the role they play in it differently. In a qualitative study of ex-convicts in the United Kingdom, S. Maruna (2001) reports on one subject who had matured, and this maturation appeared to be a pathway to desistance from future criminality. The subject stated, "My ideas, my habits, the way I see life has changed. I used to have no purpose to the day and I didn't try to do anything. Now, I have a purpose and I'm realistic. I know the pros and cons. I used to be angry . . . never used to enjoy things like nature . . . I'm more accepting now" (p. 35). Thus, the aging process, either by itself or in conjunction with other factors, can contribute to successful reentry.

Religion

Another factor that has emerged in the literature as a contributor to successful reentry is religion (Chu, 2007; Giordano, Cernkovich, and Rudolph, 2002; McRoberts, 2002; Schroeder and Frana, 2009). For some ex-offenders, finding faith or religion provided them the necessary direction and support to successfully reenter society. In a study conducted by Solomon, Gouvis, and Waul (2001), several ex-offenders cited faith as a factor in their successful transition into society. For instance, one subject stated, "God did for me what I couldn't do for myself," and a second subject reported, "I just used my faith, my discipline, and perseverance and it worked for me" (p. 7). Yet another subject stated,

> I got to the place and something said, man this is the time for you to take advantage that [sic] is being afforded to you. What I did right

then, I surrendered. My advice to anybody is for you to be successful, ex-convicts or whatever, you have got to surrender. I threw my hands up. From where I come, surrendering was a no-no. Today, I don't care if you call me a punk, I threw my hands up. And by me throwing my hands up, it allowed some things to come into my life and gave me an opportunity to do the things that I wanted to do. (p. 7)

R. D. Schroeder and J. F. Frana (2009), in an investigation of eleven men residing in a halfway house, also found religion to be a catalyst for successful reentry. One subject in their study reported,

That's one of the first times I was truly miserable. I was going through a divorce and I was drinking heavy and I meet a pastor that was right down the street from us and I started going to church—a Pentecostal church and I realized these people were sincere about what they were doing and I started going to church. I mean I quit drinking and everything and was doing quite well . . . I enjoyed having the Holy Ghost, I mean, I enjoyed having the spirit of God moving in me and God don't dwell in a defiled temple. (p. 733)

For other ex-offenders, becoming integrated with a church allows the individuals to be surrounded by prosocial associations, thereby replacing criminal associations, or allows ex-offenders to take better control of their problem behaviors such as anger or substance abuse (Giordano, Cernkovich, and Rudolph, 2002; Schroeder and Frana, 2009). One subject in Schroeder and Frana's study explains,

Anger and bad attitudes will block change from happening. . . . If you're angry you can't be happy. God don't want you to dwell on that. If you got that nasty shit in you, bad attitude, God ain't about being angry. I truly believe that. If there's any anger coming from you that's coming from you not God. . . .You don't see too many people that truly believe in living for God that walk around angry. They might get angry but they ain't going to stay angry. (2009, p. 727)

Thus, religion can provide ex-offenders with new perspectives of thinking and prosocial associations, instill new coping mechanisms to deal with strain, and serve as a foundation of support leading to successful reentry (Bradley, 1995; Seeman and McEwen, 1996).

Conclusion

In sum, the portraits of those reentering society are often much different than media portrayals. Those reentering society often face additional barriers to success based on their gender, race, or social class. Many ex-offenders clearly succeed in their transition from past criminality to future law-abiding behavior. Further, a multitude of factors contribute to successful reentry including adequate housing, gainful employment, substance abuse treatment, mental health treatment, the aging process, and religion.

In the following chapter, we present an extensive overview of the challenges that ex-offenders face on their journey to reentry success.

3

Managing Reentry Needs and Challenges

THE EXPECTATION BY MANY IN SOCIETY, BOTH CITIZENS AND politicians, is that ex-offenders should easily reintegrate upon release from prison or another community corrections sanction. For many on the outside of the experience, successful reentry is a choice, and ex-offenders are simply choosing not to succeed. An example of how choice is attributed to criminal behavior can be viewed in the 2002 HBO documentary entitled *Small Town Ecstasy*. The audience is introduced to a family living in California whose members, including the father, Scott, are using ecstasy. The film portrays Scott as having the ability to quit the use but does not due to his personal problems. In fact, his use spurs other personal problems including his arrest for possessing the drug. Following his arrest, he still is using ecstasy. However, the arrest of Scott served as a wake-up call for his children, and his son and daughter eventually choose to stop using. With portrayals such as this in the media, politicians and the public understandably attribute successful reentry, or failure in Scott's case, to a choice. However, by adopting such a viewpoint, these groups are failing to not only acknowledge but also recognize the sheer complexity of successful reentry.

While ex-offenders may be grateful for their freedom and opportunity for a second chance, successful reintegration is by no means an easy task to achieve. One does not have to look any further than YouTube and enter in a search such as "challenges leaving prison" to find a wide range of ex-offenders candidly discussing the obstacles before them as they reintegrated back into society. The 2004 PBS documentary *A Hard Straight* is perhaps one of the best gritty introductions to prisoner reentry. The film centers on three released prisoners (i.e., a gang member, hustler, and drug dealer) who struggle to succeed outside the prison walls and go "straight." From fear, lack of income, lack of job opportunities, and an absence of social and community support, the ex-offenders struggle to find the pathway to successful reintegration. Thus, there emerges not simply one challenge that stymies ex-offenders' progress in successfully reintegrating, but rather a wide range of challenges. Any one of these challenges experienced in solo would be difficult for the average law-abiding citizen to overcome but add in the ex-offender label and stigma associated with their status, and these men and women have enormous hurdles to overcome in their quest to succeed.

As mentioned in the previous chapters, research on offender reentry over the past thirty years has demonstrated that offenders' ability to reintegrate successfully is hindered by numerous obstacles such as difficulty in obtaining employment, acquiring housing, and being admitted to higher education (Allender, 2004; Cowan and Fionda, 1994; Harlow, 2003; Harris and Keller, 2005; Hunt, Bowers, and Miller, 1973; Nagin and Waldfogel, 1998; Paylor, 1995; Rodriguez and Brown, 2003; Starr, 2002; Whelan, 1973) along with serious social and medical problems (Petersilia, 2003). Newly released offenders encounter stigmatization (Bahn and Davis, 1991; J. Brown, 2004a; Funk, 2004; Steffensmeier and Kramer, 1980; Tewksbury, 2005), lose social standing in their communities (Chiricos, Jackson, and Waldo, 1972), and are in need of social support (Cullen, 1994; La Vigne, Visher, and Castro, 2004; Lurigio, 1996) and substance abuse and mental health treatment (Petersilia, 2003). The above-mentioned challenges are just some of the countless ubiquitous challenges faced by ex-offenders. In this chapter, we will discuss the myriad challenges that offenders face upon reentry. These challenges include, but are not limited to, housing, income, employment, education, substance abuse, mental illness, physical health, transportation, social acceptance, personal relationships, debt, legal complications, loss of constitutional rights, and temptation to fall back into old habits and re-offend. We should note that many of the challenges that are discussed are co-occurring. That is, typically, offenders are experiencing multiple challenges simultaneously, which further inhibits their ability to successfully reenter society.

Housing

Housing has been identified as one of the most difficult obstacles ex-offenders encounter in their reentry (Corden, Kuipers, and Wilson, 1978; Cowan and Fionda, 1994; Graffam, Shinkfield, and Hardcastle, 2008; Harding and Harding, 2006; Helfgott, 1997; Levenson and Hern, 2007; Paylor, 1995; Petersilia, 2003; Starr, 2002; Taxman, Young, and

Bryne, 2002; Wodahl, 2006). Ex-offenders often have limited credit, rental history, and finances, which restrict their housing opportunities and options (Helfgott, 1997). R. McLean and M. D. Thompson (2007) report that ex-offenders are saddled with a large amount of debt upon release. This debt includes supervision fees (e.g., jail, probation, and mandatory urine screens), court costs, victim restitution, and child support (McLean and Thompson, 2007; Shivy et al., 2007). The researchers further explain that "people released from prisons and jails typically have insufficient resources to pay their debts to their children, victims, and the criminal justice system" (McLean and Thompson, 2007, p. 7). Many of these released offenders come from lower socioeconomic backgrounds as "two-thirds of people detained in jails report annual incomes under $12,000 prior to arrest" (McLean and Thompson, 2007, p. 7). The vast majority of ex-offenders are released with a small amount of funds, termed "gate money" or "release money" ranging from $50 to $200, from the state (Wilson, 2007). For many ex-offenders, this is all the money they may have to survive on upon release as they have no other savings. Thus, the limited income and incurred debt further compound their inability to obtain housing at all, let alone affordable housing.

Some ex-offenders are fortunate enough to be able to return to their family home or reside with family members upon release. In a study of parolees conducted by M. Nelson, P. Deess, and C. Allen (1999), the researchers found that approximately 80 percent of the ex-offenders lived with family members following their release. While some ex-offenders may return to the home of their families, this option is often not available to many. If ex-offenders' family members are actively engaging in criminal behavior, then the family home is not a suitable residence for them when they are released on parole. In other cases, a breakdown has occurred in the family structure (e.g., marriage, relationships with other family members) often due to the ex-offenders' incarceration (Clear, 2007; Fontaine and Biess, 2012; Martinez and Christian, 2009). Perhaps, the family supported the ex-offender for many years, but after his or her latest conviction and sentence, family members severed ties to the ex-offender. Housing is such an obstacle for ex-offenders returning to their communities that C. G. Roman and J. Travis (2006) suggest that the question for these offenders quickly becomes "Where will I sleep tomorrow?" (p. 389). For many ex-offenders, the answer to that question is the street, and soon ex-offenders find themselves homeless (Geller and Curtis, 2011; Hamilton, Kigerl, and Hays, 2013; Roman and Travis, 2006). Without suitable housing, ex-offenders must resort to being homeless or residing in an environment (i.e., a high-crime community) that undermines their likelihood of successful rehabilitation and reintegration (Bradley et al., 2001; Clear, 2007; Kirk, 2009, 2012; Kubrin and Stewart, 2006; Rodriguez and Brown, 2003). D. S. Kirk (2012) examined residential change of parolees after Hurricane Katrina and found that parolees three years postrelease who returned to different neighborhoods in New Orleans than where they had resided during their conviction were less likely to reoffend than parolees who returned to their original neighborhoods. This finding suggests that obtaining housing is not all that matters for ex-offenders, but the characteristics of the particular community and situational and environmental context that the ex-offenders are returning to are also critical for their success. E. J. Wodahl (2006) further adds that many ex-offenders are returning to rural communities, as opposed to urban, and face even greater difficulties in acquiring and maintaining stable housing.

Many landlords are reluctant to rent to ex-offenders due to their fear for community safety or losing current tenants who may become fearful of being a neighbor to an ex-offender (Clark, 2007; Harding and Harding, 2006; Helfgott, 1997). Registered sex offenders in particular face this obstacle, not only from potential landlords but also from the authorities themselves as many states have passed legislation that further restricts their residency (i.e., not near schools, day cares, playgrounds, and parks) (Barnes et al., 2009; Chajewski and Mercado, 2009; Grubesic, Murray, and Mack, 2011). Unfortunately, sex offenders often do not have a full understanding of their residency restrictions (Tewksbury and Copes, 2013). These residency restrictions for sex offenders limit their access to affordable housing options (Levenson and Hern, 2007). J. B. Helfgott (1997) surveyed 196 property managers in the Seattle area and found that 67 percent of property managers conducted background checks on potential renters, and the crimes of particular concern to them were violent offenses (49 percent), sex offenses (37 percent), drug offenses (19 percent), all felonies (9 percent), arson (9 percent), property offenses (7 percent), and domestic violence (6 percent). Results from a survey of 138 sex offenders revealed that these offenders view such legislation as a hindrance to their acquisition of, obviously, housing but also employment and even positive social relationships (Mercado, Alvarez, and Levenson, 2008). M. Stromberg (2007) refers to this group as being "locked up, then locked out" (p. 20) since sex offenders are excluded from many housing options due to fear for community safety. P. A. Zandbergen and T. C. Hart, in a case study of ex-offenders in Florida, found "that housing options for registered sex offenders within urban residential areas are limited to only 5% of potentially available parcels and that bus stop restrictions impact the amount of livable area the most, followed by daycares, schools, parks, and attractions. The limited options to establish residency exist mostly in low-density rural areas" (2006, p. 1). Thus, sex offenders may be pushed out to rural communities, which pose their own unique challenges for successful reentry (see Wodahl, 2006).

Drug offenders are another group whose housing options may be limited more so than other ex-offenders. Status as a convicted drug offender often results in denial of federally assisted housing, a policy that has an impact on thousands of ex-offenders (US Government Accountability Office, 2005). Not uncommonly, ex-offenders who were convicted of a drug-related crime are ineligible for federally subsidized housing for at least three years (Mukamal, 2000). Ex-offenders may find that the only place they can find housing is in impoverished neighborhoods where they are less likely to find employment—another key obstacle to successful offender reentry (Bradley et al., 2001; Petersilia, 2001a; Visher, Baer, and Naser, 2006).

Employment

One outcome of the get-tough-on-crime and post-9/11 policies is that many ex-offenders have few employment prospects (Henry and Jacobs, 2007; Lucken and Ponte, 2008). The unemployment rate for ex-offenders is estimated at 25 to 40 percent (Petersilia, 2003). J. Schmitt and K. Warner, using Bureau of Justice Statistics data, report:

> In 2008, the United States had between 12 and 14 million ex-offenders of working age. Because a prison record or felony conviction greatly lowers ex-offenders' prospects in the labor market, we estimate that this large population lowered the total male employment rate that year by 1.5 to 1.7 percentage points. In GDP [gross domestic product] terms, these reductions in employment cost the U.S. economy between $57 and $65 billion in lost output. (2010, p. 1)

Other researchers have noted that possessing a felony record disqualifies the ex-offender from certain occupations (Petersilia, 2001a) and that criminal background checks create barriers to employment for ex-offenders (Harris and Kellar, 2005). The frequency of background checks for ex-offenders has increased significantly following the terrorist attacks of September 11, 2001 (Shivy et al., 2007).

H. J. Holzer, S. Raphael, and M. A. Stoll (2003) explain that ex-offenders have several characteristics that limit their ability to obtain employment or high-paying jobs such as limited education and cognitive skills and limited legal work experience. M. T. Berg and B. M. Huebner add that "many offenders lack much-needed work skills, educational qualifications, and a stable history of employment" (2011, p. 388). On the other hand, several researchers have found that ex-offenders who participated in educational programs while incarcerated have lower recidivism rates upon release (Gerber and Fritsch, 1995; Jancic, 1998; Jensen and Reed, 2007; Steurer and Smith, 2003; Zgoba, Haugebrook, and Jenkins, 2008).

A limited education further inhibits the ability of ex-offenders to obtain even an unskilled job (Freeman, 2003). In terms of deficits in education, the picture is stark since almost two-thirds of offenders and ex-offenders dropped out of high school (Travis, Solomon, and Waul, 2001). The National Institute for Literacy (2001) reports that seven in ten prison inmates function at the lowest levels of prose and numeric literacy. A. E. Hirsch and colleagues (2002) state that nearly 50 percent of offenders are "functionally illiterate." Additionally, C. W. Harlow (2003) reports that while 18 percent of the US population has not graduated from high school or completed their GED, roughly 40 percent of incarcerated adults have not.

Obtaining further education often proves difficult. The prohibition of the use of Pell Grants by the federal government for incarcerated offenders in 1994 in state and federal prisons further hindered offenders' access to higher education and their ability to obtain a college degree (Erisman and Contardo, 2005; Heinrich, 2000; Lockwood et al., 2012; Stevens and Ward, 1997). Though other sources of funds besides Pell Grants are available, upon release from prison, ex-offenders, particularly those with drug histories, have difficulties obtaining any financial aid to pursue a college education, or even knowing that financial aid is an option available to them (Heinrich, 2000). With the access to higher education blocked by an inability to obtain funds, incarcerated offenders lose an opportunity to develop skills that would enhance their likelihood of securing employment.

After long-term imprisonment, many ex-offenders find they lack the skills to search for employment via the Internet or newspapers or even fill out a job application. Many of these released ex-offenders lack the skills to construct an e-mail, utilize e-mail, or even create a resume in a word-processing program. Without a little technological savvy, their efforts to find legitimate legal employment are further hampered. If ex-offenders do secure a coveted interview for a job, they are often deficient in life skills such as knowing what to wear to the interview and how to prepare for it, knowledge that would ensure success for most job candidates (J. Brown, 2004b; Helfgott, 1997). Thus, many ex-offenders rely on personal connections to find a job (Visher, La Vigne, and Travis,

2004). However, ex-offenders often do not have many prosocial contacts that they can rely on for job referrals or may lack the ability to form social networks that could assist them in their search for employment (Shivy et al., 2007). Further, if ex-offenders are successful in landing a job, they have a "limited knowledge of workplace culture and need to develop certain interpersonal and conflict resolution skills to be able to retain a job" (Heinrich, 2000, p. 5). The absence of exhibiting proper social skills in a work environment stems from their lack of an extensive, or any, past legal work history.

Additionally, many employers are reluctant to hire ex-offenders (Buikhuisen and Dijksterhuis, 1971; Clear, 2007; Graffam, Shinkfield, and Hardcastle, 2008; Holzer, 1996; Holzer, Raphael, and Stoll, 2003). J. Travis, A. Solomon, and M. Waul report, "The stigma attached to incarceration makes it difficult for ex-prisoners to be hired" (2001, p. 31). Ex-offenders have reported experiencing discrimination in regard to employment (LeBel, 2012). Helfgott (1997) found that 95 percent of employers inquire about criminal history on applications; however, only 23 percent indicated that they had made the decision not to hire someone because of a criminal conviction, 24 percent had knowingly hired an ex-offender, the majority of whom (68 percent) said they had a positive experience with the ex-offender employee, and only 6 percent said they would not under any circumstances hire an ex-offender. Other studies suggest that employers are willing to give ex-offenders a chance; however, they are more comfortable hiring them if they have at least some prior record of successful employment or if their convicted crime was minor (Atkin and Armstrong, 2013). J. Fahey, C. Roberts, and L. Engel (2006), in a focus group study of twenty-eight employers in the Boston area, found that employers were often reluctant to be the first place of employment for an ex-offender. That is, employers were more comfortable providing ex-offenders with their second or third job upon release as prior experience would allow the ex-offenders to prove their value through an established employment track record. Additional concerns for the hiring of ex-offenders by employers surround the issue of legal liability (Lucken and Ponte, 2008). While all employers can be held liable for employee misconduct, a heightened sense of concern can be found among many employers on this issue when considering the hiring of ex-offenders, with certain types of crime of more concern to employers than others, in particular violent crime and property crimes such as theft and embezzlement (Helfgott, 1997). Thus, many employers may be reluctant to hire ex-offenders, not due to the desire not to hire them, but out of fear for being on the reverse end of a lawsuit on the grounds of negligent hiring. Employers are aware of an ex-offender's criminal history when the individual is hired, and this knowledge could more easily be used against the employer in a lawsuit—particularly if the ex-offender commits a similar crime while on the job for which he or she was convicted. Employment discrimination is another concern for this group (Holzer, Raphael, and Stoll, 2003). Holzer, Raphael, and Stoll explain, "Most ex-offenders are minorities—nearly half are African-American, and nearly a fifth are Latino or Asian. To the extent that minorities continue to suffer labor market discrimination, this will further impede the ability of ex-offenders to gain employment or earn higher wages" (2003, p. 5).

Previous research has revealed that racial discrimination in hiring is indeed a problem for minorities (Toth, Crews, and Burton, 2008). Retailers such as Abercrombie and Fitch have come under fire for discrimination against minorities in hiring for their stores (Leung, 2009). In a qualitative study of ex-offenders reentering the workforce, V. A. Shivy and colleagues (2007) report that one participant felt that racism and discrimination were significant barriers to obtaining legal employment. The participant reported,

> It's easier for White people. . . . I know what I am talking about, because I had somebody hire me straight out of prison. Didn't know me from jack, didn't know me from anything. . . . The first day I got out, I had a job, and here I am convicted of property crimes all my life. And I had some very, very good friends that I had made when I was incarcerated and, you know, a couple of them were Black, and they got out long before I did, and they still aren't working. . . . And, I learned the hard way that this is a society that is geared toward racism. It's not easy for me to say that because of where I was raised. (p. 471)

Similarly, a subject in Helfgott's (1997) study indicated that he had experienced much more discrimination in general as a result of his being African American than he had as a result of his ex-offender status.

Ex-offenders often experience legal obstacles that do not permit them to be considered for employment in particular occupations such as health care or education (Heinrich, 2000; Petersilia, 2003, 2005). Unless an ex-offender has had previous employment experience in the health-care field and obtains government waivers, then the ex-offender will be excluded from any form of employment in the health-care field (Heinrich, 2000). Other common employment restrictions for ex-offenders include government positions (e.g., political office, civil service jobs), criminal justice occupations (e.g., law enforcement officers, prosecutors, correctional officers), teaching positions at the K–12 level, child-care work, and private security (Heinrich, 2000). J. Petersilia (2005) adds that ex-offenders are often excluded from unionized jobs and face additional obstacles in meeting licensing requirements for certain job positions ranging from haircutting to even garbage collecting—those with a felony conviction are often barred from obtaining a barber's license or a commercial driver's license.

Further complicating the quest for legal employment is the formal state guidelines requiring offenders to obtain employment within a specified period of time. In Washington State, for example, residents of work release programs are required to obtain employment within ten days per Department of Corrections policy. As one can imagine, particularly in the recent state of the economy, ex-offenders find this a formidable task. With the national unemployment rate looming large at around 8 percent for the average US citizen without a criminal record, ex-offenders are at a further disadvantage in their job hunt (Bureau of Labor Statistics, 2013). After all, employers who are hiring are being inundated with applications from highly qualified individuals who lost their jobs and are also in the job market. Employers can be more selective in whom they decide to hire, more so now than in the past. This sentiment was echoed in research conducted by Fahey, Roberts, and Engel (2006), who found that employers, predictably, viewed job candidates with a criminal record to be less desirable than job candidates who did not possess a criminal record.

Substance Abuse

Previous research has established a link between substance use and criminal involvement (Anglin and Perrochet, 1998; Inciardi, 1992; Inciardi et al., 1996; MacCoun and Reuter, 2001). With substance abuse being a significant factor in the onset of criminal involvement for many offenders, it also poses a significant hurdle to reentry success for ex-offenders (Travis, Solomon, and Waul, 2001; Wodahl, 2006). A. L. Solomon and colleagues state that "more than two-thirds (68 percent) of all jail inmates meet the criteria for substance abuse or dependence, as defined by the Diagnostic and Statistical Manual of Mental Disorders, fourth edition. In comparison, only nine percent of the U.S. population abuse or are dependent on drugs or alcohol" (2008, p. 32). Other researchers have reported that, in general, up to 75 percent of all ex-offenders have a history of substance abuse or addiction (Travis, Solomon, and Waul, 2001).

Research has revealed that ex-offenders who participate in treatment while incarcerated and in community-based substance abuse programs after release have lower levels of substance use and lower rates of recidivism (Anglin et al., 2002; Jannetta, Dodd, and Elderbroom, 2011; Miller and Miller, 2010; Visher and Courtney, 2007; Wexler et al., 1999; Zhang, Roberts, and Callanan, 2006). S. X. Zhang, R. E. L. Roberts, and V. J. Callanan (2006), who examined the Preventing Parolee Crime Program in California—a program that provided a wide range of services to parolees including substance abuse assistance—found this program modestly reduced recidivism and parole absconding.

Further complicating reentry for jail inmates is their relatively low levels of participation in drug/alcohol treatment programs while incarcerated (Solomon et al., 2008). Part of this problem may stem from the fact that "less than one-fifth of convicted jail inmates who meet the criteria for abuse or dependence receive formal treatment or other programs after admission to jail" (Crayton et al., 2010, p. 21). The lack of access to formal substance abuse programs for jail inmates may stem from cuts to state correctional budgets (Scott-Hayward, 2009). That is, given the cost of offering such treatment programs and the transiency of the jail populations, correctional administrators, when faced with making cuts, may decide to first cut jail programs. However, for those inmates fortunate enough to receive treatment, how long they are able to participate in such programs has a definite impact on their success post incarceration.

The length of time an ex-offender has spent in treatment appears to be a significant factor in reentry success. Researchers have found that the longer offenders participate in treatment the less likely these offenders will commit future crimes (French et al., 1993; Lewis and Ross, 1994; Simpson, Joe, and Brown, 1997). D. D. Simpson and colleagues (1999) report that those with severe substance abuse problems have better success even with only ninety days of treatment. However, even for those ex-offenders fortunate enough to have received treatment during their incarceration, D. Brazzell and N. G. La Vigne (2009) point out that the stress following incarceration due to attempting to successfully reintegrate back into the community results in ex-offenders with substance abuse issues being at a high risk for relapse.

Ex-offenders with substance abuse histories (the majority of the ex-offender population) making the transition from incarceration to the community are in the precarious position of having to manage extraordinary stressors without engaging in old habits of substance use and abuse as a way to manage everyday stressors and problems in living. A recent qualitative study of ex-offenders conducted by L. A. Phillips and M. Lindsay (2011) further supports the idea that many ex-offenders facing the stresses of reentry are reverting to drug and alcohol use. In their study, one subject reported, "I don't cope. I did when I was younger, but once I found a drug, I just run to it. I dealt with so much at a young age, so it was easier to avoid things and get temporary relief from drugs.

Every time I have a problem, it solves it. I want something to take over my guilt and shame, but it gets worse" (p. 145). Another subject reported, "To tell you the truth, I didn't really handle it. . . . I could have handled it. I should have, but I didn't. If I don't feel like coping or dealing, I take Xanax. I don't really cope. I just use" (p. 145). Additionally, another subject simply reported, "Every problem I've ever had, I've drowned in drugs and alcohol" (p. 146).

Substance abuse problems often interfere with an ex-offender's ability to obtain employment or maintain employment. In a study conducted by Heinrich that utilized focus groups, one participant reported,

> I would just call in and make up lame excuses, because I wanted to get high even though I knew that I was supposed to be at work. After I thought about it, after I got fired, I thought it wasn't even worth it. I could have just gone in and waited until I got off to do what I had to do. But I would think about what the guys would be doing on the streets and who has this and who has that. It would be like a craving that actually just calls you and you don't want to hear anything else, so you have to go and feed that hunger. (2000, p. 6)

Clearly, the stress and strain of reentry pulls some ex-offenders into familiar, yet dysfunctional, coping patterns.

Not all ex-offenders have access to community-based treatment programs during reentry (Crayton et al., 2010; Thompson, 2004). A. Crayton and colleagues explain that "lack of insurance, conviction-based bans on receiving public assistance, or the lack of available treatment can create substantial barriers to post-release substance abuse treatment" (2010, p. 21). Without access to formal treatment, these offenders may come to rely on their parole officer, for example, for assistance (Thompson, 2004). The CCO may very well be the only prosocial individual in the life of the ex-offender, and thus, the ex-offender really must rely on the parole officer for support and guidance. Unfortunately, CCOs generally have a large client caseload and are not trained treatment providers, which clearly inhibits their ability to navigate ex-offenders onto the pathway of recovery from addiction or abstinence from drug and alcohol consumption. With community-based substance abuse programs being unreachable or unattainable for many ex-offenders, many researchers have found that these offenders will continue consuming drugs and alcohol upon release. For instance, N. La Vigne, C. Visher, and J. Castro (2004) found that 11 percent of their sample of 205 ex-offenders in Chicago consumed alcohol and 8 percent used drugs within eight months of release from prison. Some ex-offenders clearly need assistance with the prevention of relapse into alcohol and drug use (Prendergast, Wellisch, and Wong, 1996).

The problems associated with substance abuse spread into other challenge areas during reentry such as employment (Shivy et al., 2007). Therefore, the challenge of overcoming substance abuse should not be viewed in isolation but rather as a factor that seeps into other areas of an individual's life, further complicating successful reentry. Drug addiction is indeed a struggle for some ex-offenders (McKean and Raphael, 2002) and many of these individuals are also in need of mental health support (Lurigio, 1996; White, Goldkamp, and Campbell, 2006). The stress of successfully reintegrating into society is high, and some ex-offenders resort to drastic measures such as suicide in response to the stress and strain that they are experiencing during this tumultuous time (Biles, Harding, and Walker, 1999; Binswanger et al., 2007).

Mental Health

Two events at the federal level, although well intentioned, led to decreased services for people with mental health and substance abuse issues. In 1963, the Community Mental Health Centers Act was signed into law, the provisions of which led to the deinstitutionalization of the mentally ill, removing them from in-residence treatment centers to community-based treatment programs (Solomon et al., 2008). Then the federal court decision of *Wyatt v. Stickney* in 1972 stated that mentally ill and mentally retarded individuals have a constitutional right to a minimum level of care and treatment in institutions. In other words, the mental institutions had to do more than "warehouse" residents. This requirement resulted in some states releasing residents to community-based treatment facilities because the cost of providing minimum services (i.e., treatment and staffing) to those residents within the institution was cost prohibitive (Perez, Leifman, and Estrada, 2003). However, these new outpatient services were extremely inadequate. A. Perez, S. Leifman, and A. Estrada explain,

> Unfortunately, many states saw deinstitutionalization as an opportunity to save money rather than an opportunity to improve their mental health services. States closed down hospitals condemned for failure to meet the minimum constitutional standards of care for people with mental illnesses, but they did not use the money saved to develop community-based outpatient treatment centers or much-needed social services. The result has been nothing short of disaster. (2003, p. 63)

The impact of deinstitutionalization has resulted in many mentally ill individuals being shifted from state hospitals to the criminal justice system.

According to the National Association of State Mental Health Program Directors Research Institute (2000), more than 300,000 individuals with mental illness are incarcerated in jails. Crayton and colleagues (2010) report that approximately 24 percent of those incarcerated in jails show symptomatic evidence of mental illness. Persons with mental illness are overrepresented in jails and prisons, with 6–8 percent having a serious mental illness in state prisons, 7.2 percent in jails, and many more that have had contact with the criminal justice system but were not incarcerated (National Alliance on Mental Illness, 2008). L. Davis and S. Pacchiana (2004) report that the prevalence of schizophrenia and bipolar disorder are about one to five times greater in the prison population than the general population.

Over the past few decades, policy changes in the criminal justice system have resulted in those with mental illnesses being even more likely to enter into the criminal justice system and also become ensnared in it (Lurigio and Swartz, 2000). With correctional administrators unable to offer comprehensive services to those suffering from such problems due to budgetary constraints, the mental health problems for these individuals often worsen. With deteriorating mental health disorders, many sufferers act out during their incarceration terms and wind up accruing numerous disciplinary infractions, which only extend their stay in the correctional system (Kondo, 2000).

Additionally, get-tough-on-crime policies have resulted in tougher punishments for offenders and have spawned the creation of supermax prisons, which impose a strict form of near-total solitary confinement (Haney, 2003). C. Haney states that "empirical research on solitary and supermax-like confinement has consistently and unequivocally documented the harmful consequences of living in these kinds of environments" (2003, p. 130). For instance, confinement in supermax facilities and in extended solitary confinement in other facilities has resulted in a wide range of psychological problems exhibited by incarcerated individuals such as cognitive dysfunction, paranoia, and depression (Brodsky and Scogin, 1988; Grassian, 1983; Miller and Young, 1997). Since the emphasis in these facilities is on punishment and surveillance, rehabilitation is nonexistent. Thus, any offenders who had a preexisting mental illness prior to incarceration in these facilities would likely have their problems exacerbated by this type of confinement. Moreover, if offenders did not have a preexisting mental illness prior to incarceration, they may develop one due to the experiences of ongoing solitary confinement (Haney, 2003). Further complicating successful reentry for those incarcerated with mental illness is often inadequate transition planning when they are released from jail or prison (Osher, Steadman, and Barr, 2003). These offenders need a wide range of available services that will meet their needs during reentry. Unfortunately, the lack of adequate transition planning for this group increases their likelihood of recidivating. Some researchers have found recidivism rates as high as 70 percent for those ex-offenders with mental illnesses returning to their communities after incarceration (Ventura et al., 1998).

Mental health issues are indeed a challenge for many ex-offenders attempting to reenter society. Travis, Solomon, and Waul (2001) report that approximately 16 percent of all ex-offenders have a diagnosable mental disorder. The criminal justice system in all areas seems ill equipped to help those with mental illnesses on many levels (Petrila, Ridgely, and Borum, 2003). For many ex-offenders, mental health problems are not isolated but are experienced in tandem with other problems such as substance abuse. The mental health problems also cross over and present challenges for ex-offenders in other areas of their reentry such as obtaining employment, finding housing, and reestablishing family connections (Fontaine, Roman, and Burt, 2010). Thus, mental health problems often inhibit ex-offenders' ability to made strides toward success since these problems impact other aspects of their reentry.

Physical Health

For many ex-offenders, coping with physical health problems adds another layer of challenge to their bid for successful reentry (Thompson, 2004). For a larger portion of ex-offenders, physical health issues seem to be more of a serious problem for not only the ex-offender but his or her community (Patterson, 2013). J. Jannetta, H. Dodd, and B. Elderbroom explain,

> The jail population experiences much higher rates of chronic and infectious diseases than the general population, and over a third of jail inmates report a current medical issue needing attention. Individuals passing through jails account for a substantial share of the total U.S. population infected with tuberculosis, hepatitis, and HIV/AIDS, presenting a significant opportunity to improve public health. However, fewer than half of all jail inmates nationally receive medical examinations when admitted, and few of those living with infectious diseases receive care after release. (2001, p. 6)

Besides infectious diseases, a high rate of chronic diseases such as asthma and heart problems plague the jail population, and unfortunately, these diseases are rarely treated during the offenders' stay in the jail (Crayton et al., 2010).

Physical health problems and their treatment are particularly challenging as most ex-offenders lack quality health insurance and, thus, must rely on Medicaid for treatment of any health problems upon release. However, relying on Medicaid for support for physical health issues is problematic. Solomon and colleagues state, "A period of incarceration often suspends or terminates benefits depending on length of stay and can disqualify inmates from Medicaid eligibility. Activating or reinstating benefits and restoring eligibility can take several months, interrupting access to prescription drugs and putting individuals at high risk of relapse" (2008, p. 16). Thus, many ex-offenders are not receiving adequate health care to treat their ailments, which causes these offenders additional stress and strain.

The health problems experienced by ex-offenders during reentry often affect other aspects of the integration process such as housing and employment. For instance, in a study of approximately 1,000 male and female ex-offenders, K. Mallik-Kane and C. A. Visher (2008) found that many in their sample with health problems had difficulties in maintaining stable housing after release. Additionally, the researchers discovered that women with physical health problems demonstrated an uptick in residential mobility about eight to ten months after release and were more likely to report living with antisocial individuals (i.e., ex-offenders or drug/alcohol users) during this period. Further, the researchers uncovered that those ex-offenders suffering from physical health problems had greater difficulties in securing employment, and that men in the sample with such problems were more likely to supplement their income through illegal means than their female counterparts. Many ex-offenders in the sample had physical problems that were so chronic that these problems prevented them from finding work, thereby requiring them to rely on disability assistance.

Physical health problems can also contribute to feelings of stigmatization and exclusion that can alter an ex-offender's perception of self in ways that can become an obstacle to success. For example, in a study of 200 female prisoners in Russia, D. Moran (2012) found that one of the effects of imprisonment for the women in the sample was missing teeth resulting from poor and invasive dental treatment that resulted in tooth extractions while in prison. These women noted anxiety and shame associated with the missing teeth upon release that contributed to feelings of being stigmatized and excluded. These ex-offenders saw their missing teeth as a conspicuous stigma—a telltale sign like other visible markers (e.g., tattoos) that they had been in prison—and in their minds this marked them as different and was seen by the women as a disadvantage in the reentry process.

In sum, physical health problems are inhibiting ex-offenders in their efforts to successfully reenter society, but efforts are being made to mitigate this factor. J. Myers and colleagues (2005) report on an innovative case management plan in California for males and females leaving prison designed to reduce ex-offenders' chances of acquiring HIV. Initial findings from their study yielded favorable results with reductions in participants' involvement in risky behavior (unprotected sex or the use of drugs/alcohol during sex) that could lead to the acquisition of HIV. Thus, support for existing, or prevention of, health problems may help to facilitate successful reentry. Without community and health support for these individuals, the additional burden they carry in regard to their health may inevitably put them at greater risk for reoffending.

Family

In a report conducted on behalf of the Vera Institute of Justice, M. DiZerega states that "family support plays an important role in successful reentry" (2011 p. 4). Empirical research has demonstrated that family can play an important role in the ex-offenders' success or failure postrelease (Aday and Krabill, 2011; Naser and Visher, 2006; Shapiro and Schwartz, 2001). Families can provide emotional and financial support, referrals to employers, child and elder care, housing, transportation, positive reinforcement, someone to monitor health conditions, and a source of a reconnection to the community (DiZerega, 2011). C. Visher and S. M. E. Courtney (2007), in a study of ex-prisoners interviewed three months postrelease in Ohio, report that ex-offenders identified family support as being the most important thing keeping them grounded and out of prison. Previous research has indicated that family support for ex-offenders can contribute to successful employment, reduced substance use, lower rates of depression, and lower rates of recidivism (Berg and Huebner, 2011; Ekland-Olson et al., 1983; La Vigne, Visher, and Castro, 2004; Martinez, 2007; Nelson, Deess, and Allen, 1999; Petersilia, 2003; Sullivan et al., 2002; Visher, La Vigne, and Travis, 2004). Nelson, Deess, and Allen, in their interview of forty-nine male and female prisoners released from the New York State Department of Corrections, found that "people with strong supportive families are more likely to succeed than those with weak or no family support . . . [and] that self-defined family support was the strongest predictor of individual success" (1999, p. 10). In a study of 413 male prisoners returning to East Coast cities, subjects reported that they relied heavily on family members for housing, financial, and emotional support (Naser and La Vigne, 2006). More recently, M. T. Berg and B. M. Huebner (2011), in a study of 401 paroled men in a midwestern state, found that ex-offenders who had good quality ties to family members were less likely to reoffend and more likely to be employed.

As mentioned earlier, many family relationships become strained due to offenders' absence, often prolonged, while incarcerated (Clear, 2007; Petersilia, 2003). Additionally, if strain or conflict with family members existed prior to the incarceration of the offender, upon release, family members may not be willing to resolve this conflict (Petersilia, 2003). Thus, reentry for ex-offenders with strained family relations creates an additional layer of difficulty and stress complicating successful reentry (J. Brown, 2004a). Family strain is a particularly difficult problem for female offenders to overcome as they are often incarcerated in prisons located farther away from family, which results in a breakdown of family bonds (Belknap, 2007).

Further complicating the situation for ex-offenders, many of their family members may have criminal histories or substance problems, which can limit family members' ability to steer the returning ex-offender onto the pathway to reentry success (J. Brown, 2004a; Visher, Baer, and Naser, 2006). For some ex-offenders returning home, stress can be caused if family members are expecting the individual to contribute financially to the household, or parents are pressuring the individual to pursue further education or continually stressing the merits of a good work ethic (Breese, Ra'el, and Grant, 2000). In a study conducted by J. R. Breese, K. Ra'el, and G. K. Grant (2000), the researchers discovered that a major obstacle for ex-offenders to successfully reentering their communities was the pull that ex-offenders had toward criminal peer groups. The researchers ultimately concluded that family did not play a role in ex-offenders' success and suggest that prisoners may do better transitioning to a halfway house before returning home.

For both incarcerated males and females, ties with children are often disrupted. Many incarcerated offenders have limited contact or visits from their children during their confinement (Clear, 2007; Mumola, 2000). Additionally, many ex-offenders lose custody of their children while incarcerated. Therefore, upon release, many ex-offenders are consumed with regaining custody of their children. For those ex-offenders who did not lose custody of their children, some still retain a sense of fear that losing custody is a distinct possibility (Shivy et al., 2007). M. Pinard and A. C. Thompson explain that "adoption laws add pressure to returning mothers by reducing the amount of time that parents have to reunite with their children before permanently losing custody" (2006, p. 600). Other ex-offenders may suddenly be burdened with the responsibility of securing child care as well as fulfilling the other responsibilities that come with raising children, and this added obligation can complicate their successful reentry (Shivy et al., 2007). The issue of child care and its impact on successful reentry may be more of a problem for female ex-offenders as opposed to their male counterparts (Harm and Phillips, 2001). Shivy and colleagues report that "many female offenders have their children returned to them immediately upon release—before they successfully have secured housing or employment" (2007, p. 472). Absence of secure and affordable child-care options can limit the range of jobs ex-offenders can take, thus thwarting, or slowing down, their reentry into the workforce.

Despite the stress of child care, children can be a source of stabilization for ex-offenders. Some research has found that ex-offenders who spend time with their children postrelease have lower rates of recidivism (Visher, 2013; Waller, 1974). In sum, family can be a tremendous pillar of support in the ex-offenders' journey to successful reentry. However, family can also be a source of strain if conflict, unmet expectations placed on the ex-offender, and stressors in regard to reunification with family members and children further complicate the delicate transition process.

Basic Needs and Skill Deficiencies

Ex-offenders have a wide range of basic needs that, when left unmet, pose difficulties for their ability to successfully reintegrate. Besides the basic need of housing, ex-offenders are often in need of food (Helfgott, 1997; Shivy et al., 2007). For some ex-offenders the ability to obtain the basic need of sustenance is a great challenge. D. A. Mukamal (2000) explains that the Personal Responsibility and Work Opportunity Reconciliation Act, more commonly referred to as the Welfare Reform Act of 1996 permanently prohibited states from permitting ex-offenders with drug-related felony convictions to receive any form of welfare benefits, including food stamps. This permanent ban is not merely for a few years, but rather a lifetime ban (Mukamal, 2000; Petersilia, 2005). At the time of the passage of this legislation, forty-two states implemented the ban (Allard, 2002). It should be noted that some states, such as California, have initiated legislation to repeal the act in their states and restore federal assistance for offenders. P. Allard (2002) explains that this act has had a detrimental impact on low income African American and Latina women. In a study conducted by Shivy and colleagues, the reliance on receiving food via charity can be demoralizing as one subject reported, "How do you like living off somebody, eating all their food?" (2007, p. 471). Due to the inability to obtain employment and their conviction status, this need is often left unmet.

Further inhibiting the ability of ex-offenders to obtain employment is the lack of access to transportation (Shivy et al., 2007). While many probation and parole agencies provide temporary bus passes to ex-offenders to help them get around when they first reenter society, it may not be enough. The provided bus passes are often temporary, and ex-offenders are in need of longer-term solutions to their transportation limitations. This support is especially critical to those being directly released into society without any form of support services (i.e., probation or parole).

Ex-offenders need life-skills training including the development of problem-solving skills, negotiation skills, critical reasoning skills, money management skills, and independent living skills (J. Brown, 2004b; McGuire and Hatcher, 2001; Raynor and Vandstone, 1996; Roberts and Harper, 1997). In a study of Canadian parole officers, the officers reported that newly released federal offenders are in need of the acquisition of problem-solving and budgeting skills (J. Brown, 2004b). In an additional study conducted by J. Brown (2004a) where he queried Canadian parole officers regarding challenges that newly released federal offenders face, the officers identified the use of "old coping strategies" as a factor that inhibits successful reentry. According to the officers, ex-offenders may be "overcome by [the] pace of life" and feel "fear," "loneliness," "boredom," "discouragement," "lack of patience," "lack of self-confidence," or "shame" (J. Brown, 2004a, p. 28). Thus, ex-offenders who have not received any cognitive skills programming prior to release may be at a disadvantage in their ability to successfully reintegrate. Again, if basic needs go unmet and ex-offenders are not equipped with the necessary skills that any citizen would need to succeed in society, then successful reentry is less likely to occur.

Collateral Consequences

The conviction status of ex-offenders creates many collateral consequences as they reenter society, many of which were mentioned earlier in the chapter, such as problems finding housing, employment, and even food. However, other forms of collateral damage are experienced by ex-offenders. Some have referred to a conviction status as being a form of civil death or additional, yet invisible, punishment (Ewald, 2002; Travis, 2005). As explained by A. C. Ewald, "the term 'civil death' refers to the condition in which a convicted offender loses all political, civil, and legal rights" (2002, p. 1049). Pinard and Thompson (2006) explain that among the forfeiture of constitutional rights and other sanctions are the loss of voting rights; temporary or permanent ineligibility for federal welfare benefits, educational grants, public housing, gun licenses, and certain vocational licenses; and the disqualification from serving in political office, on juries, and in the military. In many states, ex-offenders never regain their voting rights even after fully serving their probation, parole, or incarceration sentences (Ewald, 2002). The loss of voting rights, referred to as "felon disenfranchisement," significantly impacts male African Americans with approximately 13 percent of this population affected by this prohibition—"a rate seven times the national average" (Ewald, 2002, p. 1053). The loss of rights and access to state and federal assistance programs has increased in the era of the get-tough-on-crime movement; however, a few states allow for eventual restoration of voting rights (Pinard and Thompson, 2006). Several researchers have called for the abolition of lifetime bans or the loss of rights for ex-offenders given that these sanctions are forms of additional punishment (see Bushway and Sweeten, 2007). Unfortunately, many ex-offenders are initially unaware of many of the rights they have lost, but when they attempt to access services available to other citizens, they become surprised to learn about it and frustrated with the myriad hurdles they now face on the pathway to successful reentry (Pinard and Thompson, 2006).

Besides "civil death," ex-offenders experience other forms of collateral consequences due to their status as convicted felons (Clear, 2007). These consequences are echoed in research conducted on sex offenders (Ackerman, Sacks, and Osier, 2013; Tewksbury, 2005). R. Tewksbury (2005), in a study of 121 registered sex offenders in Kentucky, found that many of these offenders experienced social stigmatization, loss of relationships, and verbal and physical assaults. However, in the case of sex offenders, not just the offenders themselves face these consequences, but the family members of the offenders may also experience damage due to the status of the offenders. In another study conducted by J. S. Levenson and R. Tewksbury (2009), the researchers examined the impact of sex offender registration laws on family members. The researchers found that family members experienced employment limitations, housing disruption, and sometimes threats, harassment, or property damage due to their association with a registered sex offender.

Additionally, results from the research revealed that the children of the registered sex offenders were treated differently at school or by peers and also experienced stigmatization due to their parents' status. T. R. Clear (2007) discusses how communities in which ex-offenders come from and return to can also become stigmatized. He explains, "Locations with large numbers of people going to prison also become negatively stereotyped, and this affects how the area is perceived, thus transferring the stigma to the community" (p. 128). The stigmatization may culminate in residents relocating, businesses being reluctant to open in the community, or even property values dropping (Clear, 2007). Thus, authorities must recognize that not only are ex-offenders experiencing such consequences but their family members and communities may also experience invisible punishments.

Conclusion

In sum, the average ex-offender attempting to reenter society successfully is faced with a host of challenges. Without support to obtain food, housing, and employment, ex-offenders are not likely to succeed. Additionally, family and community support play a vital role in the success of the ex-offender. Further, a wide range of invisible punishments are experienced by ex-offenders after their formal punishment, which certainly undermine not only their ability to succeed but further weaken their drive to succeed.

In the following chapter, we present a detailed examination of female ex-offender reentry and describe the similarities and differences, compared to male offenders, in their pathway to success.

4

Gender Issues

MEDIA IMAGES DEPICTING FEMALE OFFENDERS ABOUND FROM local and national news coverage to portrayals in Hollywood films. Casey Anthony, who was ultimately acquitted of the murder of her daughter, Caylee Anthony, in Florida in 2011, was plastered all over the news as a self-absorbed, heartless mother and pathological liar during her trial (Alvarez, 2011). Other media portrayals of female offenders in Hollywood films have also been unfavorable. For instance, the 2003 movie *Monster,* starring Charlize Theron, depicted the serial killer Aileen Wuornos. While the crimes Wuornos committed were serious, the film can only be taken at face value as entertainment, and, in fact, Charlize Theron won an Academy Award for her performance as the serial killer. The movie did depict some of the abuse Wuornos experienced as a child, but it failed to peel back the complex layers of abuse and trauma that she suffered during her formative years, how these experiences contributed to her commission of crimes, and the ways in which gender stereotypes contributed to her vilification and the media attention to her case. The depictions of female offenders in the media (particularly, news reports and Hollywood films) tend to be superficial and center on alleged crimes that they have committed, their trials, and sentencing as opposed to their journey after they have been through the criminal justice system—what occurs after they have served their punishment. Rarely are the stories of female ex-offenders heard in regard to their reentry into society. Y. Rainey (2001), a female ex-offender, in her book entitled *Dear Lover,* offers a brief note on reentry success. She states, "I refuse to let anything be a crutch in my not succeeding in life. I accept the responsibility for being in the position that I am right now, and I will even go so far to say I am proud to be an ex-felon because that is what saved my life" (p. 9).

Why is less known about the female reentry process than the male? Perhaps the answer stems from the fact that historically women have been overlooked in criminological and criminal justice research, thus resulting in academics labeling them as the "forgotten" or "invisible offenders" (Belknap, 2007; Chesney-Lind and Pasko, 2004). For instance, early criminologists were simply focused on the examination of the etiology of the male offender. However, in the 1970s, the feminist movement was under way in the United States, and it ignited many criminologists to begin examining female criminality and female offender reentry (Belknap, 2007).

Since the 1970s, research focusing on female offenders, such as the etiology of their actions, the identification of their needs, and the most effective treatment of underlying issues such as mental health issues and drug abuse, has burgeoned. However, while research has expanded on the topic of female offending over the last four decades, we still have much to learn and understand about their criminal patterns and needs and reentry experiences. In this chapter, we will describe the early and current theoretical explanations for female offending, sketch out a profile of female offenders, and delve into the unique issues and the struggles that women face when reentering society. For example, one catalyst for females' initial entry into offending is prior sexual abuse (Belknap, 2007; Chesney-Lind, 1989). Research is now emerging that prior abuse can contribute to females' continuation in offending and inhibit their success in reentering society. Additionally, those females who are mothers face challenges in reuniting with their children and are often ostracized by the public for committing a crime.

Theoretical Explanations

Criminologists in the late 1800s and throughout much of the 1900s were primarily focused on explaining male criminality. Criminologists of these earlier eras attributed criminal behavior to biological or social factors that were beyond the control of an individual. The exclusion of the examination of female offending is not unique to criminology. Other academic disciplines (e.g., medicine) have historically excluded female subjects from research investigations. Thus, J. Belknap (2007) refers to the oversight of female offending in criminology as part of a larger societal problem of androcentric bias.

Some of the early examinations of female offending were conducted at the end of the nineteenth century into the mid-twentieth century. Those prominent researchers offering explanations of female criminality include Cesare Lombroso and William Ferrero (1895), W. I. Thomas (1923), Sigmund Freud (1933), and Otto Pollak (1950). These early theorists' ideas about female offending were consistent with the positivist school of crime where crime was due to some individual difference (i.e., biologically determined) as opposed to a rational choice. Lombroso and Ferrero (1895) stated that the explanation for both male and female offending is due to atavistic traits, or denigration in evolutionary human development. Essentially, involvement in criminality was due to their biology: that is, these criminals were born this way. The researchers posited that females who committed crimes were masculine and exhibited an excess of male characteristics (e.g., excess body hair, moles, broad shoulders). In a departure from a biological explanation for female offending, W. I. Thomas (1923) claimed that females committed crime for the thrill or excitement and the yearning for new experiences. According to Thomas, due to societal expectations of monogamy, females have pent-up sexual energy, and this sexual tension is released in the commission of criminal acts. Freud (1933), like Thomas, viewed female offending as being linked to female sexuality. He asserted that females have a masculinity complex due to penis envy. Those females who cannot resolve their penis envy overidentify with men and will commit crimes. In 1950, Otto Pollak departed from a pure biological explanation for female criminality and attributed female criminality to a mix of biological, psychological, and sociological factors. Specifically, he pointed to the role of biology (e.g., menstruation, pregnancy) as a contributor to the development of female offending due to the psychological disturbances that they produce. These psychological disturbances push females into a cycle of offending or weaken their moral inhibitions toward engaging in criminal behavior.

Since the 1950s, many criminological theories have been put forth to explain criminal and deviant behavior for both males and females. However, notably the early empirical tests of these theories focused almost exclusively on males. Learning theories provide a useful framework for understanding female participation in crime (Akers, 1990; Sutherland, 1947b). These theories attribute initiation and cessation of criminal offending to learning processes that principally involve varying levels of exposure to "definitions" favorable or unfavorable to violation of the law (Sutherland, 1947b) as well as consideration of differential reinforcements (Akers et al., 1979) and the degree of priority or significance being attached to criminal peer associations. Thus, criminal peer associations contribute to the onset and continuation of female offending patterns (Agnew, 1991; Dekovic, 1999; Durant, Knight, and Goodman, 1997; Giordano, Cernkovich, and Pugh, 1996; Heimer and DeCoster, 1999;

Patterson and Dishion, 1985; Silverman and Caldwell, 2008). In a study of 128 female juvenile offenders from diverse racial and ethnic backgrounds, J. R. Silverman and R. M. Caldwell (2008) found that peer associations were significantly related to juvenile participation in violence. Additionally, deterrence or rational choice theories explain offending as due to a deliberate decision. D. B. Cornish and R. V. Clarke (1986) assert that decisions to engage in crime by offenders are based on the offender's expected effort and reward compared to the certainty and severity of punishment as well as other costs of crime (e.g., losing friends). The idea that females could make a rational decision to commit crimes was in stark contrast to earlier biological and psychological theories which viewed women as being incapable of engaging in rational decisionmaking (Daly and Chesney-Lind, 1988; Smart, 1977). Subsequent researchers have found that women can and often make conscious decisions to become involved in illicit activities such as robbery, drug selling, and prostitution because they decide the benefits of committing the crime outweigh the costs (Ajzenstadt, 2009; Brookman et al., 2007; Maher, 1997; Maher and Curtis, 1992). In a study of 125 incarcerated female offenders in Israel, M. Ajzenstadt (2009) found that female offenders indeed engage in rational decisionmaking about crimes in relation to their financial or emotional needs. For example, one subject, with a limited education, reported, "I tried; I really wanted to be an independent woman and mother, but every time my past came haunting me, and I could not get what I wanted, and started to look for money in a criminal way. I started to steal money from the patients in the hospital, where I worked" (p. 213).

Most control theories, however, explain criminal offending through the identification of the ways social processes influence the development of social constraints or containments (Reckless, 1961; Sampson and Laub, 1993). For example, T. Hirschi (1969), in his social bond theory, explains that individuals commit crime when one or more social bonds (i.e., attachment, commitment, involvement, belief) break down. While he asserted that his theory applies to males and females, when he empirically tested his theory, he did not bother to analyze the theory in the context of female offending. Researchers have found mixed support for the role of social bonds in explaining male and female delinquency (Alarid, Burton, and Cullen, 2000; Canter, 1982; Cernkovich and Giordano, 1987; Chapple, McQuillan, and Berdahl, 2005; Friedman and Rosenbaum, 1988; Gove and Crutchfield, 1982; Hindelang, 1973; Huebner and Betts, 2002; Smith and Paternoster, 1987).

Subsequent control theorists, such as M. R. Gottfredson and T. Hirschi (1990), assert that individuals who have low self-control (i.e., give in to impulses, take risks, need immediate gratification), coupled with ample opportunities, will commit crime and other analogous behaviors repeatedly, perhaps over a lifetime. According to Gottfredson and Hirschi, bonds to others and social institutions (e.g., employment) are unimportant to explaining the onset and continuation of criminal behavior. Empirical support for the role of low self-control in explaining female offending has been mixed (Benda, Toombs, and Corwyn, 2005; Burton et al., 1998; LaGrange and Silverman, 1999; Nakhaie, Silverman, and LaGrange, 2000; Shekarkhar and Gibson, 2011; Steketee, Junger, and Junger-Tas, 2013; Tittle, Ward, and Grasmick, 2003). For instance, B. B. Benda, N. J. Toombs, and R. F. Corwyn (2005), in a study of male and female boot camp graduates, found that low self-control may be more predictive of recidivism for males as opposed to females. Unlike Gottfredson and Hirschi (1990), R. J. Sampson and J. H. Laub (1993), in their age-graded control theory, assert that onset into criminality may be due to the presence of a latent trait, environmental factors, or breakdowns in bonds. In general, researchers state that changing social influences (e.g., marriage, employment, religion) affects whether an individual desists from crime (Laub and Sampson, 2001, 2003; Sampson and Laub, 1993). However, for African American offenders in particular, recent research reveals that marriage promotes desistance for males more so than for females (Doherty and Ensminger, 2013).

Within life course criminology, research has emerged that shows that biological factors may play a role in the onset and continuity of offending (see Moffitt, 1993; Zahn, 1999). According to T. E. Moffitt (1993), in her typology of offending, complications in prenatal development or head injury may increase a child's chances for engaging in life course persistent offending. However, females appear to be less at risk for biological interference than males (Raine, 1993). Life course persisters are more likely to be male, commit serious crimes, and exhibit versatility in offending throughout their lives. But people who generally commit crime only as adolescents, referred to as adolescent limiteds, are likely to be comprised of males and females and commit less serious crimes, though they may mimic behaviors of the life course persisters and are more likely to desist from criminality.

Since the departure from examining biology as the sole attribution to female criminality (see Lombroso, 1911), numerous criminological theories put forth since the 1950s, and the infusion of research on female offending due to the feminist movement in the 1970s, researchers have identified multiple risk factors for females' offending patterns. For example, additional risk factors besides lack of positive peer relationships, rational decisions, or absence of positive social bonds have surfaced for female offenders including prior sexual or physical abuse and addiction.

Sexual Abuse

Sexual abuse figures prominently within the life histories of female offenders. Research into offending has indicated that women in prison have a higher level of sexual victimization than the general population (Belknap, 2007; Siegel and Williams, 2003), perhaps two to three times higher than male offenders (Harlow, 1999). Consequently, research has consistently supported prior sexual abuse as a moderate to strong predictor of female offending (Belknap, 2007; Siegel and Williams, 2003). Prior sexual abuse in women has been related to running away (Belknap, Holsinger, and Dunn, 1997), entry into a criminal career (Chesney-Lind, 1989), prostitution (Simons and Whitbeck, 1991), drug use (Kilpatrick et al., 2000), and aggression (Baskin and Sommers, 1998). Numerous researchers have explored female offending and have linked prior sexual abuse to not only the onset of criminal offending patterns but also the persistence in offending patterns (Bailey and McCloskey, 2005; Belknap, 2007; Chesney-Lind and Pasko, 2004; Comack, 2005; Gilfus, 1992; Goodkind, Ng, and Sarri, 2006; Gunnison and McCartan, 2005; Widom, 1995). In a study of over 100 female offenders in a southwestern prison, E. Gunnison and L. M. McCartan (2005) found that prior sexual abuse was significantly related to persistence in criminal offending. Thus, for many female ex-offenders reentering society, prior sexual abuse can contribute to future offending and perhaps maladjustment upon reintegration—particularly for those offenders who have not engaged in any form of treatment to cope with their victimization experiences.

Because much of the sexual abuse that women experience in childhood has been perpetrated by family members, young girls find it necessary to run away from home (i.e., where the perpetrator(s) reside) and turn to a life of crime on the streets as a means of survival (Belknap, 2007; Bloom et al., 2003; Chesney-Lind and Pasko, 2004). In order to survive, females often will turn to prostitution to gain income to facilitate their survival (Silbert and Pines, 1981). M. H. Silbert and A. M. Pines (1981), in their study of 200 juvenile and adult street prostitutes, found that 70 percent of their sample reported that their prior sexual abuse influenced their decision to begin working as a prostitute. Subsequent research on female prostitution has also yielded additional support for the link between prior sexual abuse and involvement in prostitution (Bagley and Young, 1987; Boyer, Chapman, and Marshall, 1993;

Earls and David, 1990; McClanahan et al., 1999; Widom and Ames, 1994). For instance, in a study conducted by D. Boyer, L. Chapman, and B. K. Marshall, one female prostitute reported, "We've all been molested. Over and over, and raped. We were all molested and sexually abused as children, don't you know that? We ran to get away. They didn't want us in the house anymore. We were thrown out, thrown away. We've been on the street since we were 12, 13, 14" (1993, p. 16).

Without question, sexual abuse can have a detrimental impact on both males and females (McGuigan and Middlemiss, 2005; Reinemann, Stark, and Swearer, 2003; Romano and De Luca, 2000). For example, E. Romano and V. De Luca (2000), who examined the empirical literature on the impact of sexual abuse on males and compared it to the research literature on females, found that regardless of gender, childhood sexual abuse had a long-ranging negative impact on their lives. The researchers did note that females who experienced childhood sexual abuse tended to display more internalizing problems (e.g., depression or anxiety) as a result of their victimization. Women who have experienced physical or sexual abuse are at a higher risk for either chronic or recurrent depression (Andrews, 1995). Other research suggests that depression may even act as a buffer against criminal involvement. That is, females may exhibit passive behavioral problems such as depression rather than the aggressive behavioral problems evidenced in males (Karstedt, 2000). Similar results were found by D. H. Reinemann, K. D. Stark, and S. M. Swearer (2003), who interviewed fifty-seven adolescents receiving mental health services in a residential treatment center. They found that females who had experienced sexual abuse reported greater levels of depression compared to their male counterparts. Further, W. M. McGuigan and W. Middlemiss (2005) found that childhood sexual abuse can have a cumulative impact on depression experienced as an adult for women.

Other responses to childhood sexual abuse that females exhibit are substance abuse (internalized pain) and criminal involvement (externalized pain). Several researchers have linked prior sexual abuse to the use of drugs and alcohol for females (Bailey and McCloskey, 2005; Belknap, 2007; Boyd, 1993; Chen et al., 2004; Chesney-Lind and Pasko, 2004; Comack, 2005; Gilfus, 1992; Goodkind, Ng, and Sarri, 2006; Kilpatick et al., 2000; Luster and Small, 1997; Miller and Downs, 1993; Saunders et al., Widom, 1995). J. A. Bailey and L. A. McCloskey (2005) examined the link between childhood sexual abuse and later substance abuse (i.e., alcohol and drug use) and found that a relationship does indeed exist between the variables. The researchers found that the relationship between childhood sexual abuse and substance abuse held even when they controlled for other factors such as family, alcohol/drug patterns, and early deviant behavior. Their use of substances—alcohol, illicit drugs, or both—leads to long-term abuse problems. Additionally, S. Covington and J. Kohen (1984), in an examination of women who had addictions as well as women who did not, found that 74 percent of women with addictions to drugs or alcohol reported prior sexual abuse as compared to 50 percent of the women with no substance addictions.

Physical Abuse

Physical abuse experienced by females has been linked to the onset of involvement in criminal activity (Acoca, 1998; Belknap, Holsinger, and Dunn, 1997; Chesney-Lind and Shelden, 2004). L. Acoca (1998), who gathered both quantitative and qualitative data on abuse histories of young female offenders, reports that physical abuse was related to the onset of drug abuse and gang membership for young females. In a 1995 study of incarcerated female sexual offenders, M. S. Kaplan and A. Green report that female sexual offenders had higher rates of childhood sexual and physical victimization when compared to other female offenders. Additionally, E. Gaarder and J. Belknap (2002) report that, for female juveniles in their study who were accused of serious enough crimes to be transferred to adult courts, physical abuse (among other factors) at home was experienced by many. J. E. Lansford and colleagues (2002) found that early physical abuse was related to aggression in adolescence, more so for girls than boys. However, A. A. Fagan (2005) found few gender differences between early physical abuse and frequency of offending in adulthood. In 2007, Lansford and colleagues, in a prospective longitudinal study of 574 children, examined the relationship between early physical abuse and later violent offending. The researchers found that males and females who were physically abused at an early age were more at risk as juveniles to be arrested for both violent and nonviolent offenses. Further, the researchers also found that the impact of early physical abuse, along with other negative experiences, on females was more pronounced than for their male counterparts. Specifically, "females who had been physically abused were approximately 3 times more likely to have been fired and to have been a teen parent" (p. 241). More recently, R. Teague, P. Mazerolle, and M. Legosz (2008), who examined male and female offenders in Queensland, Australia, found that offenders in their sample who were physically abused engaged in a greater number of violent and property crimes than offenders who had not experienced such abuse. Clearly, similar to sexual abuse, the experience of physical abuse by females has a profound and enduring impact on their offending trajectories and may affect their lives and ability to effectively reintegrate into society in differing ways than male offenders who have experienced such abuse.

In sum, many risk factors (e.g., choices, bonds, presence of a latent trait, biology, and abuse) lead females to the onset and persistence in criminal offending patterns and can inhibit successful reentry for this group. While some similarities can be found in these risk factors for males and females (e.g., peers), some distinct differences exist for these groups (i.e., prior sexual abuse). In the following section, we provide a portrait of the female offender in the context of crimes committed.

Profile of Female Offending

In terms of the amount of crime, and types of crimes, that females commit, some distinct differences occur between female and male offending groups. When examining official statistics, males get arrested for more crimes than their female counterparts (Federal Bureau of Investigation, 2011). Specifically, females were arrested for approximately 26 percent of Index I crimes committed in 2011 (e.g., murder, rape, robbery, burglary, sexual assault, larceny-theft, arson, and motor vehicle theft) with males being arrested for approximately 74 percent of Index I crimes. Additionally, females are more likely to commit property crimes as opposed to violent crimes. In 2011, females only represented 20 percent of those arrested for violent crimes but 38 percent of those arrested for property crimes. Researchers have also discovered that females self-report less criminal involvement than males and are more likely to self-report criminal behavior that is nonviolent (Belknap, 2007; Chesney-Lind, 1989). D. J. Steffensmeier and E. Haynie (2000) state that males offend at a rate of approximately five to ten times higher than females. This finding was supported regardless of whether the researchers were inspecting official or self-reported data. Interestingly, while women are arrested more often for shoplifting, some researchers have found that women self-report similar levels of involvement in this crime as their male counterparts (Chesney-Lind and Shelden, 2004). Moreover, the Uniform Crime Reports state that arrest trends for adult females have increased (i.e., 5.8 percent) since 2002; however, the arrest trends for juvenile females have decreased (i.e., 24.6 percent) since 2002 (FBI, 2011).

As mentioned above, females are more likely to be arrested for and commit property crimes, or the Index I crimes of larceny-theft, robbery, and burglary (Belknap, 2007; Chesney-Lind and Pasko, 2004; FBI,

2011; Pollock, 2002). For many female offenders who engage in property crimes, if a co-offender is included, that co-offender is more likely to be male than female (Pettiway, 1987). Notably, some researchers have found that females often engage in violence and other property crimes with other females (see Alarid et al., 1996; Koons-Witt and Schram, 2003; Sommers and Baskin, 1993). Moreover, women are often under the influence of drugs and alcohol during the commission of a crime (Belknap, 2007; Chesney-Lind and Pasko, 2004; Pollock, 2002). Drug abuse violations also account for a significant portion of arrests for women (Chesney-Lind and Pasko, 2004). Drug use appears to be strongly correlated with their criminality more so than for males (Pollock, 2002). With the "war on drugs" campaign in the 1980s an increasing number of women, particularly women of color, found themselves arrested for drug offenses. S. R. Bush-Baskette (2000) states that from 1986 to 1991 the incarceration of African American females increased by 828 percent. In fact, Bush-Baskette (2000) notes that the "war on drugs" movement is often referred to as the "war on women." J. M. Pollock (2002) adds that the number of women sentenced to prison for the commission of drug crimes who also acknowledge having drug problems has increased.

Belknap adds, "It appears that regarding most offenses, especially serious and violent crimes, it is still a 'man's world'" (2007, p. 134). Pollock adds, "Despite a popular belief that women are becoming more violent, women continue to be underrepresented in violent crime rates" (2002, p. 43). However, females are not incapable of committing violent offenses. According to Belknap (2007), approximately 10–20 percent of all homicides committed in the United States are done so by women. Most often, when females do commit a violent crime, it is usually directed at a relative or intimate family member, such as a child or spouse, and the female acts alone in the commission of the crime (Browne and Williams, 1989; Gauthier and Bankston, 1997; Gauthier, Chaudoir, and Forsyth, 2003). Thus, much of the violent crime perpetrated by females is directed at males rather than females (Belknap, 2007). Further, M. Chesney-Lind and L. Pasko state, "Women's contribution to serious crimes of violence . . . is minor" (2004, p. 95). The researchers contend that media attention on violent female criminal activity has contributed, in part, to the perception that trends of violence for this group are burgeoning.

When race is examined, the Uniform Crime Reports, published by the FBI (2011), indicate that 69 percent of those arrested were white, and 28 percent were black. We need to recognize that while Caucasian offenders were arrested more, disproportionate numbers of African

Americans were arrested given their relative share of the population in the United States. According to the US Census Bureau (2010), African Americans represent approximately 12 percent of the total US population. Thus, with 28 percent of all arrests involving African Americans in 2010, their arrest rate is not in proportion to their share of the population as a whole. Moreover, findings from many self-reported criminal surveys do not support the official statistics regarding crime committed by those of various races and ethnicities, given that Caucasians and African Americans report similar levels of involvement in criminality regardless of gender (Chambliss and Nagasawa, 1969; Gould, 1969; Hirschi, 1969; Tracy, 1987).

Finally, in regard to age, the majority of those arrested in 2011 were over eighteen (FBI, 2011). However, researchers have long identified an age-crime curve, where those who commit crimes are more likely to be between the ages of sixteen and twenty-four (Hirschi and Gottfredson, 1983). The relationship between age and crime is consistent for both genders.

The theoretical explanations of female criminal offending presented earlier in the chapter and the profile of the modern-day female offender presented above have provided an identification of the risk factors for recidivism and specific needs that these offenders have during reentry. Clearly, reentry for female offenders is complex. In the following section, we further expand upon the reentry challenges faced by female offenders and their experiences during reintegration.

Reentry Challenges

As mentioned in Chapter 3, research on offender reentry over the past thirty years has demonstrated that ex-offenders' ability to reintegrate successfully is hindered by numerous obstacles such as difficulty in obtaining employment, acquiring housing, being admitted to higher education, obtaining treatment for mental health issues and drug and alcohol addiction, and finding support for serious social and medical problems (Allender, 2004; Cowan and Fionda, 1994; Harlow, 2003; Harris and Keller, 2005; Hunt, Bowers, and Miller, 1973; Nagin and Waldfogel, 1998; Paylor, 1995; Petersilia, 2003; Rodriguez and Brown, 2003; Starr, 2002; Whelan, 1973). K. J. Bergseth and colleagues (2011), who examined the needs of female offenders during reentry from the perspective of twenty-four community service providers, found that the providers indicated that employment, housing, and family-related needs (i.e., family support, classes on parenting skills, intervention in domestic violence, reunification with children, aid in child-care issues) were the most important needs. Given the abuse that many female offenders have endured from family members, locating housing, for example, may be more complex for this group. That is, female offenders may not be able to turn to family for help and support during reentry as they may have severed ties with their families due to previous abuse (Kellett and Willging, 2011). Additionally, failure to set realistic reentry expectations and plans may stymie successful reentry outcomes (Kellett and Willging, 2011). In a study of fifty female ex-offenders, J. E. Cobbina recounts one ex-offender's struggles to reintegrate:

> It was overwhelming . . . in the respect that I was supposed to do all these things, and see this PO [parole officer] and do all this and have these appointments set up by this and this. And it was just, like, "wow." I don't even have a car, and I don't even have a license. What the hell am I going to do? And my mom's not dependable in the respect of getting me somewhere at a certain time. If I do get a job, how do I know I can get there? . . . I worried about transportation. I worried about a job. I worried about seeing the PO. I worried about all the things that the PO wanted me to do and still to try to find time and money to eat and sleep every day and to get clothes enough to go look for a job. I wanted to try this and see my kids, and it's just a whole lot of stuff to try to do in a short period of time that the parole officer wanted me to get it done in. (2010, p. 226)

Barriers to obtaining needed services for sustained substance abuse recovery, for example, in the community further exacerbate the challenges female ex-offenders face during reintegration (Alemagno, 2001; Grella and Grenwell, 2006; Kellett and Willging, 2011; Staton, Leukefeld, and Webster, 2003).

Given the many challenges female ex-offenders face during reentry, both similar and distinct from male ex-offenders, female ex-offenders are at high risk for failing to successfully reintegrate into society (Dodge and Pogrebin, 2001). B. Bloom, B. Owen, and S. Covington report, "More than one-third of the women left prison with no job, no formal job training, no source of income, and less than a high school education, placing them at a further disadvantage" (2003, p. 7). Oftentimes, the challenges all ex-offenders face are, for females, often further complicated by the simple fact that they are women and the societal baggage that entails. Further, J. R. Scroggins and S. Malley (2010) report that current reentry programs do not meet the needs of women. The following sections outline specific challenges female ex-offenders face during reentry.

Stigma

Those ex-offenders, male or female, who are convicted of an offense face stigmatization for their newly acquired label, "ex-con" (Bahn and Davis, 1991; J. Brown, 2004a; Clear, 2007; Funk, 2004; Steffensmeier and Kramer, 1980; Tewksbury, 2005). As one might suspect, this social stigma inhibits successful reintegration (Goffman, 1963). Perhaps this concept is best explained by one particular female ex-offender:

> Let me start by introducing myself. My name is Yvonne Rainey, and I'm twenty-four years old with one child, and I consider myself to be an advocate for the most unwanted, most hated, and most discriminated, and most misunderstood social group of the world. "Ex-Felons." I became what society has labeled an ex-felon at the age of nineteen. (Rainey, 2001, p. 5)

Besides being socially ostracized for their status as an ex-offender, this group of people often find themselves solely viewed as ex-offenders and nothing else (e.g., hard worker, good parent) due to the stigma attached to the label. Essentially, the label of "ex-convict" becomes the ex-offenders' master status (Becker, 1963).

Despite all ex-offenders' positive decisions preconviction and good intentions postconviction, society tends to continue to shame them, thereby thwarting successful reintegration (Braithwaite, 1989). For instance, their label inhibits them from obtaining housing and employment—essentially all the basic requirements for successful reintegration (Harris and Kellar, 2005; Petersilia, 2001a). After all, housing and employment options are limited for those with a criminal record. The mentality of many in society is that they would prefer not to have ex-offenders as neighbors or as tenants in their rental properties (Clark, 2007; Harding and Harding, 2006). Likewise, employers, when given a choice between hiring an ex-offender or an individual with no previous conviction history, will, more often than not, unsurprisingly end up hiring an individual with no previous record (Buikhuisen and Dijksterhuis, 1971; Graffam, Shinkfield, and Hardcastle, 2008; Holzer, 1996; Holzer, Raphael, and Stoll, 2003; Travis, Solomon, and Waul, 2001). J. Travis, A. Solomon, and M. Waul (2001) note that the stigma associated with serving time hinders ex-offenders ability to be hired. The stigmatization exists for both male and female ex-offenders (see Richie, 2001).

While stigmatization may be experienced by both male and female ex-offenders, female ex-offenders may experience increased levels of stigmatization compared to their male counterparts. Belknap (2007) explains that female offenders are often criticized for stepping out of their gender role when they commit crime. That is, many in society expect men to commit crimes and perhaps brush off such infractions with the idea that "boys will be boys." However, females who commit crimes are viewed as having stepped out of their socially defined and stereotypical gender role (i.e., to be mothers, nurturers, etc.), and, therefore, their infractions are not so easily dismissed but rather are scrutinized. In a sense, female ex-offenders are "double deviants" since they not only violate the law when they commit the criminal act but they also violate established gender norms too (Owen, 1998). Thus, female ex-offenders may experience additional forms of stigmatization such as criticism of their parenting skills, designation as a "bad mother," and difficulties in regaining custody of their children that are not experienced by male ex-offenders (Burkart, 1973). In a study of paroled female ex-offenders conducted by M. Dodge and M. R. Pogrebin (2001) several subjects explained their difficulties in overcoming the stigma attached to their status as ex-offenders. For example, one subject reported, "I am doing very well. I have a place to live, but it's hard getting your kids back because nobody will believe that I have changed and I'm a different person now. No matter how much time we do, everyone always thinks it's like once a criminal always a criminal" (p. 49). Another subject, explained, "It's been tough, my sister is great letting me live with her, and all at once when people find out I was in prison they look down on me. I was going to church cause I really found God and everyone was so nice. Then, someone found out I was in prison and everything changed, no one would talk to me anymore. Now I don't go, I just pray at home" (p. 50). Clearly, the stigma faced by female ex-offenders hinders successful reintegration for this group. Dodge and Pogrebin note that female "ex-offenders rarely view themselves as blameless, but continued societal alienation accentuates feelings of guilt and hinders successful reunification and reintegration" (p. 52).

Substance Abuse Treatment

As mentioned earlier, female ex-offenders suffer from drug and alcohol abuse, which often stems from early childhood victimization (Bailey and McCloskey, 2005; Belknap, 2007; Chesney-Lind and Pasko, 2004; Comack, 2005; Gilfus, 1992; Goodkind, Ng, and Sarri, 2006; Kilpatrick et al., 2000; Luster and Small, 1997; Miller and Downs, 1993; Saunders et al., 1999; Widom, 1995). Failure to address substance abuse problems while incarcerated or relapse during reentry has been linked to recidivism for female offenders. For example, previous researchers have found substance abuse to be a more significant predictor of recidivism (i.e., technical violations) for female probationers as opposed to their male counterparts (see Olson, Alderden, and Lurigio, 2003). Unfortunately, B. Bloom, M. Chesney-Lind, and B. Owen (1994) report that drug treatment for incarcerated women is limited in many jurisdictions. B. A. Koons and colleagues (1997) explain that only approximately 55 percent of jails and 47 percent of prisons provide substance abuse treatment programs for incarcerated women. Thus, a critical factor in their reentry success is access to community-based substance abuse treatment programs and programs that are of quality. In a qualitative study of female ex-offenders, B. E. Richie (2001) recounts one woman's struggles in attending treatment and being able to focus on her recovery. The subject reported,

> I really tried to go to treatment. But I couldn't stand how they treated me. Mostly it was the men in the group who always want to get some [have sex]. They offer nicely at first, then they teased me, they just stared at me whenever I talked. It was impossible to ignore their stares. Do you know one even offered to get high with me if I give him some [sex]? So I stopped going altogether. (p. 372)

For this subject, her gender role in this program and the environment of the program were not conducive to support her sobriety, resulting in her having to recover from her substance abuse problems on her own—a difficult task for anyone, male or female.

N. J. Tiburcio (2008) cautions that recovery from substance is challenging particularly for those offenders who have abused opiates. In a qualitative examination of twenty-five former heroin users, Tiburcio reported that respondents identified positive peer support, exercise, and meditation as factors that supported their recovery efforts. One female ex-offender in Tiburcio's study, a former prostitute named Marisol, adopted a healthy lifestyle (i.e., consumption of healthy foods and exercise) where she could invest her energies in that pursuit thereby filling a void where substance use once played a predominant role. Further, Tiburcio adds, in reference to Marisol's newfound focus on being healthy, that "these substitute behaviors helped Marisol desist from prior criminal activities. Her outlook, and especially her desire to maintain as she stated a 'healthy soul as well as body,' crossed over into her behavioral patterns as well. She felt she could no longer engage (nor wanted to) in any activities that might deter her 'health' objectives" (p. 1962). Other female ex-offenders may rely on friends for social support in addition to treatment programs to assist in their successful reentry into society. In a study of female criminal desistance conducted by I.

Sommers, D. R. Baskin, and F. Fagan, one subject reported that she relied on

> a bunch of friends that always confronts me on what I'm doing and
> where I'm goin', and they just want the best for me. And none of them
> use drugs. I go to a lot [of] like outside support groups, you know.
> They help me have more confidence in myself. I have new friends
> now. Some of them are in treatment. Some have always been straight.
> They know. You know, they glad, you know, when I see them. (1994,
> p. 144)

In sum, adequate support mechanisms for substance abuse programs,
both internal and external, may assist the female ex-offender in successfully transitioning into the community. However, sometimes the ability
of the female ex-offender to overcome prolonged substance abuse issues
is inhibited or exacerbated by underlying mental health issues.

Mental Health

Previous researchers have estimated that while 10 percent of all males
in prison suffer from mental illness, 19 percent of women in prison are
mentally ill (Peters and Hills, 1993). D. J. James and L. E. Glaze (2006)
report that female inmates, in state and federal prisons and jails, had
higher rates of mental health issues than male inmates at these same
institutions. Acoca (1998) places the percentage even higher, ranging
from 25 percent to 60 percent, with an average of 45 percent, for incarcerated women suffering from mental illness. Given these percentages
reported and the earlier discussion in the chapter regarding trauma experienced early in their lives, female ex-offenders are in need of mental
health support (e.g., access to medications) and treatment, and these
needs have been identified as a serious problem for this group (Kellett
and Willging, 2011; Teplin, Abram, and McClelland, 1996). Recall that
prior sexual and physical abuse that female offenders have experienced
often results in severe depression, posttraumatic stress disorder, and sui-
cidal ideation and attempts (Belknap, 2007; Pollock, 2002). Subjects in
Richie's (2001) investigation of challenges females face upon reentry
highlight the mental health problems that female offenders face and the
need for mental health support during reentry. One subject reported, "I
have the kind of emotional problems where I just lose my temper and
start banging my head against the wall. Sometimes it gets so bad that I
stay in bed for a week, just to not hurt myself or someone else. I'm
good for awhile, then I fall back into that real deep sadness" (p. 374).
Another subject states, "I have gone crazy three times before where I

have to take pills to get my sanity back. I don't know what the pills are, but when I can get them, they help me not zone out and run away from reality. That's why I live mostly on the streets; because I zone out and can't find my way back home" (p. 374).

Mentally ill female ex-offenders are in need of basic services such as housing and employment assistance upon release in addition to mental health treatment, especially because they face additional stigma and social rejection from the community due to their mental health status, making reintegration even more challenging (Aday and Krabill, 2011; McCormick and Perret, 2010). L. K. Frisman and colleagues suggest that for mentally ill ex-offenders, "in particular, high-quality outpatient behavioral health care services—including medication management, supportive services, respite care, and vocational rehabilitation—will help reduce homelessness, recidivism, and the need for emergency room visits and hospitalization" (2010, pp. 4–9). T. M. Hammet, C. Roberts, and S. Kennedy (2001) identify five factors that can assist mentally ill ex-offenders in reentry: (1) discharge planning, (2) adherence to treatment regimens, (3) available housing, (4) quick access to benefit programs (e.g., Medicaid), and (5) access to help for managing multiple diagnoses (e.g., those having co-occurring disorders such as mental illness and substance use). In many cases for mentally ill ex-offenders, an intersection between onset of their illnesses and substance abuse problems can be identified (Rounsaville et al., 1982).

Motherhood

One significant challenge the female ex-offenders face during reentry is regaining their role as mothers and balancing the role of motherhood with other reentry demands. Since a greater number of incarcerated women are mothers and resided with their children prior to incarceration than males, the emotional welfare of their children is a concern for incarcerated females, and the worry continues upon their release (Spjeldnes and Goodkind, 2009). Richie reports that one subject in her sample stated,

> If you think it's bad for me, imagine what being in jail is like for my kids. Yes, they have suffered alright. They have no one to help them along now that I am here. No mother, no father, all of their friends make fun of them, and they don't have anyone in the world. At least if the judge is going to keep me here, he should give something for my kids. I worry that my boys are already heading down the wrong path because I'm not there watching out for them. Can someone help my children? (2001, p. 379)

Thus, upon release, many female ex-offenders are extremely motivated to make changes in their lives to enhance their chances of being reunited with their children (Baker and Carson, 1999; Cobbina and Bender, 2012; Marcenko and Striepe, 1997; Richie, 2001). In J. E. Cobbina and K. A. Bender's (2012) qualitative study of twenty-six incarcerated women, one subject expressed a desire to change and indicated that her child was the motivating factor. She explained,

> I want something better for me, and I want something better for my daughter. I don't want my daughter to grow up and be a teenager and have a mother who is either still hooked on drugs or in prison or dead because of one of the two. I want to be happy. I want to not have to worry about if I get stopped for a light, is a warrant going to show up that I've got? Am I going to go to jail? My daughter might be in the car with me. It's way too much to lose. (p. 282)

For some female ex-offenders, their children are the light at the end of the tunnel—their sole reason to make a change. One female ex-offender living in a recovery home reported,

> I've been in and out of the joint [prison] for six years now. I've tried and tried and broken more promises than I thought was possible. I've lost friends, family, money, health, and my position in the community as a responsible citizen. And then, I got a second chance to raise my kids. When I was pregnant the last time and I got into a program, the world changed for me. It's hard to describe, but basically it is because of this 5-month-old baby boy that I am clean, surviving one day at a time, and that I have hope for the future. I may never get to raise him on my own, but he is my reason for living. Who would have ever thought a baby could do such a thing? (Richie, 2001, p. 379)

Another female ex-offender reported, "I want to get [my son] back! I want to be with my kids, I love my kids. Even though I messed up, I'm still, I try to do my best for them, you know, cause I'm not messing up today" (Michalsen, 2011, p. 350). Legally, regaining custody may be an uphill battle (Mapson, 2013). The Adoption and Safe Families Act in 1997 makes regaining custody of their children impossible for some female ex-offenders. One provision of the act requires states to file to terminate the parental rights and begin looking for permanent adoptive homes for children who have been in foster care for at least fifteen months (Petersilia, 2003). Apart from the legal barriers, the strength to overcome the challenges of reunification may be too great for some female ex-offenders, greasing the pathway to failure during reentry (Brown and Bloom, 2009; Coll et al., 1998).

Upon release, however, mothers face a whole host of stressors in the role as a parent ranging from the anxiety of being reunited with children they may have lost custody of, fear of losing custody, concern for the emotional welfare of their child, and the desperation of finding housing for their family. For example, many ex-offenders work hard at kicking substance abuse habits that would inhibit their reunification (Enos, 2001). Thus, female ex-offenders who have addiction problems are saddled with overcoming their addiction, securing employment and housing, and regularly visiting their children. C. A. Robbins, S. S. Martin, and H. L. Surratt further explain that "although maternal roles may motivate substance-abusing female offenders to attain sobriety, substance abuse recovery is itself a demanding role that can compete with maternal responsibilities" (2007, p. 394). M. L. Parsons and C. Warner-Robbins (2002) add that sustaining recovery from substance abuse problems is a chief concern of females reentering the community, resulting in the reunification with children becoming a secondary goal. Additionally, C. E. Grella and L. Greenwell (2006), in a study of 483 substance-abusing women, many of whom had lost their parental rights, found that many of these women had a history of problems stemming from early childhood, which could contribute to their current lack of resources and explain why reunification with their children may be more challenging. Further, many female ex-offenders are faced with overcoming personal problems such as coming to terms with previous domestic violence victimization, dealing with an HIV positive diagnosis, coping with depression, earning money, maintaining sobriety, and trying to regain their parental rights (Arditti and Few, 2006; Michalsen, 2011). Therefore, a multitude of demands and tasks are placed on the female ex-offender upon reentry. While many of these demands are the same as those placed on male ex-offenders, the difference lies in the likelihood that female ex-offenders are the caregivers of their children upon release or have a stronger desire to reunite and regain custody of their children upon release. Richie reports on the competing demands for one female ex-offender in her study:

> I start my day running to drop my urine [drug testing]. Then I go see my children, show up for my training program, look for a job, go to a meeting [Alcoholics Anonymous] and show up at my part-time job. I have to take the bus everywhere, sometimes ride buses for 4 hours a day. I don't have the proper outer clothes, I don't have money to buy lunch along the way, and everyone who works with me keeps me waiting so that I am late to my next appointment. If I fail any one of these things and my PO [probation officer] finds out, I am revoked [probation is revoked]. I am so tired that I sometimes fall asleep on my way

home from work at 2 a.m. and that's dangerous given where I live. And then the next day I have to start over again. I don't mind being busy and working hard . . . that's part of my recovery. But this is a situation that is setting me up to fail. I just can't keep up and I don't know where to start. I want my kids, I need a place to stay, I have a job, meetings to keep me clean, and I am required to be in job training. (2001, pp. 380–381)

Hence, female ex-offenders walk a tightrope as they attempt to negotiate their recovery, other reentry challenges (i.e., housing, employment, required meetings), and the maternal desire to be the primary caregivers of their children.

For other female ex-offenders who are mothers and not suffering from addiction, securing safe housing is also a chief concern. A. M. Leverentz (2010), in a qualitative study of forty-nine female ex-offenders residing in a halfway house in Chicago, found that women in her sample sought to find housing that can be characterized as being low crime and suitable for their children. One subject reported, "You know I haven't really given that [where to move] any thought. But since you asked me that question I would like to look for a neighborhood where people are working, going to schools, striving to do better. I wouldn't want to see a drug dealer on the corner, or gangbangers. I wouldn't want to see people hanging out on the corners" (p. 657). However, those female ex-offenders who have children soon discover that their children can be a burden in their search for suitable housing. Many women seeking subsidized housing quickly learn that a barrier to entry into these homes is their children as most of the subsidized housing programs do not allow children (Leverentz, 2010). Thus, female ex-offenders who are mothers face a difficult choice to either live within subsidized housing by themselves or forgo this housing option to reside with their children. For instance, one subject reported,

I had originally put in for the town home, because I had wanted my baby daughter and my son to come stay with me, but they consider him as grown, because he was 19, and I don't really consider him grown til he is 21. So anyway that was put on the backburner so they offered me the SRO [single-room occupancy] instead of a town home, you know, so that's how it end up that I'm living in here, so I was like I'd stay here for awhile, but I'd still want my daughter to come stay with me and my son. If I'm gonna end up getting an apartment just to get the space, you know, he can stay with me til he's 21, . . . and then, but I didn't want to turn it down or nothing because you know there's other people that need to get in the program [halfway house] you know . . . so I make room for someone else. (Leverentz, 2010, p. 661)

V. Michalsen (2011), in a qualitative study of 100 female ex-offenders, found that children can both promote and inhibit desistance for female ex-offenders. However, Michalsen notes that females expressed other reasons for desistance such as avoiding incarceration, sobriety, and their own mortality, and these factors have also been identified for male ex-offenders (see also Maruna, 2001).

Conclusion

In sum, the female ex-offender attempting to reenter society successfully is faced with a host of distinct challenges that may or may not be visible. Some of their challenges are similar to male ex-offenders; however, other challenges they face in reentry are distinctly different. Clearly, gender plays an additional role in ex-offender reentry success for females.

In the following chapter, we present a detailed examination of race and social class as they relate to ex-offender success.

5

Race/Ethnicity and Social Class

INSPIRATIONAL STORIES OF EX-OFFENDERS SUCCEEDING DURING reentry are rarely publicly depicted with a few exceptions; one in particular is the Animal Planet's show entitled *Pit Bulls and Parolees*. This show depicts two groups (i.e., pit bulls and ex-offenders) in society that are viewed rather unfavorably by the general public, and the struggles each faces to reenter society. The pairing of these two groups not only serves as entertainment, but also demonstrates one positive example of successful reentry for ex-offenders. In this show, parolees are reforming their lives through working with pit bulls. Specifically, the parolees rehabilitate and train pit bulls in order to facilitate adoption of these dogs into the general public. However, the association of ex-offenders with a breed of dog that has been stigmatized as violent may have a simultaneous negative moderating effect—i.e., reinforcing a stereotype that ex-offenders, like dogs, have a propensity for violence. Another example might be the television show entitled *Dog the Bounty Hunter,* which features Duane "Dog" Chapman, an ex-offender who has successfully reintegrated back into society after serving time for robbery and murder in the 1970s and now works as a bounty hunter. However, more often than not, the success stories of reintegrating offenders are not covered by the mainstream media.

Typically, the media coverage regarding ex-offenders surrounds their failure to reintegrate successfully and the dangers ex-offenders pose to the community. For instance, in late 2011, a nine-year-old girl, Aliahna Lemmon, was killed and dismembered by her babysitter, Michael Plumadore—a registered sex-offender (LoBianco and Coyne, 2011). This unfortunate case made national headlines not only because of the brutality of the crime but also because of the perpetrator's ex-offender status. With a limited number of ex-offender success stories

87

portrayed in the media and coverage of ex-offender failure during reentry being more prevalent, the general public is misguided about the reentry process. Additionally, often missing in such portrayals and discussions is how race, ethnicity, or social class shape reentry.

Within US society, racism and classism historically have been and still are pervasive problems despite strides made during the Civil Rights Movement in the 1950s and 1960s (Barak, Flavin, and Leighton, 2001; Walker, Spohn, and DeLone, 2007). Individuals in society continue to be discriminated against for housing and employment on the basis of their race, ethnicity, or social class alone (Leung, 2009; Lui et al., 2006). The role of racism and classism has permeated the criminal justice system. For example, that a disproportionate number of minorities and members of lower socioeconomic statuses are incarcerated in the US correctional system is widely known (Harris and Miller, 2003). Given their disproportionate level of incarceration, more members of minority races, minority ethnicities, and less-well-off social classes will find themselves reentering the US society not only carrying the baggage of their ex-offender status but also facing various forms of discrimination due to other labels put on them by general society. However, the struggles that members of these groups face have not been at the forefront of the discussions on reentry. Thus, in a sense, demographic variables can, in some cases, further inhibit or, in other cases, assist offenders in reentry. That is, members of a particular race (e.g., Caucasian versus African American) or social class (e.g., upper class versus poor) may experience a smoother transition or rougher transition based on whether or not they face additional discrimination due to factors other than their ex-offender status. We explore, in this chapter, reentry experiences from the point of view of various races and ethnicities (e.g., African Americans, Hispanic Americans, Asian Americans, or Native Americans/Alaska Natives) and pinpoint the specific needs and challenges these groups have. Additionally, we will discuss how an individual's social class may assist or inhibit reentry.

Needs and Challenges of Various Racial and Ethnic Groups

African Americans

As highlighted in Chapter 4, the "war on drugs" campaign of the 1980s led to an increase in the incarceration rate of African Americans—in particular African American females (Bush-Baskette, 2000). T. P. Bonczar and A. J. Beck (1997) report that African American males are six times more likely than Caucasian males to serve at least one year in prison. These numbers suggest a significant number of African Americans are constantly reentering society from prison (G. Brown, 2010). Thus, these ex-offenders are encountering similar challenges to other ex-offenders in the struggle to meet their basic needs, such as access to food, housing, and employment (Allender, 2004; Cowan and Fionda, 1994; Harlow, 2003; Harris and Keller, 2005; Nagin and Waldfogel, 1998; Paylor, 1995; Rodriguez and Brown, 2003; Starr, 2002). While employment, for example, is difficult for all ex-offenders to obtain given the stigma associated with their conviction status, African American men and women may encounter greater difficulties in reaching success in this arena. Previous research has revealed that minorities in the general law-abiding, US society, who do not possess a criminal record, have experienced employment discrimination (Holzer, Raphael, and Stoll, 2003; Leung, 2009; Toth, Crews, and Burton, 2008). For example, research has revealed that African Americans face employment discrimination in getting hired and promoted (Queralt, 1996). Further, several researchers have uncovered employment discrimination for African American job applicants when compared to Caucasian job applicants (Beauchamp and Bowie, 1993; Turner, Fix, and Struyk, 1991; Weatherspoon, 1996). More recently, in a case that drew international media attention, a lawsuit was filed by several thousand persons of color against Abercrombie and Fitch for hiring and employment discrimination. African Americans experienced difficulties in getting hired at this store, and if successful at getting hired, they were not employed as a sales team member despite having previous sales experience. More often than not, African Americans hired at these stores would work at the store after hours as members of the cleanup crew. In 2004, Abercrombie and Fitch agreed to pay $40 million to settle the lawsuit (Greenhouse, 2004). Despite the media coverage of discriminatory hiring practices, such as the case mentioned here, still more employment discrimination occurs in US society and remains rather invisible. In short, minority ex-offenders experience difficulties finding employment (Pager, 2007), with other research showing definitively that Caucasian ex-offenders are more likely to be hired over and above their minority counterparts (see Shivy et al., 2007). Therefore, African American ex-offenders face discrimination in their quest for employment due to not only their status as an ex-offender but also their skin color.

While discrimination could certainly be an explanation for employment differences between Caucasians and African Americans, it also could be a function of the neighborhood that the ex-offenders are returning to. That is, if some ex-offenders are returning to socially disorganized or disadvantaged neighborhoods or culturally isolated neighborhoods, these factors could also provide insight into the differences in employment rates for these groups (Clear, 2007; Sampson and Wilson, 1995; Shaw and McKay, 1938). P. E. Bellair and B. R. Kowalski (2011), using a contextual analysis of approximately 1,500 Caucasian and African American ex-prisoners in Ohio, examined racial differences in serious recidivism. The researchers found that African Americans exhibited a higher recidivism rate than their Caucasian counterparts, and one contributing factor to this difference was the lack of employment opportunities for ex-offenders who were qualified for only low-skill jobs. Specifically, the researchers found that African American ex-offenders in their sample, upon release from prison, were more likely to return to disadvantaged neighborhoods where unemployment is high and low-skill employment opportunities are not prevalent. Further, the researchers found that approximately 80 percent of Caucasian parolees in their sample returned to neighborhoods with unemployment rates of 0–10 percent whereas only 55 percent of African American parolees returned to such neighborhoods. Clearly, and perhaps obviously, the environment in which the ex-offenders are looking for employment can play a role in their success in obtaining gainful employment. If African American ex-offenders are predominately reintegrating into disadvantaged neighborhoods, this lack of opportunity will certainly inhibit their ability to succeed during reentry.

Many African Americans may also face difficulties during reentry due to their religious affiliation, particularly if that affiliation is Islam. The terrorist attacks on September 11, 2001, that shook the nation resulted in a backlash against Muslim citizens of the United States since the terrorists who perpetrated the attacks followed a radical form of the Islamic faith (Price, 2002). Post-9/11, US followers of Islam have been subjected to various forms of discrimination (e.g., housing, employment), experienced violence upon their persons, had their businesses harmed (e.g., by arson), and seen their mosques become targets of arson attacks (Kaifi et al., 2011). Muslims have struggled since 9/11 with fitting into US society and being viewed as loyal US citizens. Y. Salaam (2006) states that approximately 30 percent, or 300,000, of incarcerated African Americans in 2006 belong to the Islamic faith, though exact numbers of incarcerated African Americans is difficult to ascertain as the statistics are not reported by any official government agency. Salaam reports, "The Islamic community has no structured programs, policies, or positions to help formerly incarcerated Muslims transition into Muslim society. Thus, the freed Muslim ex-offender has to not only struggle with transforming from being a jailhouse Muslim, he or she has to cope with the challenge of finding a Muslim-friendly employer, landlord, counseling, etc" (2006). Therefore, the ex-offender African American who is Muslim must cope with the stigma of their ex-offender status, likely racial discrimination, and also possible discrimination due to their faith. Discrimination based on their status as Muslim notwithstanding, African American ex-offenders have the additional obstacle of adhering to religious teachings in regard to the selection of housing and employment opportunities. That is, while housing or employment options may be made available to these ex-offenders, they will need to consider how these opportunities fit with their religious traditions. If these options are not congruent with their religious teachings or beliefs, these ex-offenders may decide to decline pursuing such options, which can further complicate their ability to succeed during reentry.

While mentioned earlier in this text, a common challenge for ex-offenders during reentry is the lack of family support. This experience is shared by all ex-offenders regardless of race or gender. However, for African American male ex-offenders, family conflict, particularly with intimate female partners, has been reported as a challenge for them and can contribute to unsuccessful reentry (Tripp, 2003; Zamble and Quinsey, 1997). W. Oliver and C. F. Hairston (2008) conducted a series of focus groups with African American ex-offenders who were transitioning from prison. Some of the sources of interpersonal conflict experienced by the men in their sample stemmed from relationships (i.e., sexual) that the female intimate partner may have engaged in while the men were incarcerated. For example, one subject reported, "Another conflict that might occur once you get released from prison . . . is that she's still having that second life. You're slowly starting to find out about it when you get the 3:00 in the morning call and then somebody hangs up. Or you catch her in the bathroom, you hear her talking about how I love you too, and you're wondering who is she talking too, and she tells you I'm talking to my mama" (pp. 266–267). Other strains reported by men in the study that contributed to partner conflict included economic pressure, the ex-offenders' lack of household authority, the female partners' challenging the male ex-offenders to "do right," the ex-offenders' displaced anger about being in prison, and parole restrictions (Oliver and Hairston, 2008). In regard to the displacement of anger, one subject reported,

A lot of times we go out, we leave prison with the ideology that we've been wronged or everybody turned their back on me. I got this madness in my heart, and I don't care who in my path I'm going to let it happen. I'm going to let you feel my wrath. Nine times out of ten that wrath happens to be one person, and that's that woman who has stuck by you, who has helped you when nobody else did. They stuck closer than your family did. (p. 269)

Some of the subjects resorted to acts of domestic violence in response to their feelings of rage and betrayal. This behavior, of course, could lead to a new conviction and subsequent parole revocation. Thus, whether it is allegations of affairs or displacement of anger toward the one they love, conflict can occur, and when it does if it is not handled prosocially, it inhibits the ability of the African American male ex-offender to successfully reintegrate.

Female African American ex-offenders encounter several obstacles in their attempts to successfully reintegrate. Similar to other female ex-offenders of different race and ethnic backgrounds, female African American ex-offenders are likely to suffer from prior sexual abuse, be fighting with substance abuse, and be struggling to regain custody of their children (Belknap, 2007; G. Brown, 2010). However, one distinct difference can be found between female African American ex-offenders and other female ex-offenders—the state of their physical health. G. Brown (2010) reports that rates of HIV transmission are prevalent in lower-income African American communities. While both male and female African Americans experience higher transmissions of HIV than other races and ethnicities, African American women have been severely affected (G. Brown, 2010; Centers for Disease Control and Prevention, 2007). In 2007, the Centers for Disease Control and Prevention reported that African American women experienced an HIV transmission rate that was twenty times higher than Caucasian women. G. Brown adds that "HIV rates for incarcerated African-American women are higher than for white or Latino women" (2010, p. 8). Additionally, this diagnosis places these women at high risk for mortality immediately upon release—especially if their medical care (e.g., drug regimen) is disrupted (G. Brown, 2010). Given this reality, many female African American ex-offenders are (1) struggling to fulfill basic needs during reentry such as employment and housing, (2) trying to get these needs met in the larger context of a society that often discriminates against them, (3) encountering specific challenges that have an impact on female ex-offenders such as coping with prior trauma, fighting addiction, and reuniting with and regaining custody of children, and (4) trying to live as best they can with chronic or even potentially fatal health problems.

Hispanic Americans

Much of the literature on reentry has focused on samples of Caucasians and African Americans, leaving a gap in knowledge for other ethnic groups such as Hispanic Americans (Martinez, 2004). Over the last decade, increased numbers of Hispanics have been sentenced in federal courts due to increased enforcement of immigration laws (Lopez and

Light, 2009). J. L. Morin reports, "In recent years, Latinas/os have been identified as the fastest rate of imprisonment of all groups in the country" (2008, p. 11). This fact is in stark comparison to the images of the crimes that Hispanics may engage in as portrayed in movies such as those featuring Cheech and Chong. The stereotype of the Hispanic male as a violent thug, as in the classic 1990 movie, *Ghost,* where Sam Wheat (played by Patrick Swayze) is robbed and killed by a man named Willy Lopez, adds to the perception by many in society that Hispanic minorities, like African Americans, are violent. As Morin notes, "in spite of the facts that belie their portrayals by the media, Latina/o youth and Latina/o immigrants, in particular, are consistently and repeatedly associated with criminality [*sic*] conduct in the media" (p. 25).

In 2007, of the federally sentenced offenders, 40 percent were Hispanic, and of the 40 percent, 29 percent were not US citizens (Lopez and Light, 2009). The Illegal Immigration Reform and Immigrant Responsibility Act (IIRAIRA) of 1996 has led to both legal and illegal US citizens being deported (Gomes, 2012; Y. Martin, 2008). Despite this legislation, a large proportion of ex-offenders reentering society are Hispanic. In 2009, Hispanic Americans comprised 21 percent of offenders under federal postconviction supervision (i.e., probation and parole) while Hispanic Americans comprised 31 percent of offenders under some form of state supervision (Glaze and Bonczar, 2011; Motivans, 2011). Given the numbers of Hispanic Americans under supervision, increased understanding of their reentry experiences is clearly needed. Hispanic American ex-offenders face the same difficulties that any other ex-offender faces in terms of locating housing and employment upon release (Martinez, 2004). Furthermore, D. J. Martinez (2004) cautions against examining Latinos/as as one aggregate group, as has been done in the past, but points to the importance of looking at understanding reentry through the lens of many Latino subgroups such as Mexicans, Cubans, and Puerto Ricans. However, identifying and distinguishing each group's challenges are difficult given the relative absence of literature on the experiences of any of these groups.

In one of the few articles on Hispanic American ex-offender reentry, Y. Martin (2008), in a series of fourteen qualitative interviews, examined reentry for ten males and four females in New York City whose nationalities were Puerto Rican and Dominican. Several subjects reported difficulties in acclimating to society and losing their ability to rely solely on themselves. One male subject reported,

> It took me half an hour to cross Riverside Drive, because I felt out of place. The cars were going too fast, and it almost made me sick. After 26 years in prison, I didn't know how to use a Metrocard. I would

walk everywhere, so I wouldn't let anybody know how lost I was. I went to buy a hot dog one day, and the vendor asked for $2.50, and I couldn't believe it. I thought he knew where I came from, and was trying to take advantage of me: when I went to prison, a hot dog was 35 cents. Shortly after, my youngest daughter had to help me to open a bank account, because I had no clue about where to start. You can imagine how that felt. (p. 223)

Besides adapting to their environment, which may have drastically changed during their incarceration, subjects also were aware of the fact that the environments they chose to reintegrate into may contribute to or inhibit successful reentry. As explained by one male subject, "Going back to your old environment is dangerous. Once I was doing fine [staying clean], I said to myself: 'let me go back to the hood and show around how well I'm doing.' That was a big mistake. I went back to smoking crack that same week. I learned the hard way to stay far from everyone. Now, I won't even have a beer. Positive peers are very important. Without that, you're lost" (p. 225). Not surprisingly, one struggle that these ex-offenders faced during reentry was securing housing, and one ex-offender in her sample took extreme measures to procure it: one subject, named Pablo, purposively ingested alcohol and drugs to secure lodging in a rehabilitation program within a hospital. Pablo explained, "They will only accept you if you have drugs in your system, . . . so I drank a bottle of rum. But it was still not enough, so I did a $20 of coke, and then they let me in. A $20 of coke is nothing, but it got me through the door" (p. 222). Martin explains that Pablo feigned a drug addiction to get off the streets and to get into a safe environment where he could find "out about the shelter system, health-care providers, job-training programs, or how to secure one's benefits and entitlements . . . some of the basic needs that the system fails to provide to those who have spent time in prison" (p. 222). Unemployment, or joblessness, has been identified as a problem for the Latino/a ex-offender populations (Cartagena, 2008). Martin (2008) found that the securing of employment was important for successful reentry, and that this factor was particularly important for the male ex-offenders in her sample.

Besides finding a healthy environment, securing housing, and obtaining employment, reentry struggles that, if overcome, can go a long way toward succeeding for all ex-offenders, female Hispanic ex-offenders identified other factors that contributed to their success during reentry. For female Hispanic ex-offenders in Martin's (2008) study, social networks played an important role during reentry, more so than for males. Martin explains that for these ex-offenders, "social networks—close friends and relatives, people that they could rely upon and with whom they felt comfortable—were a uniquely valuable resource for successful re-entry" (p. 224). Specifically, ties to positive associations and the development of bonds to religion were cited as contributing factors to female Hispanic ex-offender reentry success.

Additionally, both male and female subjects reported that successful reentry would occur when they were ready. That is, as one might expect, being ready to change or being ready to give up drugs can contribute to a positive reentry experience. One subject explained, "I was lucky with the reentry program that I got in, and I was ready to take advantage of it. The thing is that there comes a time when everybody is ready to stop using [drugs]. Unfortunately, many people don't get to that point before they're dead, or they're in prison for life. But some people hit it before that, and if the circumstances are right, then it will work" (Y. Martin, 2008, p. 226). A female subject explained,

> Being "ready" has to do with knowing that I didn't want to go back to doing the same thing. It was a matter of realizing that I wanted to change my life. I was ready to move on and do something for myself. I just had to do it for myself. I do whatever I can, not to go back. I know a lot of people that try, but they don't have any money and they end up doing things that they shouldn't. It's hard. But I've managed to stay clean, and I intend to stay this way in the future. (Martin, 2008, p. 226)

Therefore, as mentioned in Chapter 2, for many ex-offenders struggling with alcohol and drug addictions, at a certain point in their lives, they are ready to accept treatment and work to break free from their addictions. Results from Martin's (2008) study suggest that male and female Hispanic ex-offenders are similar to other ex-offenders of various race and ethnic backgrounds in this regard as well.

Another factor that inhibits successful reentry for Hispanic ex-offenders are language and cultural barriers. Numerous researchers have identified bilingual and culturally competent services offered to Hispanics in the criminal justice system as inadequate (Morin, 2005, 2008; Villarruel et al., 2002; Walker et al., 2004). If ex-offenders are experiencing language barriers during reentry, this added complication will likely inhibit their ability to successfully reintegrate. After all, ex-offenders need to communicate with those in society (e.g., potential employers) and those trying to assist them (e.g., CCOs, treatment providers). Additionally, Hispanic ex-offenders are in need of services during reentry that are culturally appropriate—that incorporate cultural values (e.g., religion) and traditions (Arya et al., 2009). That is, those helping Hispanic ex-offenders reenter society cannot be satisfied with simply employing translators and assume that, with that service, these ex-offenders understand what they need to do or that they are even getting their needs met. Rather, reentry programming designed to assist ex-offenders during reentry should be tailored to Hispanic cultural experiences and traditions. Additionally, a "one-size-fits-all" approach for all Hispanic ex-offenders in regard to the design of service programming is also problematic given the range of nationalities associated with the term *Hispanic* (see Martinez, 2004).

Asian Americans

The research literature on reentry with samples of Asian Americans is scant. This dearth may be due, in part, to the relatively low numbers of those of Asian descent in the criminal justice system when compared to other racial and ethnic groups (Oh and Umemoto, 2005). However, despite Asian Americans' smaller numbers in relation to the total prison population, A. E. Oh and K. Umemoto (2005) state that incarceration for this group has increased over 250 percent between 1990 and 2000. Additionally, Asian and Pacific Islander state prisoners committed a higher proportion of violent offenses relative to all offenses committed by this group when compared to other racial groups. As reported in Chapter 2, approximately 27,000 Asian and Native Hawaiian/other Pacific Islanders are on probation while approximately 7,000 from these groups are on parole (Glaze and Bonczar, 2011). Similar to Latinos/as, Asians, particularly noncitizens, are at risk of deportation (Hing, 2005). Given the smaller numbers and lack of attention by researchers, less is known about the reentry experiences of this group (Fei and Lopez, 2005).

One study that attempted to bridge the gap in the reentry experiences of Asian Americans and Pacific Islanders was conducted by Oh and Umemoto (2005). The researchers conducted twenty qualitative interviews with ex-offenders, social service providers, and law enforcement officers. Oh and Umemoto describe one ex-offender as follows:

> "Jong Il" is a twenty-seven year old Korean American who served three years in prison for robbery. He did not participate in the prison's voluntary pre-release class. From his point of view, the main problem about re-entry is that you need to find a way to be responsible for life on the outside. When incarcerated, he did not worry about food, clothes, housing, a bed. But upon his release, he did not know how he was going to live. His only plan was to go to a friend's apartment to have a place to sleep. Jong Il's greatest anxiety was getting older, having no skills or base from which he could operate. Because of his history of criminal

activity, he had no employment history that could be used as a foundation for seeking work. (p. 44)

Thus, for this ex-offender, finding a place to reside and gaining employment were of critical importance. This finding is consistent with the immediate needs identified by ex-offenders in general when released. Oh
and Umemoto also report that in the continental United States, Asian
and Pacific Islander ex-offenders are more likely to return to immigrant
and refugee communities. Similar to ex-offenders of other races and
ethnicities, Asian and Pacific Islanders return to environments that they
are most familiar with upon release from prison. If they are returning to
disadvantaged neighborhoods where securing safe housing is difficult
and steady employment is scarce, then Asian and Pacific Islander ex-
offenders may struggle during reentry.

Based on interviews with ex-offenders, Oh and Umemoto (2005)
conclude that family relations are the "key" to reentry success for this
group: "each ex-offender interviewee referenced the importance of family in the process of coming out of prison and seeking re-entry" (p. 54).
Culturally, the ex-offender may face stigmatization by not only family
but also their community. That is, by committing a crime they have
brought shame not only to their family name but also to their community (Braithwaite, 1989). Thus, family reconciliation and community
support during reintegration may foster reentry success. Finally, ex-
offenders reported that "successful re-entry experiences seemed to
occur where there were personal journeys, including a spiritual component" (Oh and Umemoto, 2005, p. 54). Therefore, fostering connections
to religion or spiritual exercises during reentry may contribute to successful reintegration.

Similar to their Hispanic American counterparts, Asian and Pacific
Islander ex-offenders may participate in reentry programs that do not
specifically meet their linguistic or cultural needs (Oh and Umemoto,
2005). In the state of California, for example, of the nineteen reentry
centers in the state, none offer specialized programs or services that address the needs of specifically Asian and Pacific Islanders (Oh and
Umemoto, 2005). Further, the researchers report that only five nonprofit
programs provide services to these ex-offenders. On the other hand, in
Hawaii, Oh and Umemoto (2005) report, "Eleven programs specifically
target Native Hawaiians and Pacific Islander ex-offenders. These programs offer employment and job training programs, drug rehabilitation
services, transitional housing programs, education support services,
health services, and mental health counseling" (p. 53). The researchers

add that many of these programs integrate traditional Hawaiian culture (e.g., language, art, spirituality). Another study that sheds some light on the type of services that Asian and Pacific Islanders can expect during reentry was conducted by M. T. Fei and G. P. Lopez (2005). In 2003, the researchers conducted a telephone survey of 2,000 residents in New York City with Asian and Pacific Islanders representing 12 percent of the sample and 1,000 in-person interviews with service providers. The researchers did not focus their sample on ex-offenders; thus, specifics about reentry experiences for this group, in their own words, were not reported in this study. However, Fei and Lopez report that results from interviews with service providers indicated that Asian and Pacific Islander ex-offenders would not likely find any reentry help. In fact, the researchers found that, at the time of their study in 2005, not a single service provider in New York City was focused on meeting the specific needs for this group, and only 11 percent of the service providers spoke Asian and Pacific Islander languages. This finding is rather alarming considering the increased rates of incarceration for members of this group (Oh and Umemoto, 2005).

For some Asian and Pacific Islander ex-offenders, support during their reentry appears to be present while for others it is absent. Without a supportive environment that meets their basic needs (e.g., housing and employment) as well as cultural and spiritual needs, Asian and Pacific Islander ex-offenders may struggle to successfully reintegrate back into society. Further, the wide cultural diversity that is present within these ex-offender groups means that a "one-size-fits-all" approach (i.e., only one type of cultural program) to helping these ex-offenders during reentry is likely to be unsuccessful.

Native Americans/Alaska Natives

A modicum of research exists regarding Native Americans and Alaska Natives and their needs for reentry but less is known about their reentry experiences. The minimal attention paid in the criminal justice literature to offending and reentry for these groups has resulted in an outcry where some refer to these understudied groups as "overlooked and forgotten" (Odgen, 2004, p. 63). Recall from Chapter 2 that approximately 27,000 American Indians/Alaska Natives are on federal and state probation and 8,500 American Indians/Alaska Natives are on federal and state parole (Glaze and Bonczar, 2011). Initially, these numbers may seem low and rather unalarming, but according to the US Census Bureau (2010), American Indians and Alaska Natives make up 0.9 percent of the total US population, or 2.7 million individuals. Thus, the numbers of

American Indians and Alaska Natives in the state or federal criminal justice system (i.e., prison, probation, or parole) is high and dispropor- tionate to their numbers in society. For the most part, the state or federal government does not have jurisdiction on reservations and tribal lands with a few exceptions: "where the crime took place; the status of the al- leged offender and victim (Indian or non-Indian); and the type of of- fense" (US Department of Justice, 2011, p. 2). However, the US Depart- ment of Justice (2011) reports that a majority of American Indian and Alaska Native offenders actually serve their sentences in state or federal correctional facilities—not in facilities on Indian lands. Upon inspection of data for those Native American and Alaska Native offenders incarcer- ated in the approximately eighty jails and detention facilities, both pre- trial and postconviction, on tribal lands at midyear 2009, roughly 2,100 were incarcerated in such facilities (Minton, 2011). Therefore, the num- bers for Native Americans/Alaska Natives who are reentering their com- munities is a bit higher given that many Native American/Alaska Native crime violations are handled in the tribal court system as opposed to the US state or federal court system.

One critical need for American Indian and Alaska Native ex-offenders is substance abuse treatment primarily for alcohol. Often, their depen- dence on alcohol stems from early childhood abuse (Koss et al., 2003; Robin et al., 1997). The need for such treatment has been cited as one of the most critical health problems facing American Indians and Alaska Natives—both ex-offenders and nonoffenders (Beauvais, 1996; French, 2000; Grobsmith, 1989a; Grobsmith and Dam, 1990; Lamarine, 1988; Mail et al., 2002). In a study of forty-five Native American prisoners in Nebraska, E. S. Grobsmith (1989a) found that the majority of her sam- ple currently had or had had a chemical dependency problem. Further, she found that between 91 and 100 percent of her sample committed crimes that were alcohol or drug related. Therefore, drug and alcohol addiction is a risk factor for entry into criminality. For some Native Americans seeking treatment for drug or alcohol abuse in their commu- nities, needing such help is stigmatizing. In a study conducted by K. A. Earle, B. Bradigan, and L. I. Morgenbesser, one Native American echoed this concern regarding stigmatization by stating, "It's a small commu- nity, and people fear their business will get spread, so they don't go for treatment of drug and alcohol abuse. In the community, nobody goes to outpatient, they self-medicate by drinking" (2001, p. 124). Thus, contin- ued substance abuse treatment and relapse prevention is critical for American Indian and Alaska Natives ex-offender reentry success.

These ex-offenders also have mental health needs (Earle, Bradigan, and Morgenbesser, 2001). However, their needs are often misunderstood by mental health providers or prison administrators, or their needs are not met as available treatment and interventions are not congruent with their cultural beliefs (Vigesaa, 2013). As stated by one former incarcerated Native American woman,

> The reality of psychiatry in prison has everything to do with control and management, and nothing to do with effective treatment. Most of the women I knew in county jail, and in prison, were on some sort of "medication." The guards would report to the medical staff that a woman was hysterical and needed to be medicated, especially if the woman was being sent to prison after her court hearing. Seemingly, the prison staff believes that women are more vulnerable to emotional upsets and are in need of "medication." (Ogden, 2004, p. 66)

This narrative is consistent with reports by incarcerated females of other races and ethnicities in regard to their experiences of being overmedicated (see Belknap, 2007). Thus, incarcerated Native American females may be more likely to be given medication for their needs, or at least for their "needs" as defined by others in the prison system.

Other research on the mental health treatment needs for Native Americans further illustrate the gaps that exist in regard to successful treatment for this group. In a study of mental health treatment in prisons in New York for Native Americans, Earle, Bradigan, and Morgenbesser (2001) conducted eight interviews with American Indian prisoners. Some of the ex-offenders in their sample found the mental health services provided to them while incarcerated rather unhelpful. One subject reported, "Some counselors were sincere, but there was always a lingering doubt" (p. 123). Another subject recalled, "I was forced into drug and alcohol groups. I did not believe in it, and refused meds. The psychologists did not seem to understand, just wanted to convince me as soon as possible they were right" (p. 123). These statements are disconcerting as they suggest that, while incarcerated, Native Americans are not getting their needs met. If this is the case, then Native Americans are not set up with the tools to be successful upon reentry.

One barrier to successful mental health treatment is general distrust of those who are not Native American and of treatment that is not rooted in Native American cultural traditions. For instance, one subject interviewed by Earle, Bradigan, and Morgenbesser stated, "Indians don't think they need it (mental health care), don't trust psychiatrists. They will exploit all you say, have meds, a pill for everything. Treatment would have to be traditional (Indian . . .), smudges, sweats" (2001, p. 124). Additionally, one subject stated, "Indians only want to see Indians (for mental health problems)" (p. 124). Further, another subject added, "There is a stigma to mental illness. You're considered loony. On the reservation we give sanctuary to Indian people on the run and this makes us even less likely to trust people who aren't Indian. They say Indians are abused in mental health, like boarding schools, so we don't trust any state agency" (p. 124).

This sentiment regarding the stigma and distrust in seeking mental health treatment extends to community mental health in the ex-offenders' own communities. As one subject stated, "There is an IHS [Indian Health Service] clinic on the reservation but people don't like to go to it. They say it is our clinic, but it's the government. People know what to do to fool them to get out of (private hospitals). There is embarrassment about mental problems, we are a proud people who keep to ourselves, don't admit faults. We are the underdogs already" (Earle, Bradigan, and Morgenbesser, 2001, p. 124). If Native Americans suffering from mental health issues are not getting their needs addressed in prison counseling and programming, then, upon reentry, they are likely to continue to suffer from such problems, resulting in poor reintegration back into their communities. Given Native Americans' distrust of those who are not members of their culture, their problems are likely to be exacerbated by treatment programs in their communities that are run by or affiliated with the US government. Clearly, Native American and Alaska Native ex-offenders are in need of mental health treatment, but treatment and support must be offered in ways that are aligned with their cultural traditions and by those they trust to foster successful reentry for members of these groups.

For Native American and Alaska Native prisoners, the opportunity to practice and engage in their own spirituality and religious practices can have a positive impact on their lives. Grobsmith states that "the majority of Native American inmates depend on a variety of religious and spiritual activities to aid them in their struggle to conquer the problems which plagued their early lives and the incidents that resulted in their incarceration" (1989b, p. 144). However, S. Beran states that while religion is important for this group, "many Native prisoners encounter the significant problem of being unable to satisfy their religious and cultural needs in prison because these needs are either misinterpreted or disregarded" (2005, p. 47). M. A. Vezzola (2007) further adds that many incarcerated Native Americans have been unable to fulfill their spiritual needs as they may not be permitted to practice all of their beliefs due to concerns over security. If spiritual needs are not being met within the state or federal prison system for Native American or Alaska Native offenders, then an opportunity is missed to provide these offenders with a sense of support or connection with their community upon their release.

With many American Indians and Alaska Natives being held in prisons located far away from their communities, they are likely to further lose their connection with their culture if they are unable to fully practice their cultural traditions.

Religion and cultural values as they relate to ex-offenders are indeed important, and allowing offenders and ex-offenders to effectively cultivate them can be a factor promoting reentry success for this group. B. G. Angell and M. G. Jones (2003), who examined recidivism rates for parolees over a three-year follow-up period for members of the Lumbee tribe of North Carolina living in "Lumbee country outside Lumbee country," found that those who returned to the Lumbee community were less likely to be arrested for violent and drug-related crimes. The researchers explained that Lumbee parolees who returned to their community found not only acceptance from community members and received family support, but also experienced a cultural restoration. That is, returning to their cultural roots reduced their risk of recidivism. The researchers caution that the solution to reduced recidivism is not just simply returning to live in the community, but rather the community and the Lumbee culture can actively provide pillars to reform and foster successful reentry postprison. This finding is reminiscent of R. J. Sampson and J. H. Laub's (1993) assertion that the development and building of quality, reciprocal bonds can intercept and alter criminal offending trajectories.

Conclusions About Minority Experiences

For all ex-offenders from various minority races and ethnicities, a gap exists in knowledge about their reentry experiences. While some research has emerged regarding reentry for these groups, it is limited. What is known is that all ex-offenders regardless of race or ethnicity share common critical needs during reentry such as securing housing and employment. However, some distinct differences can be observed among various races and ethnicities in their specific reentry experiences. Some ex-offenders find themselves faced with multiple layers of discrimination based on their status as an ex-offender, their race or ethnicity, and even their religion. Thus, some ex-offenders face even more significant hurdles during reentry. Other ex-offenders face difficulties within the criminal justice system—a system that may not be meeting their needs behind the iron bars and continues to fail to meet their needs when they reenter society. Yet another barrier for ex-offenders stymieing their successful reentry is their social position, or socioeconomic standing, in society.

Needs and Challenges Based on Social Class

Social class refers to the stratification of income or wealth among individuals in a society (Barak, Flavin, and Leighton, 2001). In the United States, class is typically stratified as upper, middle, and lower. The attention paid to social class in the United States is hard to ignore at any time, but especially since September 2011, as many US citizens have mobilized in "Occupy" movements to protest against the 1 percent in society who, according to them, control a disproportionate amount of the wealth worldwide and hoard this wealth, having a negative impact upon the other 99 percent of citizens (Stelter, 2011). In the media, the "Occupy" movement has been portrayed as a battleground between the "haves" and "have-nots." This disharmony, or conflict, between the social classes has been highlighted in the past by critical criminologists who have claimed that crime is a result of the conflict of various classes in society—those in power and those who are not (Akers and Sellers, 2008). Thus, the role of social class and how it permeates into the criminal justice system cannot be ignored.

While no national source of data exists for researchers to inspect in regard to the socioeconomic backgrounds of those serving various correctional sentences, it is widely acknowledged that those serving prison sentences generally come from economically disadvantaged neighborhoods (Clear, 2007; Herivel and Wright, 2003). As G. Barak, J. M. Flavin, and P. S. Leighton state, "The general pattern is that those who find themselves at the first stages of criminal justice processing are disproportionately poor, and those who emerge from the other end bound for prison are poorer still" (2001, p. 53). As mentioned in Chapter 2, many released offenders come from lower socioeconomic backgrounds and reported annual income levels at or below the poverty line prior to being detained in jails (McLean and Thompson, 2007). Therefore, ex-offenders who are reentering society face financial difficulties and are most likely not returning to families who can financially support them or communities that are advantaged (i.e., where safe housing and stable employment opportunities are plentiful). Beyond the obvious financial difficulties that ex-offenders may face upon release, their position, or class standing, may make assimilating back into society more challenging for them.

Within the literature on the relationship between social class and successful offender reentry, discussion has emerged around social capital (Hattery and Smith, 2010; Leverentz, 2006a; Sampson and Laub, 1993; Smith and Hattery, 2011). Social capital refers to the ability of individuals to secure benefits (e.g., housing, employment) through their

membership and often their specific position within a social structure
(Lin, 2000; Portes, 1998). E. Smith and A. Hattery (2011) explain that
one's social class determines housing and employment options, which
themselves can contribute to that person's access, or lack thereof, to
social networks and further acquisition of social capital. As one might
expect, ex-offenders are more likely to lack social capital than nonoffenders (Sullivan, 1989). N. Wolff and J. Draine (2004) state that incarceration experiences such as social isolation can erode social capital
that may have existed for ex-offenders prior to incarceration. This finding is particularly true for those from lower socioeconomic backgrounds. People from a lower social class find building social capital
much harder while incarcerated or even after incarceration due to their
stigmatization as "ex-cons," a fact that is further complicated by the reality that prior to incarceration, their access to social capital was likely
low. Uncovering success stories for those ex-offenders from lower
socioeconomic backgrounds is difficult in regard to reentry, both in the
literature and in the media. The media is more likely to focus on successful reentry, however, when those ex-offenders were from higher socioeconomic backgrounds. For example, Martha Stewart was convicted
in 2004 for obstruction of justice in relation to a stock sale she made
(Farell, 2004). After serving a five-month incarceration term in a federal
prison, she was welcomed back into society, and her company made
even more money than before she was incarcerated. Martha Stewart is a
prime example of someone from a higher socioeconomic background
that possessed much social capital prior to her conviction. Thus, upon
release, Stewart had a much easier time stepping back into her position
and repairing and ultimately regaining social capital.

The role of social capital and its relationship to successful reentry
has been explored in the literature. M. D. Reisig, K. Holtfreter, and M.
Morash (2002) examined social capital among adult female offenders.
Results from their research revealed, not surprisingly, that those offenders who had more education and were from higher-income backgrounds
had greater access to social capital than those offenders with less education and income. While the researchers did not specifically explore the
role of social capital and its relationship to reentry, they do caution that
those with low social capital are at an increased risk for recidivism.
More recently, after interviewing twenty-five ex-offenders, Smith and
Hattery (2011) concluded that social capital did indeed play a role in
successful reentry for offenders in their sample. Specifically, if these
ex-offenders could access social capital networks provided to them via
reentry programs, they were more likely to secure stable housing and
employment and less likely to reoffend. This finding held for African

American male ex-offenders in their sample as well. Thus, social position could assist those ex-offenders who have traditionally faced additional reentry challenges due to their race or ethnicity. In sum, based on the initial research thus far, a relationship exists between social class and successful reentry, and this relationship is present regardless of ex-offenders' race and perhaps even gender.

Conclusion

The ability of ex-offenders to successfully reenter society may not only be the result of their individual efforts and decisions and their ability to get their needs met, but may also be a function of other barriers that are often invisible. Discrimination in US society based on an individual's race, ethnicity, social class, or cultural tradition extends to ex-offenders as well. That is, ex-offenders of various races and ethnicities and social classes are reentering their communities with additional stigma and barriers that extend past their "ex-offender" status.

In the following chapter, we present a detailed examination into the successful reentry from the perspective of ex-offenders. In their own words, they personally define successful reentry, recount their successes and struggles, and provide a perspective not currently found in the literature—What makes for successful reentry?

6

Offender Perspectives

THE CORRECTIONAL LITERATURE HAS BEEN SURPRISINGLY SILENT in recent years on ex-offender perspectives in the reentry process and the transition to community life. Research in the 1960s and 1970s in the heyday of the rehabilitation and reintegration era included ethnographic accounts and insight into the everyday experience of ex-offenders (Connett, 1972; Hammonds-White, 1989; Irwin, 1970). However, focus on ex-offender perspectives and prisoner's rights that occurred during the social welfare/rehabilitation era gave way to recidivism studies in the 1980s that shed little light on a day in the life of the released prisoner. The 1990s brought renewed attention to offender reentry in the form of state and federal funding, implementation and evaluation of programs to promote offender rehabilitation, and research on ex-offenders' needs and experiences (Petersilia, 2003; Seiter and Kadela, 2003; Visher and Travis, 2003). More recently, the criminological literature on crime desistance has offered theoretical insight into the process of offender change across the life course suggesting the need for study of individual trajectories and typologies of patterns of change in crime and deviance over time (Laub and Sampson, 1993; Moffitt, 1993; Piquero and Mazerolle, 2001; Sampson and Laub, 1992, 1993).

The attention given in the news media (and the academic literature) to the high rate of recidivism, the pains of imprisonment, and the difficulties and disasters faced by ex-offenders as they reenter society after a prison sentence oftentimes overshadows positive stories of success and understanding of the real-life day-to-day experiences of ex-offenders as they make their transition from confinement to community. Far less information is readily available to tell the story of ex-offenders who actually make it in society upon release. News coverage in recent years of individual ex-offender success stories such as Dave Dahl of Dave's

Killer Bread and programs such as DeLancey Street and Homeboy Industries[1] have brought attention in the public realm to success stories
that offer hope on the heels of decades of the institutionalized hopelessness that has become the legacy of the "tough on crime" era. In this
chapter, we focus on the experiences of ex-offenders who have achieved
some degree of success in their transition from prison to community.

What is reentry success? The traditional outcome measure for criminal justice and correctional success is a reduction in crime and recidivism. However, beneath this overt marker of success is a critical mass
of personal change elements that contribute to the reduction of recidivism. In some cases, the link between these elements is clear; other
times it is not. Individuals who give up crime do so within the context
of a wide variety of behavioral, attitudinal, and life role changes (Serin
and Lloyd, 2009). Success measured through length of time between re-
offenses, commission of lower-level offenses, or phenomenological
change is rarely discussed in the academic literature or in the practi-
tioner-policy realm. The reality is that behavioral change in human beings is not black and white. Human behavior is relatively impermeable
habit that changes through a sometimes excruciatingly slow nonlinear
process (Duhigg, 2012), influenced by purposeful intervention and situ-
ational/environmental context (Ferns, 2008), and not easily measured or
understood through quantitative outcome measures like recidivism. Ex-
offenders see success as nonrecidivism, but they also describe other
measures of personal success such as enjoying a beautiful day and getting along with a spouse (Hammonds-White, 1989). These seemingly
small outcomes can potentially have deep and meaningful impact on
motivation, information processing, and identity in ways that have potential to affect a person's ability to desist from crime and to succeed
long term in the reentry process.

Previous Research

Research on offender reentry and the reintegration process has evolved
considerably in recent years. Theoretical interest in crime desistance
within the life-course literature and attention to reentry policy and practice have revitalized research on the reentry process. An impressive
body of work has accumulated regarding critical elements of importance
in understanding aspects of crime desistance across the life course and
challenges and successes in reintegration and reentry.

Crime desistance occurs when "external and internal variables align
in such a way that an offender with a history of multiple offences ceases

all criminal activity" (Serin and Lloyd, 2009, p. 347). Crime desistance is a process rather than an event that can vary based on individual agency, social structure, experience with criminal justice interventions, gender, and ethnicity (Farrall et al., 2011). Two general theoretical depictions of desistance from crime can be found in the literature: individuals who abruptly "go straight" and those who experience a steady decline in their offending behavior whereby they "glide" toward a point of zero offending (Kurlycheck, Bushway, and Brame, 2012) with the idea that the longer people go without recidivism, the better they get at not reoffending. A number of authors have discussed the turning point or "knifing off" from past criminal behavior and criminal associates (Kirk, 2012; Sampson and Laub, 1993). In their longitudinal study of convicted felons, M. C. Kurlycheck, S. D. Bushway, and S. Brame found that "instantaneous desistance does exist" (2012, p. 97). Findings showing that ex-offenders maintain adherence to societal values even while persisting in committing illicit activities and then shift their behaviors and identification with significant (law-abiding) others in line with these values in the desistance process suggest that social control theories, rather than cultural deviance theories, explain crime desistance (Geiger and Timor, 2001).

Factors that have been found to be associated with desistance include key life events such as marriage, military service, and employment (Barnes and Beaver, 2012; Forrest and Hay, 2011); relocation to a new residence and neighborhood and separation from prior contexts (Kirk, 2012); and community engagement (Wilkinson, 2005). These life events may actually increase self-control (Forrest and Hay, 2011). Other factors that can influence an ex-offender's success are personal conditions (such as mental health, substance abuse, physical health problems, and lack of life skills and employment skills), social network/environment, accommodation, legal issues and experience in the criminal justice system, lack of rehabilitation and counseling, support (such as limited access to treatment and appropriate intervention), and employment and training support (Graffam et al., 2004).

Research on ex-offender reentry and reintegration suggests that ex-offenders are presented with a situation that is the antithesis of what they experience while incarcerated and face considerable barriers in making their way from incarceration to community (Helfgott, 1997). Reentry needs consistently identified in the literature include housing, employment, vocational training, and substance abuse treatment (Morani et al., 2011). Additional issues such as a lack of centralization of services (Gowdey and Turnbull, 1978; Helfgott, 1997) and a discrepancy in perceived social distance between the ex-offenders and their CCOs may be a hindrance in the reentry process (Gunnison and Helfgott, 2011; Helfgott and Gunnison, 2008). Social and community support is another need identified by ex-offenders (Helfgott, 1997). When asked to discuss their future success in staying crime-free, ex-offenders report that success is challenged by internal barriers to change, such as social isolation, feelings of powerlessness, and lack of control over their own actions, as well as legal issues and obstacles such as an inability to obtain financial aid (Graffam et al., 2004). Others cite problems with limited access to housing, stigma and discrimination in employment, lack of access to meaningful mental health treatment, social distance between ex-offenders and their CCOs, and perceived conflicts between conditions of supervision and life realities (Gunnison and Helfgott, 2011; Helfgott & Gunnison, 2008).

Research conducted from the offenders' perspective suggests that a number of factors influence desistance and success in the reentry process such as marriage (Barnes and Beaver, 2012); experience in the military, childbearing, parenting, and friendships (Giordano, Cernkovich, and Rudolph, 2002); employment (Visher et al., 2005); social networks to assist in obtaining employment (Shivy et al., 2007); transitional experiences and decisionmaking processes (Haigh, 2009); school and family (Martinez and Christian, 2009); age-graded transitions and life events, changing roles, and statuses (Sampson and Laub, 1992); and availability and quality of vocational, educational, drug rehabilitation, halfway house, prerelease, and treatment programs (Seiter and Kadela, 2003).

There have been some recent attempts to capture the experience of ex-offenders using qualitative and phenomenological approaches (Aresti, Eatough, and Brooks-Gordon, 2010; Geiger and Timor, 2001; Giordano, Cernkovich, and Rudolph, 2002; Hammonds-White, 1989). A. Aresti, V. Eatough, and B. Brooks-Gordon (2010) conducted one of the few studies that have examined offender change from a phenomenological perspective and found that development of a prosocial identity and worthwhile employment or a new career path contribute to crime desistance—"positive conceptualization of self is developed as past events are reinterpreted to suit future aspirations" (p. 170). J. E. Cobbina (2010) examined reintegration success and failure among female offenders and found that support networks, supportive parole officers, and access to postrelease services play important roles in reentry success for women coming out of prison.

Researchers have long argued that ex-offender perspectives are a valuable addition to the perspectives of scholars and practitioners in understanding and informing policies and practices directed toward offender reentry (Connett, 1972). Recent research has acknowledged the individual pathways of offending trajectories (Maltz and Mullany, 2000) and the importance of understanding situational specificity (Horney, 2006) through alternative data frameworks that take into account the complexity of individual lives (Maltz and Mullany, 2000). These authors call for a focus on interdisciplinary, mixed method, longitudinal research that reveals the complex dimensions of the lives of individual ex-offenders. In this chapter, we present results from twenty-one interviews conducted with fourteen male and seven female ex-offenders who had been incarcerated for two to thirty years and released from one month to twenty-seven years. Interview subjects ranged in age from twenty-nine to fifty-five ($M = 40$, $Sd = 8.8$). The majority of the interviewees were white (71.4 percent, $n = 15$), followed by black (14 percent, $n = 3$), Hispanic (10 percent, $n = 2$), and Asian/Pacific Islander (5 percent, $n = 1$). The crimes for which the interview subjects had been convicted and sentenced for most recently were murder (33 percent, $n = 7$), vehicular homicide (10 percent, $n = 2$), assault/robbery (19 percent, $n = 4$), drugs/theft/forgery (33 percent, $n = 7$), and child molestation (5 percent, n = 1).[2]

Ex-Offender Background Experiences

Most of the ex-offenders in the study reported a long history of delinquent and criminal behavior with the first contact with the criminal justice system ranging from age thirteen or earlier to age forty-two, but even those who reported later convictions described earlier periods of delinquent behavior as juveniles or long-term substance abuse or repeated contact with the police as a result of driving under the influence. One ex-offender reported having no involvement in criminal behavior prior to conviction. The sample can be classified into four types of ex-offenders based on the nature of their crimes and length of sentence and crime: (1) lifers/murder; (2) long term/violent; (3) midrange/vehicular homicide; and (4) midrange/drug-property offenses. Additionally, two of the interview subjects received clemency and were released by the governor after twenty-two and thirty years in prison respectively for first-degree murder and second-degree robbery. One of these individuals was the first offender sentenced to life without the possibility of parole (LWOP) to ever receive clemency in Washington State and the other was the first three-strikes offender to receive clemency in Washington State.

The lifers included seven interview subjects who were convicted as teenagers for murder (six for first degree and one for second degree) and were incarcerated for periods of twelve to thirty years from their teenage years until their mid-thirties to late forties. The long-term/violent group included those who served long-term periods of incarceration of ten to sixteen years for armed robbery, assault, and firearms violations, or child molestation. The midrange/vehicular homicide group included two female subjects who were convicted for vehicular homicide and served four to five years as first-time offenders, one of whom reported that she had not previously been involved in any type of delinquent or criminal behavior and the other who reported a long history of repeated arrests for driving under the influence. The midrange/drug-property offense group included subjects who served shorter periods of incarceration from multiple and repeated jail or prison sentences of days/months in jail to one to four years in prison for drug and property offenses including theft, auto prowl, auto theft, forgery, identity theft, possession of stolen property, and drug offenses.

The Change Process

The ex-offenders interviewed reported that desistance from crime occurred abruptly in some cases and slowly in others. Most acknowledged that they could identify a pivotal event or memory that they associated with a change in their thinking and a movement away from a criminal identity and toward a prosocial identity. Stevan indicated that his "heart shifted" after a number of experiences during a fifteen-year period of incarceration on a three-strikes sentence:

> The light actually came on when I got tired of feeling sorry for myself . . . I was committed to not doing the same things I used to do. . . . I knew if I did, I would get the same results. . . . I knew if I tripped up it could affect those behind me . . . I wasn't going to do anything to jeopardize their freedom . . . I want to do my part to reduce the stigma of prisoner's reentering society . . . I was embarrassed by the mediaglare . . . but I kept myself on probation. . . . When I got released the media attention was so hot. . . . They not only interviewed me, they interviewed the prosecutor who supported me coming home, they interviewed the detective who arrested me on my case. . . . The detective characterized me as something that I'm not. He said, there's murderers that are more fit to be in society and what not. It stung to hear that . . . but, I couldn't feed in to that, and I used his words as more of a motivation too . . . as a motivation that, I'm going to prove this guy wrong. . . . I recently reached out to him and sent him a thank you . . . and I told him, thank you for saving my life because him arresting me at the time he did, he did save my life.

I am relying on a lot of lessons that were taught many years ago. My mother and father, they planted good seeds in me, and then older gentlemen who I met during my first and second time in prison when I was still a youngster . . . those guys planted seeds and knowledge in my head too . . . I can reflect. I can pull . . . I got a file cabinet in the back of my head and I can pull out lessons from these guys any time a situation hits. The most important lesson is, respect your freedom, and you'd rather be broke and free than sitting up in here with a few dollars on your books. . . . I was sick and tired of being in prison. I knew I could be a warden for myself . . . It took a lot to get to that point though. . . . It was internal. . . . When I knew I was in the best place is when I started seeing news stories of things happening to people out here and it would bother me. . . . It would really bother me. That's when I knew my heart had changed . . . my heart shifted, and as my heart shifted that made me more open to helping other people . . . younger offenders . . . 16, 17, 18-year-old offenders coming in. . . . Age played a role. . . . Age made me mature enough to do that self-analysis, to go to the root, to look into [my]self.

Trevor went to prison at age sixteen, was released at age forty, and was similarly affected by seeing other prisoners within the prison context. For him, the change process was a personal decision: "I don't know exactly the exact moment and date but I started looking at people in prison, attitudes, dress, and I said that I am not going to be like that. I am not going to come back to prison with fewer teeth than when I had left."

Charles told a story about a life-changing moment after years of revolving-door jail and prison stints. He said every time he came out of jail or prison he would go right back to the streets: "I would call my drug dealer and get a welcome-back bag of dope." But one day while in jail after having committed auto prowl and auto theft earlier in the day he said:

I have a conscience now . . . This is where I might get teary . . . um, I got arrested. I went to King County Jail. It was Christmas time, and I was watching the news, and I was in there for stealing cars, and you know uh, earlier that day I had been at Westlake Center in the parking garage popping locks and getting into cars and popping their trunks and stealing Christmas presents. People go into the malls, they buy stuff, they go and put it into their trunk and go to the next store, and uh, my mentality at the time was that, uh, cars are insured and people are fine, they'll get the money back, this is going to support me, and I made it OK, and, uh, here I am in the King County Jail and I just got put in the tank and into the housing unit there and the 5:00 news is on and we're eating dinner and I see this mother and her kid on King 5 News crying outside Westlake Center talking about how am I going to replace this stuff . . . and you know the kid was crying because . . . didn't know why mom was crying and this lady had no idea how she was going to provide Christmas for her kid and I took that away. . . . I know that I didn't eat dinner and I just went in my room and I cried and, uh, I told myself I'm never going to be that piece of shit again, you know? I don't ever want to be that guy again. And I'm not . . . it's heavy huh? . . . I know I was that guy. That was me who took that Christmas away from that kid at Westlake Center earlier that day. When you see the results of your actions like that, you can't hide from that. . . . That happened. I don't ever want to be that guy again. . . . It was sad. . . . It was a life-changing event.

Alise was pregnant, addicted, and under the influence of methamphetamines when she was arrested for outstanding warrants and looking at a seven-year prison sentence. Her daughter was born soon after she was arrested, and she only saw her for a moment before the state initiated the process of terminating her rights. She eventually was granted custody of her daughter again after a two-year incarceration and completing treatment. After years of drug abuse and methamphetamine addiction, delinquency and assaults as a juvenile, and adult crimes including trafficking stolen property, identity theft, forgery, obstruction of justice, theft, and car prowling, she described her transformative moment with her newborn daughter:

Losing her and not knowing what the outcome was going to be really stemmed [sic] my motivation into a positive journey. . . . That whole period I had lost any hope. It was a horrible time. I wanted to believe there was something better in this world, and when I first laid eyes on my daughter I was afraid she wouldn't know me, but she held out her arms and smiled, and I knew at that moment, that there was nothing on the streets or in a criminal lifestyle that could even compare to the love of this little girl, and so my two-hour twice-a-week visits . . . that brief moment I had with my daghter stayed in my mind and helped motivate me on those days when I was just scared and didn't know what the outcome was going to be. . . . Most horrible part of my life— losing my daughter—has now fueled into my purpose in life so I now help other parents try to get their kids back and turn their life around who have lost their children to CPS [Child Protective Services] so it's cool how that stuff turns around.

Brandon's change process began the moment he found himself in shock at being sentenced to four years for assault with a deadly weapon at age seventeen: "My friends and family were in the courtroom as if they were at a funeral watching me close the casket [sic], and I woke up the next morning in prison and realized that I was not dead, and I asked myself what you would do if you came back to life today—and I would change everything and that's exactly what I started to do." Felise described a combination of key circumstances that motivated him to want to change:

> I finally grew up . . . There is a time that I think, everybody has that time, that "Wow" This is not something you need to be playing with no more, and uh I put through the effort and studied law. . . . yeah . . . tired of it . . . When [I] started getting into a psychology book, I found out that, wow, I had a problem, as far as alcohol, anger . . . and looked back to my court records and everything . . . , You kind of find the path, or the pattern, you were going, and I got involved, highly involved with laws and then studied some of the things that was right there in the law library. In the law library, I knew then that this is not for me anymore, looking up cases, and seeing other people's cases. . . . It was six years before I got out . . . and then from there on it was books, books, books, books, books. And, uh, it is true, education can get you in places . . . and so I stuck it out . . . um, I don't know I just find it more that I see is a problem and I need to fix it, then I'll do it . . . I do do it. . . as long as I'm not hurting anybody or taking anything from nobody, I'm OK, I'm OK . . . and if I need to do this because this is the way my life has got to be, then I'm going to do it. . . . Yes . . . the thinking changed a lot, the thinking process, the mentality. . . . I think overall it was everything. . . . When I went back to the court records and read some of the things that people say about you that are not true and how they sit there in the courthouse and paint the picture of this very very, uh, violent or killer on the loose in the state of Washington or wherever that may be, and . . . you know you start seeing how people can truly make you feel and I don't want to go through that process ever again, being put in the position where people are saying things . . . but it was also a good experience for me because I got to learn that people do talk and people do things that you might not like and you might not agree with and you got to let it go and let it roll off your shoulders . . . there was the solving of my anger . . . that's when I knew if I could sit here and listen to somebody tell me who I'm not . . . you get frustrated, you get angry and you want to do something about it. You might want to punch them in their face, but I couldn't because I was in court. So I asked myself if I can do that right now, why can't I do it for the rest of my life? . . . So, I learned my lesson. . . . So overall everything from cultural, from family, it's a combination of experiences and I think that made it solidify my decision that I'm a lot more than just you sending me to prison as not fit for society, and I can fit, and I'll prove it to you.

Similarly, Donny, who had been out of prison for over nine years, described a personal choice to make a change toward the end of a sixteen-year sentence for armed robbery and possession of firearms: "What happened for me is that I got tired of dealing with the violence, screwing up—I decided to flip the switch."

Some of the interview subjects reflected on a more gradual process of change. But those who explained their change in thinking as abrupt and those who described a more gradual process noted that their change in identity toward more prosocial thinking was associated in some way or another with the aging process. Kim was in and out of prison over five times during a twenty-year period with his last stint being a six-year sentence for assaulting a police officer. He described his process of change:

> It wasn't until [my] most recent incarceration that I started to take an active thought process. Before this I came out with the attitude I was going to do everything right, but sometimes I find that listening to everything the authority tells you to do is not always the right thing for a particular individual. . . . Getting older has something to do with it . . . switching on.

Donny said that part of his motivation to remain prosocial is a fear of going back to prison: "I was getting older. I didn't want to deal with the violence. It had marred my thought process so much I was sick of it. To tell you the truth I was actually scared to go back to prison. A big tough guy like me, I didn't want to go back." Stevan said about his process of change, which began about three years into his fifteen-year incarceration:

> Getting that life without parole sentence made me look in the mirror to dig in my soul to make me figure out how, you know you may not get out, but if you are you better be ready because you don't want to come back. So it was after that life sentence I started getting myself ready, and when the lights did come on and I was allowed to reenter society, I was armed with tools. I had learned skills to address my addiction issues that I was carrying. I had got a lot of good community support behind me. . . . I had learned patience. Those were things than I lacked in [the] past. I'd always got out and never had a plan. . . . A lot of people look at transition reentry as one thing, but your transition should begin before you get out. I learned that after trial and error. I finally got it figured out and said to myself well if I get a chance to get out I'm already going to be in transition mode. . . . In 1997 I was at Walla Walla and, um, I started . . . seeing younger and younger offenders coming into the prison and I started reaching out to them trying to encourage them, 'Hey, let's go to this AA group,' and I'm knowing they're getting out and if they don't deal with the situations that led them there, they're going to come back. So along with pulling them with me I started doing things for myself . . . going to all the support groups—the NAs, the AAs, anything I could get. You know . . . the light actually came on when I got tired of feeling sorry for myself and wiped the tears away.

The Reentry Experience

The ex-offenders in the sample ranged considerably in terms of the length of time they had been out of prison—from Kim who had been released one month prior to the interview to Jane who had been living successfully in the community in the same job for twenty-seven years. The issues the ex-offenders faced at the front end of the reentry process were more likely to involve culture shock and frustrations in getting basic needs met, such as housing, employment, and transportation, while the issues after many years postrelease tended to be struggles with achieving an identity as something other than a criminal after living crime-free in the community for many years.

While all of the ex-offenders indicated that the basics such as food, clothing, housing, and employment were the primary needs they had upon release, most had found a job, some relatively quickly (many while in work release) and others after plugging away at it for a while. They held jobs ranging from restaurant work to youth advocacy, machinist, welder, tree cutter, and case manager and counselor positions. Most were also enrolled in college or graduate school or had completed college (or in one case a graduate program), and most were also engaged in some form of volunteer activity. All had been involved in some form of prison program, inmate organizations, or leadership roles while in prison, and in many cases these connections provided opportunities for employment, educational opportunities, or volunteer and advocacy positions upon release.[3] However, some of the interview subjects described difficulties in finding a position given the nature of their crimes. Jill had been in prison for four years on charges of identity theft, possession of drugs, and violation of a drug offender sentencing alternative sentence, and after being out for two months, she described the difficulty in finding a job with her particular crime: "When I was in work release and was hired at Ross, I was 100 percent honest and disclosed. On the third day they pulled my till and escorted me out and said they couldn't hire me due to my criminal history."

The day-to-day challenges faced by the ex-offenders in the initial stages of the reentry process ranged from difficulties in getting set up with necessary identification and credit to dealing with new responsibilities and adapting to differences between the prison culture and free society. Trevor had gone into prison at age sixteen, was released at age thirty-four and had been out for ten years. He recalled, "My biggest challenge was opening a bank account, grocery store, stuff like that. Dealing with people, doctor's appointments, car appointments, driver's license. I was thirty-four and never had a license." Greg explained the logistical difficulties in getting set up with identification, banking, and other everyday necessities:

> I mean nothing shocked me, but everything surprises you . . . I mean just shopping, um, going to places, I mean how to learn how to bank, Department of Licensing. . . . I couldn't get no ID for the first month at work release due to [the] fact that I was never in the Department of Licensing system. . . . There were so many hoops I had to get through to get an ID. You got to get your birth certificate, you got to get your social security number, I had to have the Department of Corrections write a letter and sign a statement that that's who I am. The whole world was new to me. I went in when I was fifteen so I had a fifteen-year-old's grasp on life. I come out when I'm forty-five, have to find a job, have [a] place to live, have to learn how to drive, learn everything that most eighteen- and nineteen-year olds are supposed to know, but then I'm forty-five and trying to learn. I mean the shock was a forty-five-year-old man trying to get a permit, a driver's permit.

Similarly, Gerald recounted,

> I missed the whole computer era, the whole cell phone era. Everything to me was totally space age. . . . I went in in the 80s and come out in the late 2000s and you know everything had changed, even the cars had changed. . . . I was still just trying to get acclimated to being on the outside . . . to be able to go to the store, just to have money in my pocket. I hadn't seen money in over two decades, other than being in the visiting room with coins, but I never had any money. . . . To be able to answer the phone for a change . . . sleeping on multiple sides of the bed rather than on one side. It took me six shots to the Department of Licensing to get a Washington State ID. . . . They said they need three pieces of ID, so I showed them my prison ID, and they said that is not good enough, so I showed them my birth certificate, but I needed two other pieces, so I said, "I don't know what to tell you. I don't have nothing else." . . . "So we can't give it to you." . . . I wanted to go [to] continue education. Little did I know I didn't apply for the voluntary draft at age eighteen so I couldn't qualify and apply for loans. . . . Only thing they gave me was $40, all $5 bills . . . and 20 of that was to get my Washington State ID. . . . It took a letter from the governor's office to get a Washington State ID. There was even a picture with me and Governor [Christine] Gregoire that I'd show them and they said it wasn't authentic. . . . And then I had the Department of Corrections write a letter to say he was with us for the last twenty-seven years. It took a whole year for them to finally give me approval just to get financial aid to allow me to go to school.

Kim described his experience in the weeks since his release struggling with day-to-day challenges and transportation from the rural area he was released to and difficulties in meeting the requirements of community supervision to take the bus, apply for jobs, and return at a designated time:

> Total shock at the price of food, how expensive everything has become. Part of the problem with the prison system is that they remove the circulars from the newspapers so you have no idea what anything costs. You don't know what clothes cost, you don't know what food costs, um, there's limited rental information in newspapers depending on where you're incarcerated at and where you're going to be released to. . . . Getting used to doing everything that the prison did for me . . . learning how to budget for food, what foods to buy, how to find the best return for what you're spending on the food so that you don't buy something that's really expensive . . . just learning how to get around, learning what buses to take at what time in order to maximize the amount of time you have available so you can do a job search or get to the Worksource and get to the college and then go back to the Worksource and then go back to the house so that you don't miss the bus and have to walk because I live in a relatively rural area. . . . There haven't been any real difficult struggles for me, but there have been an accumulation of small little tasks that amount to . . . well, I call them adventures. For example, getting my Washington State ID has taken me over a month because they don't give it to you when you release from prison. You go to apply for a job and I've used my prison ID a couple of times, but it just creates a whole negative atmosphere, so then I had to go find this guy at Community Action who in turn decided they could help me pay for my ID and then I went to a food bank and I found at the food bank I could volunteer there. I wanted to volunteer at the food bank because I wanted to use that for references so that I could create my own job history and also wound up getting Community Action to pay for my food handler's permit card. And then I'm going to take the food handler's card to the food bank and the food bank reimburses me for the card and then I take the money back to Skagit Community Action so that they have the money. And the reason why I do all that is because that way they can help someone else. But doing all that, and continually taking each little step—taking the bus down to pick up the check, then taking the bus down to get your ID, and hoping you have enough time to wait at DMV before you have to get on the next bus to get back to where you live at . . . the logistics of traveling . . . all the little red tape and all the little nit picks.

Pat went to prison at age seventeen, was released at age forty-four, and had been in the community for two years. He obtained a job while in work release at which he was still employed, but he described difficulties in obtaining credit: "The only problem I did have was being accepted for credit. I had no credit so when I tried to purchase something that needed a credit score I was denied because I didn't have a credit score." Because of his nonexistent credit score, he had a difficult time obtaining a cell phone, and dealing with the credit issue represented a nuisance that ended up taking up more time and being more of a frustration than it seemed to be worth. Alise spoke of the difficulty in finding herself the parent of a toddler: "My lack of parenting skills made it difficult. . . . All of a sudden I was the mom of a seventeen-month-old toddler."

Jill, a former meth addict under federal and state supervision who had been out for two months, struggled with the logistics of meeting state and federal supervision conditions: "It's hard for me right now because I'm on two different types of probation and getting drug tested by four different places." Felise, eleven months postrelease, shared difficulties in connecting with his mother due to community supervision restrictions: "I can't leave [the] country to see Mom. She is in Samoa. I'm not financially set to take myself there or bring her here. Sometimes I just meditate and get rid of things I don't need to be thinking about."

Technology was raised by a number of the interview subjects as a surprise after living in a world with no access to computers, cell phones, or the Internet. They described coming out of prison and hearing about Google and Facebook and not knowing what people were talking about. One interview subject described seeing people talking to themselves while walking down the street and then later finding out that they were talking on phones. Sarah was in college and had been released five months prior after serving almost five years on a vehicular homicide charge. She said, "When I first got to the college and people were constantly looking down and had their ear buds on and their phones, I wasn't used to all that." The technology issue was particularly challenging for those who had been in prison since before this technology was available. Gerald, who went into prison at eighteen, was released at age forty, and out for three years, explained, "It was a total different era after twenty-two years. I missed the whole computer era, cell phone era. Everything was totally space age. I went in, in the eighties and came out in the later 2000s. I didn't have any experience. I was trying to adjust and get acclimated." Dawn was in prison for four years and enrolled at the University of Washington within ten days of her release, but found the technology challenging: "Going back to school, technology had changed. . . . The stuff they were doing on computers I was way behind on that, so having to ask for a lot of help. In prison, some Excel but no practice using Internet or that type of stuff." Dolphy recounted his experience with cell phones after being released after twenty-two years in prison: "Cell phones—*hahaha*—oh my god. I didn't have a clue. Once you figure out a couple buttons but at first I'm hanging up on people not knowing what to do or texting."

Switching modes from prison life to life on the outside was a salient issue for many of the ex-offenders, in particular those who had recently been released after long-term imprisonment. Dave, a former gang member who completed a fifteen-year sentence for murder and had been out for just seven months, explained the process of going from free society to prison and back again. He described how he felt when he first went to prison at age nineteen.

> It was pretty scary . . . especially because none of this was like planned out, it was just, you go to a place for one reason and it turns out to be something else. . . . I was so drunk that I passed out in the hospital because I got stabbed myself. So I woke up and I'm already chained up to bed, and I woke up to this situation. There's no other word to say, it was just scary. It was. You're losing everything. You done lost everything. If you talk about how the whole time in, like how you change, from then until now, you know everything changes. Not only do you get older but all your emotions and feelings and concerns start shutting down because, you know, you're at this place where there is nothing really good to move forward to, you know? And yeah, you get to a point where what was important is not important anymore, and your values on say even like—I had two kids myself so when I first went in, my oldest was like the one that brought me tears to my eyes, I mean he was like my everything. But with the years I got to forget about that. You know, not because I wanted to but because like I'm not around so you get to forget that you're actually a dad . . . you used to love someone so much, and now you become to be this . . . like I said you begin to start shutting down.

Overwhelming sights and sounds and interactions faced in the first days and weeks postrelease were noted by many of the interview subjects. Greg, who had been released only sixteen months prior to the interview after doing thirty years in prison on a murder conviction at age fifteen said about his initial days postrelease: "I had a depth perception problem. What I mean is like this world out here is so huge. . . . I still get lost. . . . Everything looks the same. The world is huge." Several also described initial difficulties in interacting with people they met on the street. Donny described his experience in the first weeks he was released after sixteen years in prison:

> Rude people . . . that was a problem for me. . . . I got out and punched [people] a couple times. They flipped me off in traffic. Pushed me to the point to go out of the vehicle and punched them. It threatened me. You better hope the light does not turn red, and it turned red a couple of times. I've learned to deal with that stuff. People are going to be rude and obnoxious. . . . I understood if I did that I could go back to prison for a long time. It clicked eventually you're being a dumb ass.

Dave, who had spent fifteen years in prison, shared a similar story:

I remember when I first got my ID from work release . . . all these noises, people, I just got stuck looking at everything. I'm so used to my ID I was wearing it on the streets. Four times within three or four hours I kept putting my ID back on. Pretty crazy. . . . For me it was like . . . I see the cars . . . run me over. . . . It was that crazy. Lasted for a couple of months . . . maybe a week to that extent. . . . To this day I walk around maybe being too careful. I got out and got a job and started going to Bellevue CC [Community College]. I was still in work release when going to school. In school you got all these people that don't know anything about the life you've been in, so people bumping into you. I had to remind myself they don't know. . . . And had to remind myself every day that I'm not in prison no more. . . . One day on [the] bus on the way back from school, this guy without knowing I was be-hind him he had a big backpack on and turned around and he hit me in [the] face. My first reaction was to grab him and push him. I realized it wasn't right and I went back to help him out. He looked at me, "What's wrong with this dude?" I don't forget that because my first reaction was to act that way. Reminding myself all the time I'm not in there no more, I'm not in there no more. Trying to change everything you know from the last decade to readjust yourself.

Gina remembered:

Well when I first got to work release and I had to go down to get my ID, um, of course I got lost on the bus and got lost walking to the bus stop and was in total panic mode because I didn't know where to go. I didn't know who to talk to and didn't have anybody to really ask on the streets. You know when you've been incarcerated as long as I was, you don't ask people too many questions. So that kind of was scary. And when I got back from getting my ID I called my mentor in tears because I was sick, I was sick to my stomach being out with the pub-lic, being out without the fences, being out where there was normal people. Um, I can't go into a Starbucks and order a coffee because I don't know how to even do that. Even now, if somebody doesn't order it for me, I have no idea. I'm also a full-time student at Seattle Central Community College and I'm in an honors class at the University of Washington. So, the first time I walked into the bathroom at UW, the toilets flush themselves, and that was very very strange for me. I was totally freaked out about that. And then washing your hands in the sink. You put your hands under the sink and the water doesn't turn on and I thought, who broke the handles on the sink? It's crazy because you look at all these things and you think, what in the world? Just being on the bus and being around all of those people. It's very over-whelming. I remember going into Walmart even and feeling over-whelmed to the point where I had to walk out and leave my basket of stuff because I was so overwhelmed with all the people and the bump-ing into each other and they're rude. And if you're rude in prison, you don't stay rude long. You just don't, you know, um, and in prison to be

honest I had it pretty much made because I worked full-time, I pro-
grammed full-time, I was involved in my church activities, in Toast-
masters, in the IF Project, and I was a horticulture TA so I was outside
in all the gardens in the vegetable gardens and the rose gardens. They
even trusted me to go and work on the outside of the prison to work
in the gardens without being supervised . . . and I'd been there long
enough that people knew who I was and I knew who they were. And
then coming out when you don't know anybody or anything, um, it's
hard. I moved right down the street from my work release because I
didn't want to change bus lines.

Pat recalled situations at work when he would forget that he was no
longer in prison, which sometimes made it difficult to communicate nat-
urally with his boss: "Funny part is I view my boss as either a corrections official or corrections officer, so I don't really talk to him or associate with him that much. Even though he's not. It's just a mind-set I've
been stuck with."

Dawn had difficulties making decisions when released after a four-
year sentence for vehicular homicide:

Making decisions was a big challenge . . . because you don't get to
make choices in there [prison] so the first time I went to the grocery
store and there was like eighteen different kinds of ice cream and
cereal, and just like making decisions was really really overwhelming . . . um, making decisions about, I don't know, everything. . . .
That was big and has gradually gotten better. I sought out counseling
for a while but it's very expensive and I think I just wasn't able to
maintain that. I just know, I don't know, I just deal with it and it is
something I'll have to deal with for my whole life. And it kind of like
just comes in little spurts. And I'll get depressed or sad, and I'll know
that those emotions are there, and I'll deal with them, in a healthy
way, or as healthy as I can, not like going out and self-medicating.

Greg shared his thoughts on the differences between the cultural
norms in prison and free society: "People out here are different . . .
[than] when you live in a closed society of men. It's more respectful.
It's not that I feel disrespected out here, but it's just the caring aspect
out here. People don't care about each other. In prison you have friends,
people care for you."

Trevor similarly describes the differences between prison culture
and free society:

The worst place to gain outside knowledge of how the world actually
works is being in prison . . . you know being in a medium or maximum security facility. You get no sense of what the real world is like.

. . . Through prerelease I got a little taste, a little more, and I tried to absorb everything I could . . . and then I chose different idols to look up to . . . not idols, you know mentors. I talked to people and tried to emulate people that were successful. And then you know work release was another step. . . . I guess the biggest challenge now that I think of it . . . it creeps in to this day, is the fact that the way of thinking in prison, whether by the inmates or by the staff, is not applicable in the free world at all. . . . The attitudes, the way you deal with people, um, how you address people, all that stuff, none of that in prison is applicable to the free world. If someone owes you money, you don't go beat them up to get it, you know what I'm saying. I think that's probably the biggest challenge, and then when somebody gets mad at you or you get mad at somebody else, you know how you deal with that anger isn't the way that you would deal with it in prison. . . . You know somebody can call you a punk or a bitch in the free world and it's really not that big a deal. It's not worth, you know, going to jail for by beating them up just because they called you a name.

All of the interview subjects recounted that this initial shock of the different cultural norms, the surprise of all that had changed in society during their imprisonment, and the nuisances of navigating the initial logistical issues of obtaining an ID, bank account, and cell phone gave way to other issues. All said that they adapted once the initial shock wore off and credited their ability to adapt to their experience adapting to the prison environment.

On the other side of the reentry process were issues raised by the interview subjects who had been living crime-free for many years. Five of the ex-offenders interviewed had been living in the community as law-abiding citizens for five or more years. These interview subjects struggled with different issues, in particular the desire to be free of the criminal identity and the ex-offender label. In fact, the issue of the ex-offender label came up more for those who had been out for several years, and most had prepared for the stigma and had a personal resolve to manage it constructively. Stevan said, "I've never been one to be too worried at someone looking at me as an ex-offender because we are all just a decision [away] from being an ex-offender."

However, those who had been out for an extensive length of time expressed difficulty in witnessing the "us versus them" divide in the workplace, news media, and peoples' attitudes. Jane had lived crime-free and in the same job as an administrative assistant for twenty-seven years, a position she obtained while on work release shortly after being freed from jail. She said she was so afraid to lose her job that she worked extraordinarily hard, put in extra hours, and never complained: "I have always been scared to death of losing a job. Part of it is because I have done unemployment fraud and therefore can't get unemployment." Jane described a thirty-year relationship with her drug-addicted boyfriend, whom she eventually married. She spoke of years struggling to be "normal" with a stable job that she was afraid to lose for fear she would not get another one. She lived a double life going to work every day, acting as if she was "normal," while going home to the chaos of a drug lifestyle. Eventually, her husband stopped using drugs and things calmed down; however, she described an enduring feeling of never being completely free of the ex-offender label while witnessing goings-on in her workplace such as the implementation of background checks for new employees and an individual who had gotten fired for being an ex-offender:

> Keeps dinging you all the way down the line . . . and then here . . . all the things that have happened here to other people. When I was hired here, they actively hired people like me. After three to four years no more hiring. Then they started that committee, and then the thing with [the co-worker who was fired]. . . . It just took a total turnaround. . . . It made me feel scared. Before it got like that, I talked to people, but afterwards not. . . . Legally they didn't do anything to me because I did not lie, so I never told people very much. . . . It has been twenty-seven years. I talk [only] to individuals I trust.

Others echoed this ongoing challenge to live in free society and be respected as a law-abiding citizen. Kim said, "We're all going to be living in your community. Most of us would rather live as members of the community. . . . [The term] *offender* is really offensive . . . same thing as calling someone an idiot. . . . Well, who have I offended lately?" Gerald offered a particularly poignant perspective on this:

> *Offender* is a horrible term. I don't even like that word being used around me. . . . Also when you make that reference to a person as ex-offender, it always puts you in a certain class of people that is rejects of society. So when you call a person an ex-offender it treats you as, I used to be a reject but now you're allowing me to come back versus now I'm a taxpaying citizen. Just because I made some mistakes in my life, does that mean I am always going to be that ex-offender? They don't call a military person an ex-military; they call them a veteran. You know, so it's a classification that you put on someone to always have that label on them that they'll never escape. . . . That makes you feel like you're putting this label on me with intentions of actually labeling me because you want to make sure that you . . . it's almost like you're leaving that mud on me. At what point am I no longer an ex-offender? And you know you put that on people because the first thing they do is talk about is your conviction you know so you can't trust this person because he is an ex-offender. It has so many different negative connotations on you that anyone that knows you're an ex-offender is not going to give you a fair shot at believing or trusting you.

Trevor explained how, after ten years being in the community crime-free, getting along is sometimes more difficult than when he was first released. As a welder, he said he cannot work at some job sites, and that this restriction is particularly difficult given he has achieved a great deal of stature in his position after many years in the field. He also had had difficulty traveling that caused him embarrassment:

> I can't work in some hospitals because of my criminal record. I can't work at Boeing, can't work on military bases. To me that's the wave of the future—everyone is going to be in a catalog. . . . I can't go to Canada. I've been to Canada twice and got caught the second time. I went on an Alaskan cruise and it stopped in Victoria and they called me because they did a random background check and told me never to come back to Canada again.

He also described the difficulty he had in sharing his past with the family of his girlfriend of ten years:

> You come across as someone on the outside. No one knows, no one can guess. . . . It depends on what kind of relationship I have with the people. I have told close friends . . . but sometimes it gets weird. . . . If I'm close with a person, it's a huge part of my past. I never lie. If someone asked I would tell them. . . . I don't tell [girlfriend's] family. . . . [Girlfriend] is okay with me telling them, but that would be a mistake. She has four sisters—two are republican and two democrat and one a religious freak. . . . She would probably dub me unfit for the family, and her mom is not receptive. Half believe in the death penalty. . . . That death penalty thing is close to home. When I was in court and sixteen years old, they considered the death penalty. To even mention that and for anyone to believe in that is a little off. They're not part of the forward thinkers—that is old school. So that creates a gap or a divide in our relationship. . . . It just creates something that you're aware of and they're not, so it's kind of like you're hiding something from them . . . but they've never delved into my past. If they asked, I would tell. I still may do it someday.

Echoing Trevor's sentiments about the ongoing difficulties ex-offenders face even many years postrelease, after nine years, Donny said, "It's hard every single day."

The Role of the CCO in the Reentry Process

The interview subjects were asked whether or not their CCOs contributed to their reentry success. Of the twenty-one ex-offenders interviewed, seventeen (81 percent) indicated that their CCOs contributed to their success and four (19 percent) indicated that their CCOs did not contribute in any way and actually made the process more difficult. Of the seventeen who indicated that they had had at least one CCO who was helpful, three (14 percent) indicated that they had also had one or more CCOs who had been a hindrance to the reentry process.

By and large, the ex-offenders interviewed indicated that the single most constructive thing a CCO could do to help them was to trust them. The ex-offenders recounted example after example of situations where they were surprised when their CCO trusted them, understood them, and gave them a break. They seemed to particularly appreciate it when a CCO was willing to listen, to go out of his or her way to understand, and to be flexible with a policy that may not neatly apply to the individual situation. Sarah spoke of a CCO who trusted her but whom she let down when she violated her supervision conditions: "She was great. . . . I apologized for letting her down. . . . She basically trusted me and I totally let her down. She was awesome."

Many of the interview subjects expressed appreciation for CCOs who treated them individually, saw them as human beings and not monsters, seemed to actually care about them and their situations, and were flexible enough to work with them to make their situations manageable. After serving thirty years in prison, Greg was surprised at how helpful his work release CCO was:

> I was shocked to be honest with you . . . by him, because DOC [Department of Corrections] has always put a negative face in my mind about me transitioning out. But then I went to work release and I met this CCO. . . . He took me everywhere. . . . He took me to the mall. He said, you need to realize what a mall is. . . . Large crowds still make me uncomfortable. He showed me how to apply for jobs . . . how to hunt for jobs. . . . It's just the overall feeling of he cared.

Kim was enthusiastic about his CCO, whom he had just been assigned to after being released from a six-year incarceration one month prior:

> CCOs can make an incredible difference based upon the manner in which they work with the client. They can make a significant impact, but then there are challenges for the CCO, burnout, limited amounts of resources for a large caseload. . . . The CCOs that I've been with at this point in time don't necessarily stick to what I call the bureaucratic response. That's sometimes atypical of certain CCOs that feel that they have to stick to the law and rule of policy. I believe that my CCOs that I've worked with currently have an understanding. They'll still hold you responsible for something if you happen to do something that's not

appropriate but at the same time they're going to say well if this is going to work for this person and it's not totally outside the rules or the realm of possibilities then I'm going to allow to have it, for example me coming to Seattle for the interview, it allows me to network with individuals. Intelligent flexibility . . . they think about the individual and say ok this person needs this and this person it may not be so appropriate for.

This "intelligent flexibility" was mentioned in one way or another by all of the interview subjects who described their CCO as supportive. Dawn recounted her experience with a CCO who supported her in participating in a study abroad program despite the difficulties in getting international travel approved: "I wanted to study abroad in Peru. My CCO was monumental in getting that approved. He was very helpful." Donny was encouraged by a CCO who "cut him some breaks":

I had one CCO and he actually did . . . cut me a couple of breaks. . . . He was a nice guy, very patient with me. I can say that much. He encouraged me, told me I was doing good, just those few words were big, boosted my ego. I went out and got a second job because I wanted more praise. I was cut some breaks. That did help me out a lot.

John shared how his CCO's flexibility after a lapse in judgment and violation of his supervision conditions motivated him to change:

He forgave the drinking incident. He's allowed to throw you in jail . . . can throw you in on hearsay and a nineteen-day to thirty-day investigation. He had all the rights to throw me in because I told him. He could have violated me, but he chose to overlook it and treated me fairly. I valued that immensely and never broke anything since. I really did appreciate that. There is probably a rule that they can forgive the first violation. . . . To me it was big. . . . [He gives me] praise on the schooling. He doesn't have to talk to me the way he does. . . . He really is interested in me . . . asks for my report card. I could be another number but he treats me fairly. I'm on the dean's list every quarter. For me I don't need obnoxious praise, and I don't need someone yelling at me like my obnoxious father.

The ex-offenders also appreciated CCOs who listened to them, seemed to understand their situations, encouraged them, and were knowledgeable about their interests and resources in the community and the programs and activities in which they were involved. The ex-offenders saw these CCO strengths as key contributions to their success. Beatrice appreciated her CCO's listening: "I appreciated her because she was

different from other probation officers. She would listen and she helped
. . . every time I would go in and visit her. She allowed me to travel to
Florida. That blew me away. . . . She was very supportive." Dave spoke
favorably about a new CCO he had recently been assigned to: "I actually like him because he knows what I'm trying to accomplish. He
knows the programs I'm involved with." Felise suggested a similar experience with his CCO: "He helped me . . . he helped me by the fact that
he listens to me, that he heard me, and aware that I'm going, I'm going
somewhere. I'm going to be somebody and I'm going to be somewhere
so he basically believed in me, and I truly believe in myself too." This
individualized attention and desire to know the ex-offenders as more
than who they were on paper were seen by Dolphy as key strengths of
the best CCOs and an area where improvement was much needed for
many CCOs who do not approach ex-offenders in this way: "There is
definitely a disconnect [for some CCOs] because they are caught up in
a system that's already in place and caught up in a job . . . instead of
seeing what the individual needs or the things they need for this individual to be successful. I don't think a lot of people take the time to assess
the individual instead of just process the number."

Several of the interview subjects had had experiences with more
than one CCO and reflected on the differences they saw in the officers'
professional style that made officers who trusted them stand out from
those who did not. Trevor had been out of prison for ten years after
serving eighteen years in prison. He received his sentence prior to 1984
and was under community supervision under the Indeterminate Sentence Review Board (Washington State's old parole system) and had experience with multiple CCOs. He described his experience when he was
first released and his appreciation for a CCO who trusted him:

> I had two CCOs and thank god I didn't have the first one very long.
> One I didn't have long . . . met her two to three times, and she was
> mean. . . . She wanted me to take UAs [urinalysis], breathalyzers, lie
> detector tests, the whole deal that I would have to pay for. . . . They try
> to keep you broke. . . . I got this other CCO and she was very trusting,
> a long leash, no UAs because I was in the union and they insure drug-
> free. And she didn't feel the need for a lie detector. CCOs have their
> [finger on the] pulse of the underground crime society so they usually
> hear about people. I think she helped because she trusted me. If I'm
> going to do something wrong she's going to hear about it. I was okay
> with that. She was very smart and seemed like she treated me with re-
> spect. I've heard horror stories. . . . [I appreciated her] not giving me
> a bill for UAs breathalyzers and lie detector tests, and if I wanted to
> go someplace, I just had to let her know.

Dolphy also shared his experience with dramatically different CCOs:

> [Work release] CCO [X] was huge in my success. He drove me around the city. He really talked to me about things. Put me in uncomfortable places to get used to them and was always there to talk to or to show me you know the right way to do something or help me with my communication skills, um and brought me to the postprison education program, so he was helpful in a number of ways. But once you're released onto the streets you fall under a field agent CCO, to where the guy that I ended up with . . . let me backtrack a little bit, so when I was getting ready to go to work release I submitted an address and then this guy went to my mother's house, talked really bad about me, talked really bad to her, made her cry, and then rejected my release address, so they turned down my release address which means normally I wouldn't have got out of prison. He was just really mean, and he was talking about me, he was talking about my childhood, and she didn't make the best choices as a mother when I was young. . . . She told me all this and I was really angry about it. . . . So they refused my release address. . . . And later, when out again, ended up with the same CCO again . . . sat there with him for two hours with him telling me all this crap about how he's going to watch everything I do. . . . I'd better not even think about messing up because he will send me back, and he wanted me to move. . . just all this negative stuff. I don't feel like that's a very positive environment to be in. . . . He was just super-negative even though I was doing all these positive things.

Another theme in the ex-offender responses regarding their CCOs was that it was particularly helpful to have a CCO who treated them like a human being. Gerald described his CCO: "She's the best. I have only had her. I call her a friend. She doesn't treat me like an ex-offender. . . . She's not judging. She's just a good human being. She treats me like a human being rather like a client. . . . Genuine respect. . . . If there was ever a such thing as the way CCOs should be, she is a model for that." Similarly, Jill spoke highly of a federal CCO whom she found particularly supportive: "Her attitude was helpful. . . . For me it's really important to be able to have a CCO that doesn't talk down to me, that treats me as a human."

The few interview subjects who did not see their CCO as contributing to the reentry process indicated that the officers to whom they had been assigned were unnecessarily punitive or (in some cases) mean. Pat, who had spent twenty-eight years in prison from age seventeen to age forty-four on a murder charge and under indefinite community supervision under the state Indeterminate Sentence Review Board, felt like he was treated with an unnecessary amount of suspicion: "I'm supposed to be a member of society now, but I'm still treated like I'm a convict by the CCO and parole board." Pat recalled his experience with two very different CCOs:

I had . . . three CCOs at work release. . . . [X] and now one who was so like a police officer that he annoyed the hell out of me [Y]. He's so much like a cop, vest, gun on the side . . . like a cop. He has been more lenient but I still view him as a cop. [X] I viewed as someone I could get along with, but he got transferred and I got stuck with [Y]. Yes, I could do without any of them.

Similarly, Chris described two different CCOs:

It was a horrible relationship that I had with my first CCO. This was in 2000. He'd come over to my house and I'd have 40 ounce bottles all over the place and empty weed bags and I'm sure I had an attitude because I didn't want to see him and I knew he was going to take me to jail or something you know, but with [more recent CCO], she was always professional and, uh, I don't know like . . . she wasn't like, oh, patting me on the back all the time or anything like that but she was very, I don't know, I don't know what the word is but she was a person who was on the other side. She was a cop basically and the idea that we could have a nonadversarial discourse between us, it gave me confidence in myself so that even in the eyes of the law, which she was to me, that, um, if I kept my nose clean I would be OK . . . I have a lot of respect for her. She did her job really well. But I did my part too, you know. Yeah, she was cool. . . . I have an example . . . she was impartial . . . she helped me out by getting me information, and she wasn't like, "We're right, you're wrong." It was refreshing because she seemed to take what I said at its merit and investigate it and not just relegate me to some lying inmate. . . . I didn't really think that anybody in there [Department of Corrections] would actually help me at all, but it wasn't that way . . . it was the way that she didn't choose a side between DOC and me when I was trying to get things figured out.

Taken as a whole, the ex-offenders saw at least one of the CCOs they had worked with as a positive force in their reentry process. Alise described several CCOs and the different ways in which they contributed to her success:

I've had a total of three . . . DOC CCOs. . . . Well, they didn't arrest me so that was cool. The first two were women and I was more comfortable opening up with them. One was a man and I know he is proud of me. I hope if they remember how horrible a person looks on paper change is possible. . . . When it came time for networking for resources he might have been the one to say CPC [community psychiatric clinic] for counseling. We can attribute just having to check in as important for me. . . . The CCO in Kent . . . wow . . . I just didn't feel judged and I think she appreciated the fact that I told her I almost just robbed a car and I need help. . . . I had a probation officer too. She contributed to my confidence because she took me off on a really early release. . . . Every time she saw me, her face lit up. . . . She had a very nurturing demeanor and . . . I just really thrived with her personality because it can be very intimidating checking into agencies for your criminal stuff. I kind of took on a feel [like] I'm less than you. . . . They think you're up to something. . . . Part of the changing process is changing the mind-set [and] is realizing to do what you need to. They're doing their job and hopefully the majority don't have the mentality of peer judgment.

Thus, the CCOs who extended trust, were flexibile, listened, seemed to understand, and were knowledgeable of the community resources were seen by the ex-offenders as contributing to their reentry success in some cases in ways that were personal and powerful. Interestingly, the few ex-offenders who said they did not have a CCO who contributed in any way to their reentry success still had positive things to say. This sentiment is reflected by Brandon's recollection of his CCO when he was initially released after a four-year sentence: "He was just funny, cool, burnt out by all the drama all the inmates give him. One time I got a job interview selling knives. . . . He was supercool. He was just there, but he was nice and he would always praise me. He was super supportive. . . . I want to say yes [that he contributed to reentry success], but no, because I was going to do that [succeed] no matter what."

Reentry Success

The interview subjects reported a range of successes in obtaining employment, finding housing, forming relationships, making links to the community, experiencing personal growth, contributing to the community, and managing their everyday experiences. The group as a whole was overwhelmingly positive in their recounting of the reentry experiences. Even when recounting hardship and extreme frustration, every one of them did so with a positive tone and a considerable amount of personal dignity, in some cases in the face of particularly difficult experiences. One interview subject (Trevor) made a particularly important point regarding his definition of success that is indicative of the sentiment of the sample as a whole: "Being successful on the outside is relative. If being successful to somebody else is just not going back to prison, to me that is not being successful. You could be living in a cardboard box. . . . For me to be successful is to live out all my dreams and to live a very happy positive life and doing the best I can."

Greg described his success in obtaining a job in under a month after being released after serving thirty years: "I was fortunate it only took me less than a month. It was like three weeks. I learned a trade when in prison and I continued on outside. I was a water jet operator in prison. I did that for eight months at the company I worked for. I'm a CNC [computer numerical controller] machinist. They pay me well now. I love it." Pat talked about how nice he found the task of taking care of a cat after not being able to have a pet during his twenty-eight years in prison: "It has been a positive thing to be able to care for an animal. . . . That would be one of the immediate affection things where you can interact with an animal, and it shows . . . I don't know if it's unconditional love from the animal but in the prison system you don't see that at all from anywhere." Stevan described his postrelease lifestyle: "I work hard. Five days a week. Volunteer work, outreach work. . . . I surround myself with positive things."

The number one factor the interview subjects highlighted when asked about the factors they believed contributed to their success was relationships with one or more people. They spoke of volunteers in the prison who had influenced them, prison staff (in one case a superintendent), CCOs, and other criminal justice and social service professionals who went out of their way to understand, reach out, and help them. They also talked about family members who allowed them to stay with them when they were released, spouses or partners who stuck by them in prison and postrelease, and their children who they were able to reunite with in some cases after many years. They cited employers who gave them a chance, property owners who were willing to rent to them, instructors and professors in and outside of the prison who believed in them, and people in the community who accepted them. Those who were not able to build relationships inside prison that extended to the outside and who did not have family in the area to release to had a particularly difficult time in the initial stages of reentry. John said, "It was a cold start." Gina's comment is particularly illustrative of the feelings that many of the ex-offenders expressed about making the identity change moving from a long history of feeling like an outsider and the importance of having relationships that support and affirm this change: "It's not me against the world. I've always considered myself an outsider looking in, and I'm not. That's false."

One of the things that appeared to be critical in the success of many of the interview subjects was the degree to which they were linked with organizations and programs that allowed them to make connections with people on the outside. Gerald indicated that the single most important factor contributing to his success was "support. Absolutely support. . . . People being there and caring for you. Genuinely caring for you so that even if you fail, there's someone there to help you rather than criticize you." He described how he met people in prison who supported him as he went through the process of seeking and being eventually granted clemency:

> When I was in prison, I was president of the Black Prisoners Caucus for four years and the vice president of the Concerned Lifers Organization, and both of those groups allowed people from the community to come inside and be a part of whatever project we were working on, and that allowed me to meet a whole lot of different people, like teachers, regular folks, professors like yourself, political leaders. I was able to build relationships with a lot of different people, a lot of church folks. Also a part of the youth-at-risk program inside that brought a lot of different people in from the community. . . . [At clemency hearing] fifty to sixty people from the community who supported me showed up.

Others highlighted this critical role of friendships and social networks in succeeding upon release and the importance of interacting with positive, prosocial people. Donny explained how hard initially breaking free of old relationships was, knowing he needed to be engaged with a different sort of social network; "When you start over new. You literally have to erase your past." Greg said, "It's who you surround yourself with."

A number of the interview subjects suggested that their ability to stay in a stable relationship and have patience with other people was the direct result of having had so much taken away for so long. These ex-offenders felt that the deprivations they had experienced in prison gave them an appreciation for people and experiences and the details of everyday life that others seemed to them to take for granted. Pat said, "A relationship is pretty much sacred, in a sense. . . . You hold onto it as best you can because you never know what could happen next." Donny expressed a similar view: "In prison, you learn to take care of things . . . this is just with objects, but it goes through with other things too . . . it's in your persona after that. . . . You take care of everything you have. . . . You value it very much, because there could be a point that it could go away, you know, the guards may come take it or something like that . . . I don't think of anything as short term I guess . . . I view everything as long term, and that's the way it should be." Both Donny and Pat had been involved in stable relationships on the outside since their releases and indicated that their ability to stay in their relationships was a direct result of their experience of imprisonment.

Another salient theme was the amount of hard work and diligence that the interview subjects had expended in making the transition from prison to community, the personal resolve to succeed, and the degree to

which the experience of imprisonment had given them psychological
strength to adapt to free society upon release. Alise described her experience coming out of a two-year period of incarceration and in-patient
drug treatment and transitioning into her roles as a mother and college
student:

> My daughter and I living on our own. . . . It was stressful turning
> around. I'm hard on myself. I hold the bar high because so I'm fearful
> of the other side. . . . I go, go, go, go, go. It's a challenge to just
> breathe and remind myself that I've come a long way. I feel there is so
> much I need to accomplish so my daughter and I have the best possi-
> ble chance at this. It's constant faith versus fear . . . getting rid of my
> anxiety. I think I do a pretty good job of trying to manifest my recov-
> ery on top of working part-time, full-time student, and full-time mom
> of a three-year-old. It's too much sometimes. . . . It's learning how to
> say no to too many things so I don't drive myself crazy. For all the
> holes in my brain from meth, I have a straight 4.0. I'm a firm believer
> in education counteracting a criminal history and through education
> those of us formerly incarcerated are able to reach our full potential. I
> will walk with a degree next month.

Others linked their ability to adapt to free society and to constructively
navigate the challenges of reentry to the skills and experience they had
acquired through imprisonment. John received a cancer diagnosis
shortly after being released from a ten-year period of incarceration for
child molestation. He said of his prison experience that it was "such a
low in my life that it makes these things like cancer seem like nothing.
I just did ten years of incarceration."

   This notion that the hardships of imprisonment facilitated adaptation to the challenges faced upon release was echoed by Trevor: "It's
hard for me. . . . You know what? Life is hard. It's hard to stay in shape.
It's all hard but you got to do it. . . . Prison is a life challenge. Most people in the free world don't have a life challenge where it's between life
and death, so when out it's a little different, not on top [of the prison hi-
erarchy] anymore. Just another citizen, very small in a pool of sharks."

   Several of the interview subjects were high-profile cases. Their stories had been in the local news media at the time of their crimes and at
the time of their release. All of these ex-offenders felt considerable
pressure to succeed and felt that a lot of people were watching them,
and counting on them, both inside and outside of prison. They had also
been through a great deal of setbacks for years in their attempts to seek
release. Two of the interview subjects received clemency—Stevan was
the first three-strikes offender to receive clemency and Gerald was the
first offender sentenced to life without parole to receive clemency in

Washington State. Both Stevan and Gerald were well respected in leadership positions while in prison and described many years of false hope and alternating periods of hopelessness and an excruciating process of trying to maintain hope and personal resolve to make the best of the situation. Gerald described the day he was finally granted clemency, becoming the first such offender to receive clemency, and told he could leave the prison at age forty after twenty-two years of being incarcerated:

> I was granted release April 9, 2009. . . . They let me out that night. . . . It was funny how that happened because I was sitting in the dayroom ready to go out into the yard. . . . It was just after lunch, around 12:20, and my counselor comes up to tell me Gerald stay here because Superintendent [X] . . . want to talk to you. And usually when you hear those kinda things you thinking something's wrong. I got confronted like that a few times and got put in segregation . . . so I'm skeptical, I'm thinking, what does he want to see me about? But she would not tell me and everybody's sitting around saying. What did you do? And I'm saying, I don't know. . . . I'm forced to stand here and not leave the unit. So when one o'clock came they called the yard and everybody went to yard. But I can't go, and she came back out and she said, no, you stay here because the superintendent called me and he wants you in the unit to come down and talk to you. . . . So, I'm nervous, I'm worried thinking like, oh my god what are they going to accuse me of now? So, I go to my cell . . . a correctional officer comes to my room to see if I'm still there, and I'm thinking when's the goon squad coming? At some point they're going to arrest me and put me in the segregation for some type of investigation, as I've experienced for many years. So, finally around you know 1:15 they come and knock on my door and say the superintendent's in the sergeant's office and want you to come out there. So I comes out of my cell, I walks down the tier, but when I turns in the hallway I see a couple officers, . . . I cracks a joke like go on and get your handcuffs because I know you all are about to handcuff me. . . . But nobody says a word. So I walk into the sergeant's office and the superintendent's there and he tells me, have a seat. He says, "Gerald, have a seat," and I was like man . . . because I see a bunch of papers rolled up in his hand which are usually segregation orders and I said, "Whatever it is you guys are going to do to me, just go ahead and do it." And he says. Gerald, have a seat. So I sat down and he unrolled the paper and says, "I just want to be the first person to tell you, you're a free man." And I was like, run that by me again? And he unrolled the papers out of his hand and he showed me "the governor has granted you clemency, but there are conditions that you must agree to, [and] you must sign." And I'm dizzy at this point. I'm looking at this man, I'm sitting here looking at this paper that I can't even read the words on the page. My eyes start . . . I looks around . . . I mean, I'm not even on earth at this point. I'm just like, What? I'm not getting this. He said, "Gerald, your clemency was granted by Governor

Gregoire this morning, you must sign these conditions." There were fifteen conditions . . . I gotta do UAs, I gotta report to my CCO, and all these things, and I looked at the paper and I'm reading it, and I see her signature granting me clemency on April 9, and he said, "Is there anyone you want to call?" And I was like sure, I wanted to call my lawyer first. So he slides the phone over to me, but as soon as I dialed my lawyer's number she answers the phone and the first thing out of her mouth, "Are you sitting down?" and I tells her . . . I already know, and she's like "Our whole office is celebrating" but then I handed the phone over to the superintendent and I don't know what she asked him but she must have asked him, "What is the process, how long is this going to take for Gerald to be released?" And he said, out of his mouth, "I'm walking Gerald out of here today." That was my first time realizing how soon . . . he was actually going to release me that night. So, at 5:00 that night, he walked me out of the prison. Oh my God that was like . . . I don't even know how to describe that day. I was just so excited . . . and then of course he walked me out. . . . And usually you know, staff usually go out the left side of the gate while prisoners go to the right to the visiting room. . . This was my first time actually being able to go to the left out the gate . . . and walked out the door. First stopped by his office. He shook my hand, gave me his card, and he said, "If you got anything you want to talk about . . . whatever, just give me a call." He shook my hand, and he said, "Good luck." And I walked out the front gates of the prison for the first time after 22 years.

While high-profile interview subjects like Gerald represent rare cases and their experiences in the reentry process may not be generalizable to the general ex-offender population, their experience offers insight into the reentry experience for ex-offenders who have received some degree of media attention. Stevan recalls: "When I walked out this time, I walked out a high-profile individual. . . . I was the first three-striker granted clemency. I didn't feel pressure because I had a plan. . . . I knew I was carrying the torch . . . if I tripped up it could affect those behind me." Gerald expressed appreciation for the chance at release:

I am just so grateful to be given an opportunity that I prayed about for so long, and all of a sudden it is thrown in my lap, that I know I'm doing whatever I can to take advantage of it because I know how easy it is to be snatched away from you, same way it did last time. That's what I am grateful for. To be able to get up and go when I want to versus when I am being told to. To be able to make choices rather than choices being made for you. To be an adult, a responsible adult without being perceived as irresponsible. And I know that I'm going to run into some hurdles. I'm just hoping that people help me get through them rather than judge me and just refer to me as an ex-offender. That will devastate me.

Gerald, Stevan, and other high-profile interview subjects who had spent many years in prison shared this feeling of responsibility to the people they knew in prison and their networks of support, and were determined to succeed.

Suggestions for Enhancing Reentry Success

The interview subjects were asked what suggestions they could offer regarding things that could be done in the prison and the community (and by ex-offenders themselves) to enhance reentry success. Suggestions included more understanding of ex-offenders, changes in policy by departments of corrections, changes in policies and practices in the community involving background checks, creation of mentorship programs involving people who had similar experiences, reduction of the stigma of incarceration, implementation of transitional programs that better connect prison and community life, environmental/ecological changes in the community to inhibit rather than encourage offenders' slipping up, assistance with resources and instructions regarding the nuts and bolts of making the initial adjustment to the community, improvements and opportunities for education, and willingness to give ex-offenders a chance to succeed until they prove otherwise.

Of these suggestions, several rose to the top as the most critical for most of the interview subjects: (1) transitional programs that bridge prison and community and that encourage the development of a community of support; (2) public education that reduces the stigma of incarceration so that ex-offenders are given a chance; (3) assistance with the logistics of the initial adjustment phase and awareness of the reality of the situation for ex-offenders during this time; and (4) increased opportunities for education.

The consensus among the interview subjects was that more needs to be done to develop and maintain transitional programs that bridge the gap between prison and community by providing inmates in prison opportunities to connect and build relationships with people on the outside, including individuals who have experienced a similar situation and who they will be able to count on as part of their support network upon release. Chris suggested:

> What I think is important . . . a person needs to have support from people in the same boat. Can't just be somebody who wishes them well. . . . A person has to surround themselves with people and realistic options

[for] a better life. Otherwise, you're just joking with people about their life. A person can mean well and still fuck somebody up. . . . A person who's going to be successful is going to have appropriate support, and a lot of it because he might not always want it. . . . You can't have just one person providing the support. It has to be a community of support.

From the perspective of the ex-offenders, such programs would take into account the differences between the prison subculture and free society, would provide mentorship to assist ex-offenders in making the transition from prison to community, and would assist in providing realistic options and logistical details that will be helpful in a concrete way upon release. Trevor suggested:

Real-world applicable skills . . . social skills . . . it's hard to focus on the right way to treat somebody when everyone around you [says] it's okay to treat people bad, it's OK to do that . . . treat everybody around you like crap and you'll get, you know, you'll get kudos for that. You know, I mean, if you can beat someone up, you become higher on the food chain in prison . . . you know and dealing with candy bars and cigarettes and black-market drugs and all that stuff. There is no applicable . . . that doesn't apply to the outside. And so you get caught up in this way of thinking and then when you get out on the street, everything you learned in prison about how to survive doesn't translate into the real world. . . . I'm not an expert on the psychology of inmates . . . but the thing is that if somebody isn't shown the way to treat other people, and the way to just interact you know in the free world, then they're not going to know anyways. You see what I'm saying? So if somebody is trying to reconstruct their lifestyle and the way they think about things, if there's no opportunity to grow, then it's just going to wither on the vine and they're just going to go back to whatever they were doing.

Charles added:

There needs to be programs outside that connects with the inside, some kind of connection with business owners. That is the most important thing. I went to so many interviews and they ask you about your past and as soon as you tell them you have a felony record, the light goes off and the interview [ends]. I went on over 100 interviews and could not get a job. My rap sheet is twelve pages, so that might make a difference, but it is just insane, you know? . . . There needs to be something rock solid. . . . You're coming here, you're going to stay here, and I have these interviews for you, and you're going to pick which one you want, which one fits you the best. You know? And here you go. I guarantee you there would be 98 percent change in the people coming out of prison if they had something like that. They come out with nothing. They have no hope, no hope whatsoever.

This notion of need for mentorship to teach ex-offenders ways to reconstruct their lifestyles to conduct themselves in ways that will foster successful adaptation to free society was echoed by most of the interview subjects, as were the issues regarding the antithetical nature of the prison culture.

The interview subjects who had been out the longest expressed a greater level of frustration over the lifelong stigma associated with the ex-offender label. Their (and others') suggestion was to make attempts to reduce the stigma of incarceration through public education. In fact, most of them indicated that it was for this very reason that they chose to participate in the study.[4] Stevan said, "I really hope the book highlights the fact that until society understands that all people are redeemable if put back in the right environment with the right support around, they are capable of turning their whole life around while incarcerated and not." Jane indicated what she would like to see:

> Gotta have stability. They gotta have a job and a house. . . . If you come out with nothing, you know, it's an exceptional person that comes out with nothing and makes something out of it. . . . You need a job and a house, or a place to live, stability . . . life skills. . . people understanding, people's attitudes. . . . It is an attitude. . . . For example, why are we even asking students whether they've got criminal records? I have no idea what the logic behind that is. Um, I understand for employees a little bit more, but I don't even agree with that. . . . That's a whole attitude, and I don't understand the reason for it, especially with students. . . . There was a . . . you know those news things many years ago now, it was channel 7 . . . it was about the UW. . . . The reporter was doing this expose on students at the UW and their records and they had some enormous statistics about how many people were at the UW with criminal records and what it could mean, you know there were rapes and there were . . . he just named all kinds of horrid crimes of course, which maybe five of them had a record with a horrible crime, um, and made it sound so extraordinary like if your child went to the UW, they were in so much danger from the other students, the whole spin on it . . . and I'm sure the stats were skewed just to make it look that way, and that's just the kind of thing that comes out of places all the time. You just gotta shake your head . . . that kind of stuff is bombarding them all the time, you just wonder how does anybody think they could stay straight?

Most of the interview subjects expressed a desire to be given the benefit of the doubt and to be seen as potential law-abiding, contributing citizens, at least until they prove otherwise. This opinion was expressed by Gina, who said:

> When we come out . . . I'm not saying I wasn't manipulative because I was. . . . I get it . . . but there's also another side to us . . . when we

don't feel we have to fight our way. Love us with iron fists. Love us but let us know we're held accountable. Rent to us on a month-to-month basis. Give us the opportunity to get a job . . . [and] make it easier for us to be a part of society.

The number of interview subjects who articulated difficulties in the initial stages of the reentry process highlights the need for increased attention to the logistical details in the first days and weeks postrelease. Kim offered a suggestion regarding the need for awareness of the situational/environmental factors that have the potential to increase the temptations for ex-offenders coming out of prison and hinder reentry success:

I think the most important thing is the continuation of the transitional process from when you're released from prison to when you go to the community. And there's a big break in that. Essentially when you get released from prison, it's here you go, and you go to the CCOs office. There's very little community interaction to get you ready for who you're going to be working with, who you're going to be talking to, who you need to network with or get to know so that when you do get released that day you know instantly that I can go see, for example . . . that I can go see Jessica down at Community Action and she can help me with getting my bus pass, she can help me with getting a Walmart card so I can buy some hygiene items and some clothing. Those are the type of things that would help an individual stay out much more effectively than all the treatment programs that you can give them inside the prison system. It's the continuation of what you started in prison, you get a person towards a right path, has to go out along the whole way. . . . I wasn't even given a map of where my CCO's office was or where my release housing was. I was basically put on a bus with a bus pass and a phone card that was good for two phone calls and sent on my way. Took the bus to Seattle, transferred in Seattle and got on a bus to take me to the Mount Vernon station, and from there I called my CCO on the phone. And my CCO came and picked me up, actually it was her partner that came and picked me up. I took the Greyhound bus. . . . They don't put you on the bus . . . here's what's funny. When I got dropped off at the bus station, there were two other guys with me, and the first thing is you're out, you want to walk to the local store to get something to eat or whatever, and what's funny is that, we walk to the local store, and I pick up some beef jerky and a soda, and one of the other guys picks up a forty [ounce] of Olde English 800. And I'm thinking geez . . . I'm thinking like really? And the reason why it's interesting is that the store does this on a daily basis where people come out of prison and they go there and they buy stuff. And that's one of the things where I think that if CCOs become aware of it, they could just go to the store, talk to the owner, and say "Listen, if a guy shows you a DOC ID, please don't sell him any alcohol."

This suggestion that situational aspects in the community made an enormous difference was also mentioned by Elise:

We're talking about removing the felon box if possible, access to appropriate housing, a onetime fee for background checks—there are a lot of units that charge you like $30 to do a background check for all so there is a committee that is trying to have a onetime fee. When you are getting out, trying to get back on your feet, that low-income, poverty component where do you go. I mean you end up hitting so many walls, so many barriers. . . . Agencies [should recognize] that there's a lot of us not trying to reoffend. We're trying to be better people. . . . Stop cutting programs and reduce stigma that a felon is a bad person.

A final suggestion that there needed to be more opportunities for education was made by many of the interview subjects. Many shared stories about how a teacher in the prison had influenced them, gave them confidence they never had, and encouraged them to work to obtain an academic degree upon release. They also related how their educational success contributed significantly to their self-esteem and hope for themselves for the future. Dawn said, "I think education is a great thing. . . . It's really hard to get a job, and it's a positive thing, feeling like accomplishing, actually doing something. Helps people if they get involved in something that's positive." Brandon concurred: "I don't have a lot [to] hope for in prison, I mean . . . the only good thing I had in there was education. They wouldn't let me see a psychologist. They wouldn't let me see a counselor. All the programs I tried to get initiated were just rejected. . . . I don't know maybe a prep class. . . . I had zero idea what I was getting into when I stepped out that door."

Conclusion

The ex-offender perspectives on the reentry process offered here provide a rich source of information about the reality of the situation for ex-offenders making the transition from prison to free society. The findings presented highlight a number of issues important for understanding the reentry experience regarding the process of desistance, the nature of the reentry process, the factors that contribute to reentry success, the role of the CCO in reentry success, and ex-offenders' perspectives on ways to enhance reentry success.

First, the desistance process identified by the ex-offenders in this study is consistent with the research literature suggesting that desistance is a process that is the product of the alignment of external and internal variables (Fox, 2013; Serin and Lloyd, 2009) and a slow, nonlinear process (Duhigg, 2012) that is influenced by situational variables and environments that create opportunities for change (Ferns, 2008), and can vary based on a range of individual, social, and structural factors, experience with criminal justice interventions, and gender and ethnicity (Farrall et al., 2011). While some of the ex-offenders in this study could identify a particular moment they saw as life changing, most articulated a more gradual process of change that involved an internal identity shift and personal reflection and resolve, a merging happenstance and good fortune in making connections and building relationships that assisted them in the reintegration process, and opportunities in the community and the criminal justice process that provided them an opening to succeed. This complex process over time is consistent with past research that identifies a gradual process of desistance (Geiger and Timor, 2001), leaving open the possibility that some individuals do, in fact, experience abrupt change as noted by Kurlycheck, Bushway, and Brame (2012).

Second, the findings suggest that the reentry process is characterized by a range of needs and challenges that change over time. Much of the literature on offender reentry focuses understandably on needs and challenges in the first ninety days postrelease (J. Brown, 2004a, 2004b; Gunnison and Helfgott, 2007, 2011; Helfgott and Gunnison, 2008), and a few studies focus on the needs and challenges of ex-offenders three, five, ten, or twenty-plus years postprison. Findings presented here suggest that ex-offenders face challenges many years postrelease and that needs and challenges at the onset of the reentry process change as time goes on. These findings support those of C. Visher and J. Travis (2003) that highlight the dynamic dimensions of the transition from prison to community that include individual characteristics, family relationships, community context, and state policies. Ex-offenders coming out of prison are initially faced with culture shock and struggle with getting their basic needs met, including food, clothing, housing, and employment. Once these initial needs are met as time goes on, sometimes many years, issues such as overcoming the ex-offender identity and being seen as a law-abiding citizen still linger. One of the most troublesome issues of all becomes the perception among ex-offenders that they are never fully seen as law-abiding citizens worthy of the same respect as others who have not been in prison. This information is important, in particular regarding the use of the term *ex-offender* in academic publications, the news media, criminal justice and social service contexts, and everyday life.

Third, the results regarding the perceptions of the ex-offenders on the factors that contribute to reentry success are consistent with those in the research literature that highlight the importance of social networks

(Shivy et al., 2007), family ties (Giordano, Cernkovich, and Rudolph, 2002), transition programs and strategies that straddle prison and community (Seiter and Kadela, 2003), and the role of education in building self-esteem and enhancing success (Matsuama and Prell, 2010). Furthermore, although only seven female interview subjects took part in the study, all of them spoke of issues pertaining in some cases specifically to women and to the unique situations female offenders are faced with, in particular the role of children in the desistance process, the limited housing opportunities for women coming out of prison, the complicated relationships between drug use, criminal behavior, and romantic relationships with men, child custody issues, and the difficulties in reconnecting with and regaining custody of their children. While this study did not focus specifically on issues related to the reentry of female offenders, the findings support the call for greater attention to the special issues faced by women in the reentry process (Cobbina, 2010), female desistance (Gunnison and Mazerolle, 2007; Uggen and Kruttschnitt, 1998), and the relationship between attachment to children and desistance (Michalsen, 2011).

The findings regarding the role of CCO contributions to the reentry process provide much needed information regarding the role of the CCO in assisting ex-offenders in making the transition to community life from the perspective of the ex-offender. The insights and experiences shared by the interview subjects in this study provide valuable information that can be used to improve training for CCOs and to shed light on the ways in which they are perceived by their clients. The results offer additional insight into the perspectives of ex-offenders and the views they hold about their CCOs. The finding that most hold favorable views of their CCOs adds important information to help make sense of previous findings (Helfgott, 1997; Helfgott and Gunnison, 2008) on the discrepancies between perceptions of ex-offenders and those of CCOs, in particular with respect to the issue of social distance and the ability of CCOs to understand ex-offenders' needs and challenges. Whereas previous research found that ex-offenders perceived that the social distance between their lifestyles and experiences and those of their CCOs was a possible hindrance in the reentry process (Helfgott, 1997) while their CCOs did not see this as an issue hindering their success (Gunnison and Helfgott, 2007, 2011; Helfgott and Gunnison, 2008), the current findings help conceptualize the issue and suggest that CCO trust, flexibility, and the willingness to listen, understand, and provide individualized case management goes a long way toward mediating any other issues that could potentially hinder CCO attempts to assist offenders in the reentry process.

Finally, the ex-offender suggestions on what could be done in the prison and community to enhance reentry success offer a framework for future work to improve the current state of offender reentry. This information provides additional qualitative data to supplement findings of evaluation studies of reentry programs (e.g., Fox, 2013; Seiter and Kadela, 2003) and may help make better sense of these findings. For example, using the Maryland Scale of Scientific Methods, R. Seiter and K. Kadela (2003) reviewed thirty-two evaluation studies of reentry programs. One finding was that education programs received mixed results in terms of reducing recidivism. The results presented here from the perspective of the ex-offender clearly show that education has played an enormous role in increasing self-esteem and motivation for the ex-offenders in this study and has also had the effect of greatly expanding the social networks of those who have ventured into postprison higher education. This is just one example of the importance of a more nuanced understanding of aspects of the offender change process and the necessity of examining outcome variables beyond recidivism as well as the indirect impact of reentry programs on factors that influence recidivism.

Future research is needed on the variation in the experience of ex-offenders in the reentry process. M. D. Maltz and J. M. Mullany (2000) offer an alternative data collection framework that utilizes subject-defined variables in narratives to map out an individual time trajectory showing life-course events. This framework allows for the complexity of the lives of individuals to be examined for causal connections and to be more meaningfully understood. The narrative information gleaned from the interviews in this and other qualitative studies of the lives and experiences of ex-offenders could be mapped in such a way to more clearly understand the variations in the life-course trajectories of ex-offenders as they move further in the reentry process. This approach, in conjunction with Helfgott's (1997) suggestion that ex-offender transition and adaptation be examined from the framework of ecological mapping, would be an interesting area for future research. Examining the differences in the postprison life experiences of ex-offenders as they move further out in the survival curve and make the transformation from offender to ex-offender to nonoffender identities would also be an interesting and important direction for future research. The findings presented here that show very different concerns and challenges three, five, ten, or twenty-plus years postincarceration highlight the need for future research in this area. One consideration that deserves further attention is P. J. Hirschfield and A. R. Piquero's (2010) suggestion that as the mass incarceration movement increasingly has an impact on a greater number of people, the more incarceration will become "normalized" and the more likely the possibility that the stigma of incarceration will be reduced. We find this to be a reasonable and hopeful speculation. Future research is needed to examine the impact of these cultural forces on desistance and reentry.

Notes

1. These stories show ex-offenders with histories of long-term imprisonment for serious and violent crime and gang membership (e.g., Homeboy Industries) involved in highly successful business ventures who have made significant life changes in personal and business arenas. See Delancy Street (http://www.delanceystreetfoundation.org/), Homeboy Industries (http://homeboy industries.org/), and Dave's Killer Bread (http://www.daveskillerbread.com/daves-story/video.html).

2. For a detailed description of the data collection method and interview schedule, see the Appendix at the end of the book.

3. Programs that the interview subjects had been involved with in prison included inmate clubs such as the Concerned Lifers Organization, Black Prisoners' Caucus, United Asian Coalition, Indians of All Tribes, Hispanic Culture Group, University Beyond Bars, the If Project, the Post-Prison Project, Alternatives to Violence, the Citizens, Victims, and Offenders Restoring Justice Project, and the Creative Expressions Project. Several of the ex-offenders had also been involved in a program that brought youth into the prisons, gang outreach, and advocacy for women in prison who have lost custody of their children. The number and nature of these involvements for the interview sample as a whole was extensive and played an instrumental role in linking them with similar sorts of involvements postrelease.

7

Practitioner Perspectives

THROUGHOUT THE PRECEDING CHAPTERS, PREVIOUS RESEARCH has been presented regarding ex-offender reentry challenges from the perspective of ex-offenders themselves (see Cobbina, 2010; Dodge and Pogrebin, 2001; Earle, Bradigan, and Morgenbesser, 2001; Y. Martin, 2008; Oh and Umemoto, 2005; Oliver and Hairston, 2008; Richie, 2001). The use of qualitative methods to explore ex-offender reentry by our predecessors provided a solid foundation for understanding ex-offender reintegration. Yet some gaps still remain—specifically in regard to pinpointing success factors for ex-offenders reentering society. Thus, in Chapter 6, a deeper analysis of ex-offender perspectives on reentry success was presented through the examination of original research collected by the authors. As presented in Chapter 6, ex-offenders cited numerous examples of situations in which their CCOs contributed to their reentry success. These examples suggest that, from the perspective of ex-offenders, CCO trust, flexibility, and the willingness to listen and understand and provide individualized case management go a long way and enhance their ability to succeed in the reentry process. However, examining ex-offender reentry success from the point of view of the ex-offenders may not paint a clear picture of what ex-offender reentry success looks like. By examining just one viewpoint on reentry, researchers may miss the identification of key success factors. For instance, in previous research conducted by J. B. Helfgott (1997), ex-offenders reported that CCOs did not understand their needs during reentry and many could not even relate to their CCOs. However, E. J. Latessa and P. Smith (2011) suggest that CCOs do indeed understand the needs of ex-offenders and play a vital role in assisting ex-offenders in their transition back into society. Therefore, CCOs' experiences are valuable in understanding what factors make ex-offender reentry successful.

Previous research has found that offenders feel that their CCOs cannot relate to them since they have not "walked in their shoes" (Helfgott, 1997). Subsequent research explored the social distance between offenders and CCOs (Gunnison and Helfgott, 2011; Helfgott and Gunnison, 2008). In this chapter, we present research from practitioners' perspectives including presentation and analysis of results from nineteen qualitative interviews with CCOs. These interviews were conducted to examine perspectives from those who currently work in the system to better understand what they think about offender reentry success, and to ascertain their opinions as to what is needed to assist offenders in reintegration.

Previous Research

As mentioned earlier, in 1997, Helfgott examined the relationship between ex-offender needs, through surveying transition agencies, employers, property managers, colleges and universities, the general public, and ex-offenders to determine the extent to which ex-offenders' needs were being met during reentry in Seattle, Washington. The results of her research yielded the identification of many needs that ex-offenders have during reentry. One unexpected finding was ex-offenders' reports that CCOs did not understand their reentry needs. In fact, many ex-offenders in the study did not see their CCOs as a resource in the reentry process. One offender stated, "They [CCOs] just want you to tell a good lie . . . [and] they have no understanding of what it's like," suggesting that if CCOs were "[taken] out [of their environment] . . . they wouldn't be able to survive on the streets" (Helfgott, 1997, p. 16). However, a missing component of her study was data on CCOs' views of ex-offender reentry needs and challenges as well as their perception of whether or not officer-offender social distance influences the reentry process.

Subsequent researchers have explored whether criminal justice professionals are aware of ex-offenders' needs and the challenges they face upon reentry (J. Brown, 2004a, 2004b; Graffam et al, 2004; Graffam et al., 2008; Gunnison and Helfgott, 2007). For example, J. Brown (2004a) examined perceptions of federal parole officers regarding ex-federal offenders' needs in Canada and found that federal officers are well aware of the needs faced by offenders. J. Graffam and colleagues (2004) also examined the perceptions of needs of ex-offenders in Melbourne, Australia. However, the sample was made up of twenty-two criminal justice professionals that did not include CCOs. E. Gunnison and J. B. Helfgott

(2007) examined 132 state and federal CCO perceptions of ex-offender needs, the value officers' placed on the specific needs, and the opportunities available for offenders to meet their needs in Seattle, Washington. The results of the research revealed that CCOs identified needs and challenges that were consistent with those identified in the literature. Additionally, the researchers uncovered gender differences in the identification of needs and challenges facing newly released offenders. Specifically, female CCOs rated needs and challenges for offenders significantly different than male officers. In another study, J. B. Helfgott and E. Gunnison (2008) surveyed 132 CCOs and found that social distance was significantly related to officer identification of some offender needs, offender challenges, and officer attitudes toward offenders. However, social distance did not play a large role in officer ability to identify offender reentry needs, and officers do not collectively perceive officer-offender social distance as a hindrance in the reentry process.

To further explore CCOs' perspectives on offender reentry, Gunnison and Helfgott (2011) reported results from narrative survey responses from 132 CCOs. Some CCOs reported that successful reentry is due to a rational choice to make a decision to change. For instance, one officer reported, "Prosocial living is a choice just as crime and drug use is a choice" (p. 295). Another theme that emerged from the research revolved around officer attitude. That is, the CCOs' attitude may contribute to or hinder offender reentry success. As one officer stated, "Sometimes depends on the CCO if they have a superior attitude or not, if the CCO believes he/she is better than the offender, then offender will see that and act accordingly" (p. 296). When the CCOs were asked whether social distance played a role in reentry success, overwhelmingly they reported that social distance did not play a role in offender reentry success. In response to this question, one officer reported, "No! The offenders will find all kinds of excuses to lurk behind. It's the offenders that would want to change and the community corrections officer's situation does not matter here" (p. 295).

In sum, research has emerged on practitioners' perspectives on reentry. Much of the previous literature on practitioner perspectives has focused on CCOs' ability to identify needs and challenges. However, gaps still remain. Specifically, CCOs have not been asked to pinpoint success factors for reentry, recall specific cases of ex-offender reentry success, and identify what is needed *right now* to foster successful reentry. In the remainder of this chapter, results of research from nineteen interviews with CCOs will be presented to attempt to fill in the gaps in the literature on successful reentry. The majority of our sample was male (57 percent) and overwhelmingly Caucasian. Our sample also included one African American, one Hispanic American, and two Asian American CCOs. Additionally, our sample ranged in age from twenty-nine to fifty-four years of age with an average age of forty years. Further, our sample had a range of years in service spanning from one year to twenty-nine years with the average being 8.5 years of service.[1]

Definitions of Reentry Success

Each CCO provided a unique definition of reentry success, though some overlap did occur. Several CCOs defined success as an absence of re-offending. Chris T., a CCO with eight years of experience, stated, "I'll keep it simple. If they are coming out of prison and don't return or get convicted of anything else, that's a success." Kristyn, a CCO with five years of experience, stressed the safety of the community and no reoffending as the foundation to her definition. She reported, "I would say at base level with my job, success is if the community is safe and the person doesn't reoffend. When I say reoffend, I mean when they get out and they relapse. I don't consider trespass a criminal offense. I mean a serious violent crime. Crimes similar to their original offense." Another CCO, Chris B., with six years of experience, shared a similar definition but acknowledges that one's definition may include both negative and positive factors. He stated,

> The first thing that pops into my head is a negative definition. Which is not going back. Not screwing up, not going back to jail, not continuing in the patterns of behavior that led to that in the first place. I try to reframe that in my head because when you start with a negative, when you start with a list of don'ts, you have nowhere to go. You need a list of do's. To me, successful reentry is building a life with a number of different things, building a prosocial life; building a support space of friends and family; people to hang out with and socialize with who are not involved in a lifestyle which is going to get you in trouble. Getting a job, being successful in a lot of the more traditional sense of the word that we as society think is a sign of what is life, what you have to do. Getting a place to live. Creating a life that is absent of those behaviors which sent them to prison in the first place. It's hard to get away from that total negative, but it's there.

Other CCOs defined reentry success in positive terms or increments made in the life of the ex-offender. Thomas, a CCO with eleven years of experience, suggested that any small improvements in the life of the ex-offender are an example of reentry success. He explained,

It so depends on where they started. I think the one thing I've learned at least working with this population is defining success really tends to be in very small increments. I don't think there is any one thing that you can pinpoint, and I would just say that quality of life is improved. It's improved from wherever it was before they came into the criminal justice system. Whatever led them to be in the criminal justice system. Somehow we've made an impact so that they've gotten some insight as to how it is they got there.

Several CCOs also recognized that reentry success is different for each ex-offender. Jacob, a CCO with five years of experience, illustrated this point with his response:

Well, that's a difficult question because success for some offenders is completely different for another offender. You have someone with an extremely lengthy criminal history and success for them is that for the next year that they're off of supervision they don't commit a new felony offense. Where you may have another person who has mental health issues and just to get them stabilized on medication and have them actively participate in the community, that's a success. As so it's hard to, you know, put it all in one box and say that's success. Each offender is kind of a different story all to themselves. So, it's really the way you look at it that you try to increase their strengths and decrease their deficiencies or their risk factors.

Fred, a CCO with eight years of experience, stressed this notion that success is intertwined with the tools that ex-offenders are given. He noted, "To be successful is for them to reconnect and get the tools to reconnect back into society. Not all ways work for the same person. For one offender, the tools will work; for others [they] will not." Thus, successful reentry may hinge on the ability of a CCO to identify the deficiencies that an ex-offender has and link that person up with the appropriate resources in order to facilitate success. In sum, a wide range of definitions of reentry success were provided by CCOs. One important realization is that CCOs did not all agree that success was defined by recidivism, or especially lack thereof. All too often in the field of criminal justice, researchers are focused solely on recidivism rates as a measure of success. Thus, if empirical examinations of reentry success fail to investigate other forms of success during reentry such as family reunification or employment, changes in the way the ex-offender thinks or the types of strategies used to manage behavior, length of time between offenses, or changes in the severity of the types of offenses or violations an ex-offender engages in, then the picture of what makes for successful reentry is conceptually incomplete.

The Making of Successful Reentry

Through our interviews with the CCOs, we learned that successful reentry involves a number of factors converging together to make success. While we found some overlap in responses, opinions also differed. Congruent with previous research on factors that can hinder or assist in reentry as presented in earlier chapters, housing, family support, sobriety, and mental health assistance were often cited by CCOs as the foundation pieces to successful reentry (J. Brown, 2004a, 2004b; Gunnison and Helfgott, 2007; Helfgott and Gunnison, 2008). One of the CCOs we interviewed, Thomas, described how having a basic need met such as housing can free ex-offenders to focus on what they need to do to be successful:

> The first and probably most important thing is that they have housing. That they have a safe place that they can be so they can focus on the things that are going to make them healthy, mentally and physically. Focus on, if they have family, to make sure that those relationships are strong because that's their support network. If they can focus on gaining insight into their mental illness, because obviously 90 percent of the time, it's driving their involvement in the criminal justice system. You know, not accepting the fact that they are mentally ill and not taking their medicine, whatever it might be. So housing tends to be the common dominator that we found for folks kind of as the starting point.

Several other CCOs referred to housing as being an important factor in successful reentry. Jacob responded, "Stable housing, that's a huge thing. Having a place where they can go home to, and that [they] can relax [in], they can build upon. Whether that's with family or by themselves because sometimes offenders, they have families that aren't the most prosocial and not going to lead them into a positive direction. So, stable housing." Kristyn, a CCO with five years of experience, explained,

> What is huge for this population in particular is housing; I mean that is important for anyone, but when you're working with people who have chronic mental illness and such a lengthy history, it is another compounding factor that keeps them from doing well in addition to being a convicted felon, in addition to having a history of homelessness; then they have this chronic mental illness and probably, maybe a drug or alcohol addiction with it. . . . I've seen housing be an amazing component to someone's success and turn people's lives around in a way you never thought . . . like a motel room would even do.

Other CCOs explained that adequate finances and employment are also necessary for successful reentry. Lori, a CCO with eleven years of experience, stated,

They need assistance in probably whether it is employment or getting the financial assistance that they are going to need. If they are applying for SSI [supplemental security income], if they need help with applying. Some don't need help applying; they just need to know where to go. Or assisting them in getting employment so they can pay those bills and have that stability. Finances, as with everybody, if you don't have money, you don't have what you need in life. You don't have food, the roof over your head. If you don't have those, you're going back to what you know to get those.

Besides basic needs being met, some CCOs indicated internal factors such as attitude as being important. Chris B. stated, "Attitude. I think primarily some of the important things are a positive attitude. I don't mean that as 'Yay! Happy, perky!' I mean a decision to do what you need to do. A lot of offenders that I see get out, they haven't decided to change. They haven't decided to be successful." Brad, a CCO with four years of experience, explained:

Honestly, it's really going to boil down to the individual. We can help them along the way as a CCO or as a counselor or as a mental health therapist. But honestly, that drive for change needs to come from inside. If it's not coming from inside, you're not going to be able to force somebody . . . just like you can't force somebody to look through your own eyes or viewpoint. That's the bottom line. It's that need or want to make that positive change in their lifestyle.

Thus, from the perspectives of CCOs successful reentry may be a combination of having basic needs met and intrinsic factors. These themes will be explored in greater detail later in the chapter.

Success Stories

When we interviewed the CCOs, we asked them to recall success stories of ex-offenders that they worked with. The success stories they were able to recall were few and far between. Some CCOs could not recollect whether any of their former clients were successful, or if CCOs could recall success stories, they usually only remembered one or two clients who were successful on supervision or shortly thereafter. Brad, however, recalled several success stories in his burgeoning career:

He was in prison for manslaughter as well. He was drunk and accidently killed a cop in an accident. Really kind of turned his life around. Before prison, he was kind of like, getting by, getting drunk and really dealing with his personal demons. I think he did seven years in prison, made it out to the work release, and found some work at the car dealership, and last I heard, he's one of their top salesmen. He actually works for Korum's down in Puyallup. He's doing really well for himself. He got married, living in Federal Way. He came up to see me about a month ago, just to let me know how he's doing. That was really neat. Another gentleman, he's been in the system for years, years, and years. Multiple felonies, multiple causes. Recently got out a couple years ago, maybe a year and a half ago. I used to call him "Slim." Longtime drug offender, not necessarily an addict himself but he would revert to a lifestyle of dealing because it's quick, easy money. We got him working at the Woodland Park Zoo when he was on work release and he stuck with it. He came by a couple weeks ago and told me, "Hey, just letting you know, I made it up into management and I'm doing really well and still at the zoo." It happens a lot more than people realize. That people really do make that change and really do well.

Other CCOs recalled interesting success stories and the role of sobriety in those stories. For example, Lori stated:

Alex was one of the most prolific car thieves in Snohomish County. There would be times when I was supervising him, I would get calls from local police saying, "Do you know where Alex is? We've had a rash of car thefts lately." Usually it was, "No, he's on warrant status," and all of a sudden there he was in one of the cars. He was one of these guys who had nothing in their life, dad wasn't in the picture, mom had addiction, and so he basically raised himself. He didn't have any family members. He did have a wife and a girlfriend who happened to meet the day they were both giving birth to his sons. They met, they became friends and decided to raise the boys together. . . . He'd come into my office and we'd speak for a couple hours, "How about doing it this way?" I tried to get him into programming. I will talk about programming; I'm very pro-programming. He'd come to programs for a couple days, and he would be off using his drugs again. He was a real methamphetamine user. He finally got popped or arrested again for another car theft, and this time he received a drug offender sentencing alternative or a DOSA sentence. . . .

He was finally just realizing that "I have really got to get my act straight or I'm never going to have the life that I want to have" with his family. So he took a DOSA sentence, moved out of Snohomish County, moved down here to Seattle, did the treatment as required through DOSA. He stopped in the office. It's been about a year ago. . . . He stopped by and gave a clean UA [urine analysis], and he stopped in to see a couple of us CCOs who he had also worked with. He came in and he was telling me he had a friend who financed him to have his own car repair shop. This was a guy who had been taking apart cars and rebuilding them for years. He got the tools for this car repair shop. His ex-wife and ex-girlfriend both allowed him to start having contact with the boys, and he actually had the boys for Christmas that year. He had been clean for two and a half years. A huge turn around. It was really cool. As we were walking out the door and saying good-bye, he pulls the door open as he says, "You know . . . all those talks we used to have, they worked." He closed the door and walked off. It was really cool. He really needed that extra shot, which he got through the DOSA program. But evidently something that I had said along the way, some of those thoughts helped him somehow, or he wouldn't have made such a point to tell me that it helped.

Another CCO, Rebecca, mentioned the role of sobriety and avoiding criminal associates and even noted how perhaps age played a role in success, with middle-age ex-offenders doing better—although some seemed to be ahead of the curve:

> One in particular right now and I have regular contact with him. Initially, he looks terrible on paper, he was a meth addict, he was involved in a lot of residential burglaries, manufacturing and dealing meth, so messy, so one of those situations, that we don't see people come out of very easily. He is one of the few people that I have seen come out of prison actually commit to completely changing their environment and people they spend time with and not falling back into the same behaviors. It's easy to hang out with the people you always hang out with. He made an active choice to stay away from them which is hard because Seattle is small. He went all the way through supervision without any violations, which is very impressive. He has been out for one year. He is now active in the community. He was one of those fellows that we did not expect to succeed. He is in his early thirties. We don't see them as being successful as those in the forties. They are tired. They're done. They don't have the same energy—they tend to age out. He was younger and was able to make a change.

CCOs also mentioned the role of family support as contributing to successful reentry. Jacob recalled,

> I had a guy that was a repeat offender, extensive criminal history. When released, he released to his in-laws' house with his wife. While he was in prison his wife got clean and sober and had moved back in. She regained custody of their children. And so when he released, his release plan was to move back in there. His father-in-law really worked hard on getting him programmed, and it was almost like he had a second CCO with him all the time. And he was able to start his own business. . . . He was on supervision for two and a half years. By the end he was selling cars. He was basically buying them from auctions, repairing them, and selling them and doing quite well. He was in college . . . oh, just a total success story.

For other CCOs, the success of their clients may be due to finally getting the mental health assistance that they need. Kristyn recalled,

> I can think of another guy and he hasn't been on supervision for a long time. He was another guy who was very, very psychotic, always experiencing symptoms even when medicated. He was a violent, violent guy. He had an assault history and attempted murder. So he was definitely high on our radar of people to watch. Because if he stopped taking his medication, he [would] go south pretty quickly.
>
> The problem with him that he, like a lot of people with pervasive mental illness, he would start to feel better and think that he could go off his medication. So he wouldn't show up for a couple of days and we'd get a call from Minnesota saying he was trying to get benefits there, and from Orlando, Florida. He just hopped on a bus and [had] gone all the way across the country and trying to get benefits. Then we would have to issue a warrant for him, extradite him back here. I think for him what was huge is that he moved into some partner housing that we have up in the U District, and the woman that owns that housing is this ninety-year-old woman who is the sweetest person you can ever meet, and she loves helping people out. So he moved into this housing and I think it was that and finally just coming to [the] realization that [to] keep doing what he was doing; it wasn't working.
>
> Oftentimes, people will be ordered to twelve months of supervision but if they're not complying it gets stretched out to two years to three years. He was that kind of guy. It was looking like it was going to take him six or seven years to finish eighteen months. But as soon as he got linked up with housing, he started volunteering and got a cat. . . . He's another person. He has lived in the same housing for [the] last six years. He's never committed a new crime, nothing, not even trespassing. He's been done with supervision for years.

Denise, with over twenty years of experience in the corrections field, stated:

> I can think of a client I had who came into my program. She's a mom of three kids. They're like eight, ten, and sixteen. Her husband was also convicted and went to prison. . . . She finally determined that what she needed was mental health help. She didn't necessarily know what; she just wanted to go talk to somebody just to kind of get some things out. In about a year's time, she had gone from her primary goal in life was how to get on her husband's visiting list in the prison to "I'm not sure I want to stay with him. I'm not sure he's the best interest for my kids."

Thus, from the perspectives of CCOs, reentry success can be enhanced through ex-offenders receiving mental health care. Once ex-offenders are more stabilized mentally, then they appear to be better able to tackle the many challenges that await them on their path to successful reentry.

Role of CCOs in the Reentry Process

As highlighted in Chapter 6, the majority of ex-offenders in our study reported that their CCOs contributed to their success. For many CCOs, building rapport and trust with their clients is one method that they utilize to enhance success. Kelley explained,

> I meet with my people when they come to my caseload. I meet with them weekly or biweekly so that I get to know them and they get to know me so they feel a little more accountable to me. If you build some sort of rapport with that person, they're less likely to fail to report and go on warrant status, and then you have no way to intervene in drug use or get them into in-patient treatment. If they disappear, you can't work with them. You can't help them.
>
> When they come in, I give them the opportunity to be honest about what's going on, just to tell me if they've used and to talk about what happened surrounding the use, who they used with, what the situation was, why they think it happened, what led up to it. So I help them sit there and have them trace it all the way back to where it started from so they can realize triggers and things like that. Then they know if they use, it doesn't mean that I will automatically throw them in jail. We can get them into in-patient treatment or have them go to their out-patient three times a week instead of one time a week, go to more sober meetings, things like that. But I do have an open communication style with them so that they feel, they're scared about going back, because I can do that. But they have some amount of trust and the fact that even if they do go to jail, they know why and they know what's going to happen. There's always the opportunity to get treatment and help for the problem. Because throwing someone in jail, it doesn't solve the problem; the problem is still there when they get out. So you have to do the jail time but have something in place to deal with the actual issue when they get out. Sometimes, I'll go to the jail and take someone up out of the jail and put them on a bus so they can go to treatment.
>
> I think a lot of it has to do with building rapport. I've had a lot of people say that they actually didn't necessarily like working with me in the beginning because I do say, "Here's your rules. You will follow them. Here's what happens." But in the end, I think that they, after they've reported for a while, they do understand that my job is to, I feel, try to keep them in the community and transition back in so that they aren't this revolving door of in and out of jail. When that happens, that what makes my job worthwhile. If I was just arresting people all

the time, I would have been a law enforcement officer. That's not what
I love to do; I like to see people successful.

In reflecting on a successful case, Fred noted that building rapport with
his particular client was the key to his success:

> I don't know the extent of the history of all the CCOs he had previ-
> ously. I truly cared and I showed him that by my actions not just by
> giving him lip service. I let him know up front what would be his con-
> sequences of his actions. The rapport, the way I treated him. He told
> me that he appreciated that. I did not treat him like the scum of the
> earth. This is a man talking to a man and held him to that standard.
> Those who were doing something positive in his life, I would build re-
> lationships with them. I encouraged his son to be patient and keep en-
> couraging his dad. Be a prosocial outreach for his dad as he did not
> have a lot of positive people around. I showed his dad the difference
> between positive people around you and those people that don't mean
> any good. How many of those people actually visited you in jail? . . .
> Your son called you in jail and your girlfriend visited you. Those two
> people actually care.

Building rapport and sometimes sharing a bit about their own backgrounds is one method that some CCOs utilize to break down walls and
assist their clients:

> I am not afraid to let them know about my background that I have had
> a drinking and alcohol problem. I have never gone to prison or had
> some of the childhoods that these people had, but I do know what it is
> like to have an addiction issue. I know how hard it is to get off that
> stuff. I had a problem with Jack Daniels and cigars and I can tell them
> what I went through personally to get off that stuff. I tell them how
> hard it was for me and what it took for me to get over it and that it
> does not happen overnight. Relapse is the road to recovery. It is very
> rare (and that is why I get mad when I see people get arrested for
> every dirty UA) because it would be rare for you to get someone
> straight out of prison that would give you nothing but clean UAs for
> twelve months straight. Most will have a relapse period, and it is how
> you attack. Do you attack that relapse with knee-jerk reactions to send
> them to jail? Or what is their attitude? Are they coming into the office
> being an asshole with me about it or work it through? Are you not
> going to try? That rapport . . . sometimes you can have a person that
> has a really bad attitude when they first come into your office because
> of their past experiences with past CCOs. I will say, Drop the attitude
> at the door. You don't know me. I will work with you at the intake.
> That does not mean you can give me twelve dirty UAs in a row but I
> will work with you for two or three.
> I see my job as trying to keep you out of jail, not put you back in
> jail. A lot come out of jail with this attitude "You are setting me up for

failure." I am trying to keep you out of jail, not to send you there. I know you can do it because I did it. Also, I don't come from a rich background and I know what it is like to be one paycheck from the streets. I have never been homeless, but I came close twice . . . real close. Being able to relate to them and tell them, you know, I cannot 100 percent understand your situation. In their intake we look at employment, financial history, family history, education history, employment history some of them have been through hell. I won't completely understand, but I understand somewhat. It is the glass half empty, half full attitude. They have this perspective that this will happen. You have to change their perspective on things. And those things may happen if you keep making those same poor decisions. Some CCOs have them do thinking error reports. I don't. I have them talk it out—what were you doing when you did that, what should you have done. A lot of them are impulsive: "Where is my next hit?" Try to get them out of this negative day-to-day lifestyle and to a positive week-by-week, month-by-month lifestyle. Try to get them a long-term approach lifestyle.

I can tell you about this guy who failed. He used this street term: "Once a street so and so (n word) always a street so and so." He had an alcohol, cocaine, and gambling addiction. He had won a lawsuit from the Department over something that happened in prison, and I would work with him and would say, "You can take that money, invest it, buy a house," but instead he was blowing it in the casino and he would admit that is what he is doing. He had eighteen months of community custody. For twelve months, he would do okay most of the time but one slip, one dirty UA, he then would go to one out of four DV [domestic violence] classes. But he had this attitude that this is my life and we caught him with two guns, so he is going to federal prison probably for twelve to twenty years because he has a criminal history. I thought I was doing well. But he is a perfect example of an entrenched person. But you try. I have a lot of stump speeches. It is about how to act and utilize prosocial coping skills.

Other CCOs indicated that they offer support to ex-offenders through providing guidance and pointing their clients to services in the community that may assist them. Denise stated,

Everybody in my unit calls me "the mother," so I go in there and I guess I mother people. I don't want to excuse their bad behavior and I want to hold them accountable, but at the same time, I want them to feel that they can come and talk to me. I want you to call me and I want to talk to you about drug use before you start using again. I want a chance to intervene. I want a chance to teach you the different things you can do, show you different behaviors. Refer you to different counselors, or if it's an NA [Narcotics Anonymous] meeting or whatever it is. Sit down with you and have an opportunity to find out what your individual specific needs are, maybe get some background on where things come from, although I'm not certain if it's important enough if you were abused as a child. It's kind of where are you today and where can we go from here to shift your thinking one degree in a positive direction and get you going in a different direction.

Jacob recalled one successful story regarding a female offender and how he and fellow CCOs supported her. Thus teamwork and going the extra mile appeared to make all the difference in her case.

> I had a female offender. When I first met her, the first time I ever arrested her, it was because she had a hatchet in her hand, and it was a pretty scary situation, and over the course of about a year and a half of going back and forth to jail, at the end, she finally kind of got it. And she had been a victim of abuse. She had been raised in a poor household and it's almost like we became part of her family. We wrapped ourselves around her and really worked hard on helping her get to the point where she needed to be. I remember Christmas Eve a few years ago. She was beaten pretty bad by her boyfriend and the first person she called was myself and my partner. We're the ones that got her into a nice safe home that night. It was on Christmas Eve and we stayed and worked until about six-thirty to seven o'clock, just kind of helping her. I think by building that kind of relationship and forming that [idea that] someone does care and we're not here just to arrest you. Because I think for a long time, that's what she thought I was there to do. And when she got to that "No, I'm actually here to help" that it changed the situation around.

The ability of CCOs to make connections with their clients is critical in the reentry process as often the CCO is the only prosocial individual in the life of the ex-offender. Results of our research reveal that CCOs utilize various methods to reach out to their clients on an interpersonal level and contribute to their success. For example, CCOs that can build trust and establish rapport with their clients are one step closer in fostering successful reentry for their clients. Additionally, using arrest as a last means of resort for their clients who make mistakes as opposed to using arrest as their first "solution" may also be key in not only building trust but also contributing to keeping their clients on the pathway to success. Finally, CCOs that have the ability to bridge the gap between themselves and their clients may be more likely to "reach" those clients who may have put up a wall between themselves and their CCO.

What About Social Distance?

As mentioned earlier in the chapter, previous research has identified the issue of social distance between ex-offenders and CCOs and explored whether social distance plays a role in ex-offender reentry success (see Gunnison and Helfgott, 2011; Helfgott, 1997; Helfgott and Gunnison, 2008). With regard to social distance, several CCOs believed that the perceptions of social distance by ex-offenders about their CCOs may be due to the nature of the CCOs' role—to maintain professional boundaries between themselves and their clients. Chad, a CCO with four years of experience, explained that he avoids explaining his background or personal struggles with his ex-offender clients for the most part. However, he acknowledges, that he may share some of his personal struggles in certain cases: "There's been a select few, if I'm really trying to get through to them." Other CCOs do recognized that ex-offenders may perceive social distance, but the CCOs work to break down these barriers through establishing good communication and rapport with their clients. Kelley, a CCO with eleven years of experience, stated,

> No, I haven't walked in their shoes. I think that is something they feel a little bit of, of course. Especially when I was in West Seattle, I would set everything up, and we would sign all our paperwork, and the offender would look at me and go, "Oh, okay well thanks. Now can I meet my CCO?" . . . It's a matter of, with my guys, I tell them. I haven't been through what you've been through. I don't have an addiction issue, you know. I didn't grow up the way you grew up. Everybody's issues are their own and we all have something. I think once you, I think I talked about this before, we do establish some rapport with people, and I think when they see that I don't judge them for the things that they did before, or choices that they've made. Then, they can understand that I don't come from where they come from, but I'm certainly not judging them because of it and that helps.

Michael, a CCO with nine years of experience added that the "best thing to do is to establish rapport" to get past any perceptions of social distance by ex-offenders.

Several CCOs pointed to rational choice as a factor in reentry success. Will, a CCO with two years of experience, stated, "My opinion is that it's really up to the person. Yeah, a lot of that can be rational choice. We've all made choices in our life. We've all made bad choices in our life. That's what life is all about, making choices." Rebecca, a CCO with eight years of experience, responded,

> Absolutely, yes. I mean at some point they have to take it upon themselves to recognize it is ultimately their choices. A whole load of circumstances that get them where they are but it is their choices that can get them to the next step. The guys that do well on supervision, and gals, traditionally are the ones that I perceive have made the choice to actively adjust their behavior themselves. It is trying to get people to

fit into a mold that they don't fit into—I think that is what they see for the most part, that we sit on the other side of the desk and we don't have any perspective and that we are trying to tell them to be more like us, but there is no way. They live their own life, have their own experiences, so it is more a matter of them recognizing that they can, still in that whole chaos that could be their environment, make the choice to not make their matters worse.

Other CCOs recognized that rational choice both may and may not contribute to reentry success. As Jodyne, a CCO with sixteen years of experience, put it: "I think it plays a role. I think the fear of failure plays a role in the choices they make. Some have never had a driver's license so they think, 'What if I fail? Then what?' Rational choice could play a role but sometimes they don't have a choice either." Ashley, a CCO with one year experience, responded:

Even my own offenders will tell me flat-out, "It is always our choice. It's no doubt it's our choice." But that's partial. I think people are going to do . . . based on many factors. Like, how they were raised, what environment they're still in. How desperate they are to survive. The easy answer that anyone can say, that it's a rational choice. They either do or they don't. Of course it is; however, life isn't always as simple as black and white.

In sum, many CCOs recognized that social distance may exist between CCOs and ex-offenders or can certainly see how ex-offenders may view the presence of social distance. It appears that right from the get-go, that first initial meeting between CCO and ex-offender, the CCO is trying to strip away such perceptions through communication and building rapport with the client. However, as previous researchers (e.g., Swanson, 2009) have noted, CCOs also make the conscious choice to maintain social distance as a psychological mechanism to maintain professional boundaries in their work with their ex-offender clients. Additionally, CCOs view rational choice as a piece to the puzzle in what makes for successful reentry. However, most CCOs stopped short of pinpointing a rational choice as the only factor in successful reentry.

Primary Factors Obstructing Success

In an attempt to have CCOs pinpoint the exact factors obstructing ex-offender reentry success, we asked CCOs to identify those key factors that block ex-offender success during reentry. Not surprisingly, many of the responses centered on key needs not being met such as housing and employment. Siobhan, a CCO with nine years of experience, stated:

> Housing. Having support, some come out with nobody that's prosocial to you. I think funding: a lot of them have no money. But the way DSHS [Department of Social and Health Services] is now, they really don't qualify for a lot. Some do. They cut the funding so much. I think for me, if I show them, you can get job skills, there's more opportunity for employment. With the economy the way it is, people with degrees can't get a job, let alone someone who has no work history. I think they need job skills. I know they cut a lot of programs in the prisons.

Another CCO, Thomas, reported that lack of or inadequate housing and employment and a lack of educational opportunities are hindrances to successful reentry:

> Not having housing is the probably the biggest thing. When you have to worry about that, if you're out couch surfing, you don't have the time or energy to focus on things you should be focusing on. I think for the mainstream groups of folks, I would say access to educational opportunities. I just think about some of the programs we had at CJC [Community Justice Center], we had Life Skills to Work program, which seemed to be very effective. Class was always full but it was a resource that went away. I think making that kind of entry level or introductory thing into the education arena and not making it intimidating; I think the educational system can be intimidating, trying to get into it, trying to navigate how to get the funding for it and what have [you] . . . it can be very intimidating and overwhelming. There's no doubt that access to work and work that's going to be able to pay the mortgage. If you've got a felony on your record, it's a lot tougher to get a job, it just is. So I think that's an obstacle for many. If you're somebody, I don't know what the percentages are, but if you're somebody [who was] dealing drugs or running drugs, you're making a lot more money than if you were working at McDonald's or Safeway or something like that. So, it's kind of tough to compete with. I think education and work seem to be the things that seem to be tough, that I hear, just in the hallways and what offenders talk to other CCOs about.

Jacob also pointed out the role of employment and how minority ex-offenders find obtaining employment difficult. For instance, he noted, "I think the fact [is] that some of the employers won't hire ex-felons. How do they expect to find work if the moment they put out a job application and have to put [an answer to] have you committed a felony? It stacks against them. There's research out there, even for minority offenders, how that it's even more difficult. It's crazy." Another CCO hinted at the fact that race complicated the ability of the ex-offender to obtain employment: "I have another guy out of work release, another gentleman, well spoken, appearance wise looks old due to his life. He had a difficult time, African American male, for the first few months. He had a hard time getting a job."

Several CCOs also reported that access to treatment or the bureaucracy involved in securing treatment is a major obstacle to ex-offender reentry success. Chad explained,

> A judge orders these guys in this state to do treatment that there is no way that they will be able to afford. Following the law. . . . If I just follow the law, I am to throw them in jail for not doing their treatment, which is completely, completely insane. Two of the worst ones are DV treatments, DV guys, domestic violence guys are the worst offenders to handle. Bar none. You can't tell them anything; you almost always have to have a male CCO because they can't take orders from a woman. But they all have to do treatment, and the treatment is really expensive, and we don't offer it. The treatment we offer is chemical dependency, and then there's sex offender treatment, which is thousands and thousands of dollars, and none of these guys can get hired. I have two guys right now that are supposed to be going to treatment, can't afford it and are doing everything right. My hands are tied. . . . I mean, I'm not going to arrest them. But they can't find work.

Lori added: "Bureaucracy. When they have to wait for four to six weeks to get into in-patient treatment, and they're meth addicts, they're not going to make that appointment to get that next level, and it's not anything against the treatment program. We don't have the space, the funding, all that kind of stuff." She added regarding the bureaucracy surrounding getting mental health needs met: "Or they go to jail for thirty days and lose their medical coupon and it takes them three to four weeks to get their medical coupon back before they can get back on their medication. By that time, they have spiraled downhill enough that they've gone out and done something else."

Other CCOs, such as Kristyn, pointed to difficulties in navigating the system and ex-offender attitudes as major obstacles:

> I think, I think this is going to be a really broad answer. I think navigating the systems. There are so many systems that you need to navigate. When you are handed down your judgment and sentence from a judge, they often do an appendix of specific evaluations and conditions you need to comply with. So to come from prison out to the community and the state has been in a budget crisis for the last several years, and [the prisons] are losing many, many of their programs that were sort of targeted for getting the people ready for the community. Knowing where to start with DSHS and getting your benefits; knowing how to find a mental health agency; knowing where to get a DV [domestic violence] evaluation, and how you're going to come up with the $900 to

do it; how are you going to get around navigating the bus system? Those are just really . . . I think all the different things that, not having a computer to look any of this stuff up. If you're moving into Seattle for the first time, figuring out the city . . . I think [is] a huge obstacle. And then once you have encountered several frustrating situations or failures if you want to call them that, I think that it's pretty easy to shut down and throw up your hands and think, "I'm not doing well with this. I'm a month out of my transition, and I've already come up against this many obstacles. I have hit my head up against the wall this many times trying to figure stuff out and I feel like I'm not getting anywhere." I think a lot of times when people get out of prison they want it to happen overnight and that becomes frustrating and a big obstacle.

Chris B. added:

Attitude, a sense of entitlement. Again, that revisits what is the most successful thing is attitude. The most important thing is attitude. One of the biggest barriers is just someone's personal attitude. I don't want to repeat myself by saying entitlement. Entitlement is a big one. I see a lot of offenders who get out and feel that "you locked me up, so now you have to give me a fresh start." They feel like somebody should be giving them everything from bus tickets to come report to food to lodging to "give me a job."

In sum, several of the factors identified by CCOs as contributing to unsuccessful reentry are consistent with previous research on reintegration. That is, housing, employment, and education are critical needs for ex-offenders, and a lack of fulfillment of these needs will likely contribute to failure during reentry. Additionally, the CCOs identified other contributing factors not previously mentioned in the literature. For instance, the bureaucracy of the reentry process for many ex-offenders and the attitude of ex-offenders are factors that have not been previously addressed in the empirical literature on reentry. Interestingly, previous research by Gunnison and Helfgott (2007) revealed that CCO attitude may hinder reentry. However, the narratives from the interviews of CCOs in our sample revealed that *ex-offender* attitude as opposed to CCO attitude plays a role in ex-offender reentry success.

Primary Factors Contributing to Success

The CCOs interviewed identified key factors that contribute to successful reentry for ex-offenders. One CCO suggested that for success to occur, ex-offenders need to be willing to change and have the necessary support systems in place to facilitate change. Thomas reported:

I think, probably number one they have to be in a place where they want to do something different. I guess it doesn't matter what treatment you provide them, they have to be in a place to kind of accept that. They have to have a good support system in place, people they can rely on that are going to help them get through that transitional period of having the temptation of going out to use or maybe not wanting to take medicine, and kind of keep them on track, keep them on that path.

Siobhan added:

Housing, community support, job training, family. If people have people that hold them accountable, they know that people care. They know that they are not just going to let themselves down but those people in their lives. That could be their kids, or moms, parents, cousins, whatever. I wouldn't just say housing, I mean, yeah, housing seems like "of course." But it's not. A lot of guys get out and have housing and they're not doing really great. I provide you housing and the hardest thing for people to have and it's still difficult. And jobs, it's very difficult for a lot of convicted felons, sex offenders to find employment. So, if they can't get any kind of employment, they are stuck in a place where they have no money coming in and no place to stay and I think that ends up where they don't kind of beat that obstacle.

Other CCOs pointed to an effective reentry plan and support system as keys to successful reintegration. Kristyn explained:

The prison is unfortunately losing some of these programs for a while, and I think we're building them back up. I think a huge thing is talking about reentry and preparing offenders for reentry before release. So I just think preparing people and giving them information and talking to offenders about what they think the world is going to look like, that's a huge thing. I think that as staff, we're not having the conversations with offenders like, "What do you think Seattle's going to look like? When was the last time you were there? Ten years ago? How do you think it might be different? Do you know how you're going to get around?" Just having that conversation, because a lot of those things are things they are probably not thinking about when they're sitting in prison. They're not thinking about how they're going to get from place to place when you do release. You're thinking about what's going on in prison. So I think conversations are . . . starting them early definitely is beneficial.

I think once people are out, I think a support system is a huge thing. A lot of people have that. They don't necessarily have family and friends waiting for them in the community that can help; some people do and that's very, very fortunate. A lot of people we work with have histories of violence within the family, so their families might want to be supportive but they have "no contact" orders in place so they can't be. So figuring out a different support system, a support system of choice and that might not be peers, it might be case managers and counselor and CCO, but I've found that getting an army of people who have a particular offender's best interest in mind is sort of intricate [*sic*] to them doing well. I can only speak to our population with this. To an average CCO this would not be the same.

One of the things we're really, really aware of and make sure to do is to congratulate people for really small success. It sounds kind of trivial but telling people they did something well or thanking them for coming into the office, saying that you appreciate them doing something. I don't think people who have gone through the criminal justice system have experienced that a lot. I think they get told a lot of what they are doing wrong, what they're doing is bad. But I think thanking someone for showing up or saying that you appreciate something or congratulating them on completing a group actually goes a long way. It keeps them feeling good and like they are succeeding and I guess that's more about rapport and relationships. It works well for a lot of people who are pervasively mentally ill.

The perspectives of CCOs make clear that factors contributing to reentry success go way beyond the needs previously identified in the literature. Sure, housing, employment, and treatment are critical needs that help build the foundation upon which successful reentry can be built. However, providing just the basic needs for ex-offenders appears to not be enough to promote successful reintegration. Rather, other factors such as an effective reentry plan that includes a support system and perhaps words of encouragement by CCOs may be other contributors to how and why ex-offenders can succeed during reentry.

What Else Is Needed to Promote Success?

We asked the CCOs what else they thought could be done to foster successful reentry for ex-offenders. Chris T. pointed out the lack of quality treatment:

Quality of providers that are out there. Across the board, whether it's chemical dependency, sex offender, and mental health. Just from working with all of them, there's just some people that just shouldn't be doing this stuff. I see a lot of providers in the sex offender level. I'm a lot biased there. There's a lot of people out there that shouldn't be doing it. And the definition of what exactly are they providing, sometimes they just sit in a chair. Who really knows what they're providing.

> I read a progress report and I am thinking what are they doing? And then you get another report from another provider, and I can see that this person's doing clinical work. I don't know what all these words mean. There's a gap amongst providers. A lack of, actual lack of services. Because not everyone can access services.

The need for wraparound services was also mentioned by several CCOs. Brad explained, "Wraparound services for every guy coming out. Honestly, I'd say the first forty-eight hours of release, that's the most crucial time. Unfortunately, the prison system is so overloaded that we can't provide that for everybody coming out of the prisons." For some CCOs, funneling additional monies into programming is a much-needed priority for ex-offenders today. Kelley explained,

> I think money needs to be put into programs to support the offenders when they get out and then once they're off supervision. They'll be in a better place if they'd have mental health treatment or . . . look at the sex offender population, their treatment is just so expensive, and you know, the treatment when they're on supervision and they're compliant for the most part and they do well, it's something that's really positive that these guys need to be in and need to go through, but if you can't afford it, you're in violation and then you can go back.

Other CCOs identified the need for mentors and community support. Denise, a CCO with one and a half years of experience, reported:

> They need connections, connections with people. Mentors are good things. Women's groups, church groups are great places to refer people to for fellowship. I don't mean you need to go in and find Jesus because you lost him or whatever. There's a bunch of jokes about that. I'm a pretty spiritual person myself and not overtly religious, and sometimes I'm even uncomfortable with that when it comes in my office, but they're great connections. So you get in there, and you get involved in a group that meets once a month for a potluck and then you see . . . or go to a NA meeting, and they have a camp-out weekend. You need to connect with people. We need to have a sense of community around people. As much as we need to tell people what's wrong about them and what we won't accept, we need to tell them what's right and we need to tell them, "You can have my help if you need it."

Additionally, other CCOs mentioned the need to celebrate the success of ex-offenders who have reintegrated. For instance, twice a year at the Everett Community Justice Center, a "Celebrate Success" dinner event is thrown, and ex-offenders are invited to have a meal and be praised for all of their success. As Lori puts it, "we're so punitive, that saying, 'Hey, good job' goes a long, long way."

Conclusion

To summarize, CCOs utilize a broader definition of reentry success than the typical definitions used by criminal justice researchers. Primarily, criminal justice researchers have defined success as lack of recidivism, but the scope of this definition clearly needs to be expanded to include other measures of success. By not capturing other indicators of success, the picture of what makes for successful and meaningful reentry from a holistic perspective is conceptually incomplete. Consistent with previous research, CCOs in our study provided critical factors for ex-offenders' success during reentry. However, we should note that while most of the factors identified by CCOs were extrinsic to the ex-offender, such as housing and employment, the CCOs also identified intrinsic factors as well, such as ex-offender attitude. Additionally, CCOs identified other situational/contextual factors for ex-offenders' success during reentry that either have not been discussed in the previous literature or have been only minimally addressed. For example, the establishment of a solid reentry plan and the building of a strong support system (family and community) were identified as additional factors that contribute to ex-offender reentry success. The findings of this research also reveal that the establishment of rapport between the CCO and the client may also be a contributing factor as well, but that the ability of CCOs to establish and maintain this rapport is a special skill that requires a nuanced view of the CCO role and the ability to navigate professional and personal boundaries to make careful decisions about when to give ex-offenders small breaks that may go a long way, which ex-offenders on their caseload they are able to connect with by lessening the social distance barriers, and so on.

Much work still needs to be done to promote ex-offender reentry success. The current state of the economy has made obtaining treatment or paying for treatment more difficult for ex-offenders. Many agencies that provide treatment for ex-offenders have faced budget cutbacks as well. This situation has resulted in longer wait times for ex-offenders to obtain treatment, perhaps contributed to less quality programming provided to ex-offenders who receive it, and a reduction in much-needed wraparound services for this group. Further, perhaps even engaging in small steps such as celebrating the successes of ex-offenders may be yet another contributor to sustained, long-term, ex-offender success in reintegration.

Note

1. For a detailed description of the data collection method and interview schedule, see the Appendix at the end of the book.

8

Policy Implications

EX-OFFENDER REENTRY HAS EMERGED AS AN IMPORTANT TOPIC within the corrections field over the past decade. With the passage of the Second Chance Act in 2008, the process of offender reentry has come to the forefront of discussion among criminal justice researchers, practitioners, and policymakers and in the general public. With over 700,000 people coming out of prisons annually and 2.9 percent, or one in thirty-four adults, under correctional supervision in the United States (Glaze and Parks, 2012), the issues faced by ex-offenders, criminal justice professionals, community agencies, and citizens in the reentry process need to be seen as central to discourse on crime and justice and criminal justice policy and practice. We can no longer hold the discussions about offender reentry behind closed doors, perhaps exclusively between CCOs and their clients, or sweep the topic under the rug or stuff it in the end chapter of a community corrections text, but rather offender reentry has become an issue to be carefully examined as the implications of such research are far reaching.

As discussed in the previous chapters, the pathways to successful reentry are complex and are typically fraught with a range of short- and long-term difficulties for ex-offenders. However, successful reentry is indeed possible despite the focus on failure in media news reports, in pop cultural portrayals, and within criminal justice research, where the emphasis has been on aggregate recidivism rates as the primary empirical outcome measure. Additionally, reentry success may look different when viewed from the perspectives of CCOs and ex-offenders. Recall that CCOs defined reentry success differently for various types of ex-offenders, rejecting a "one-size-fits-all" approach to both assisting ex-offenders in the reentry process and determining their success or failure based on an overly simplistic outcome measure of recidivism (generally evaluated in terms of reoffense, commission of a technical violation, re-arrest, reconviction, or reincarceration). On one hand, success for one ex-offender, CCOs explained, may be not being rearrested while success for another ex-offender may be the cessation of a pervasive drug habit or an increase in the amount of time between technical violations while on community supervision, or personal progress in recognizing situational cues that trigger spiraling-down behaviors that may lead to antisocial or criminal behavior. Further, CCOs often cited different success factors for different types of ex-offenders. For example, several CCOs defined the obtaining of legal employment for sex offenders as a huge milestone for this group given the tough economy that ex-offenders are currently trying to find jobs in but also because of the social stigma associated with their criminal offense.

Human change is not linear or instantaneous. We know from the accumulation of empirical research on desistance that personal transformation from an antisocial and criminal lifestyle to one of a law-abiding citizen involves an identity shift that brings with it changes in thinking, development of insight, and self-narrative (Stevens, 2012). Persistent lifestyle patterns that are influenced and reinforced by substance abuse, early childhood trauma, social and economic disadvantage, mental health issues, and particular environmental and situational contexts are extremely resistant to change. Crime desistance is occasionally abrupt, but more often, it is the product of a long drawn-out history of many unsuccessful attempts at change.

With the current widespread interest in "evidence-based" policy as the "Moneyball" approach[1] to the historical failures of the correctional system (Cullen, Meyer, and Latessa, 2009) and the growing amount of empirical research in the academic literature on crime desistance (Farrall et al., 2011; Geiger and Timor, 2001; Kirk, 2012; Kurlycheck, Bushway, and Brame, 2012; Maruna, 2001; Sampson and Laub, 2003; Serin and Lloyd, 2009) and principles of effective correctional interventions (Andrews and Bonta, 2010), the time has come to boldly reexamine the policies, practices, and methods of measuring success in offender reentry. S. J. Listwan, F. T. Cullen, and E. J. Latessa observe:

> There has been a growing recognition that it is irresponsible to simply release tens of thousands of inmates from prison and to place them into parole officer caseloads that are too high to allow for meaningful intervention and re-entry. In a way, this has been corrections' "dirty little secret"—a practice that simply is indefensible from a public policy standpoint. Beyond lack of resources, there is no way to justify the unsystematic dumping of offenders back into society, since it jeopardizes both the successful reintegration of offenders and the protection of public safety. (2006, p. 19)

Dealing with corrections' "dirty little secret" requires the identification of evidence-based strategies to guide reentry policy and practice. In particular, working toward more successful outcomes in this arena means utilizing the research on offender desistance, ex-offender and CCO narratives, and the risk, need, and responsivity principles in correctional interventions to develop appropriate reentry policies and practices. The historical focus on recidivism as the only mark of success flies in the face of the desistance literature, and the policies and practices that have contributed to high community corrections caseloads and lack of meaningful interventions have not sufficiently attended to the burgeoning knowledge base that has accumulated over the past thirty years on "what works" to change offender conduct.

The ex-offender and CCO perspectives presented here highlight the need for individualized assistance in the reentry process and rewarding ex-offenders for intermediate successes such as behavioral indicators (e.g., getting a job, completing a substance abuse treatment program, getting a college degree, repairing relationships with family members, completing a parenting class, regaining custody of children, engaging in service to the community, and development of prosocial relationships) that are not readily reflected in aggregate recidivism rates. Referred to as "intelligent flexibility" by one of the ex-offenders interviewed for this book, this recognition that all individuals coming out of prison may not be released to the same playing field, with the same skills, needs, and risks, or into the same situational contexts with the same players is a critical piece of the puzzle in assisting ex-offenders in making the transition to free society. While most of the current sentencing practices in Washington State, across the country, and at the federal level involve some form of a determinate sentencing structure, this one-size-fits-all approach is not appropriate at the reentry stage of the criminal justice process. Furthermore, individualized intervention and attention to what might be viewed as "small" changes in ex-offenders' thinking, behaviors, or interactions have the potential to turn into the "big" recidivism changes and cost reduction that policymakers and the public ultimately seek as a measure of reentry success.

With regard to our research investigation, we should note that this study has a number of limitations. The sample of nineteen CCOs and twenty-one ex-offenders under supervision in northwest Washington is small and local, and the findings may not be generalizable to other populations. Furthermore, the snowball sample method used for recruiting ex-offenders resulted in individuals from particular sources and networks that may not be representative of the ex-offender population as a whole. In fact, most of the ex-offender interview subjects in this study were actively involved in prison programs, educational programs, and community outreach. Thus, as a group, they were a self-selected, highly functional subpopulation of ex-offenders. Findings from this population are certainly warranted given that focus on ex-offenders who want to succeed is a smart use of resources and attention; however, future research should also attempt to examine other, less-motivated subpopulations of ex-offenders.

Despite these limitations, the results of our research are consistent with previous research on reentry. That is, successful reentry can be achieved if ex-offenders are given the necessary tools that they need to succeed. The purpose of this chapter is to provide a discussion of the steps that are currently being taken or need to be implemented to foster offender reentry. Specifically, in this chapter, we will outline factors in ex-offenders' success and the many reforms needed to cultivate that success. Further, we will highlight the complexity of reentry and the unique needs groups have based on their gender, race, or social class. Attention will be paid to the few states that offer employment or service fairs as a new and innovative way to assist this group.

Success Factors

As outlined in the previous chapters, factors that increase the likelihood of reentry success revolve around getting ex-offenders' basic needs met at the initial stage of the reentry process. If ex-offenders can secure housing, employment, and food, then this accomplishment lays the foundation for success. Although getting these needs met can be difficult given the multiple barriers that ex-offenders face in regard to job restrictions, exclusions from public assistance, and a reduction in the number of housing options available to them due to their criminal record (Mele and Miller, 2005; Petersilia, 2005). In the case of housing, simply ensuring that ex-offenders obtain housing is not sufficient. They also must receive the appropriate treatment for other conditions such as substance abuse or mental illness (Culhane, Metraux and Hadley, 2002; Haimowitz, 2004; Worcel et al., 2009). Recall that R. J. Sampson and J. H. Laub (1993) propose that individuals who build social capital in areas such as employment are more likely to desist. Thus, the ability of ex-offenders to obtain employment is a huge factor that sets the stage for their potential success during reentry. C. E. Kelly and J. J. Fader (2012) note that many employment applications are online, and therefore ex-offenders not only need access to computers but also need training in the use of computers including Internet navigation. R. Apel (2011) cautions that giving ex-offenders jobs or helping them find jobs is not enough, but rather a clear need exists for the enhancement of employability of ex-offenders. That is, ex-offenders need job skill enhancements in order to reduce their chances of job termination and recidivism. E. J. Latessa (2012) stresses the importance of targeting offenders' attitudes and values about work. Without forming a connection to work, ex-offenders are not likely to hang onto their jobs for the long term. Additional obstacles, often invisible, further complicate the ability of ex-offenders to build social capital and get their basic needs met. That is, ex-offenders often face discrimination based on their status as ex-offenders as well as due to their gender or race. The public often supports services to assist in ex-offender reentry, but eventually discussions tend to shift to which offenders, if any, are the most deserving of assistance (Garland, Wodahl, and Schuhmann, 2013). Additionally, when these initiatives hit closer to home for even advocates, such as building affordable housing for offenders in their own neighborhoods, support often wanes (Garland, Wodahl, and Mayfield, 2011). Furthermore, stigmatization is an issue experienced many years postincarceration that affects individuals who have succeeded in building lives for themselves as law-abiding citizens.

As highlighted in Chapter 5, minority ex-offenders are saddled with discrimination from general society based on race/ethnicity as well as their status as ex-offenders, which can stymie their chances of securing housing and employment. Additionally, services beyond those that simply meet ex-offenders' basic needs are also required. Previous research and CCO and ex-offender narratives have indicated that many ex-offenders reenter society with substance abuse problems and mental health issues (Petersilia, 2005), and when they return to the community, they need support services to assist in their transition. As J. Petersilia (2005) points out, however, the stagnating economy has contributed to the reduction or elimination of support services provided by state and federal correctional agencies and their community partners. With budgets being slashed throughout the correctional system at large and in the agencies that have supported ex-offenders in the past, members of this population find themselves in a severe conundrum. On one hand, they are mandated by the court to obtain treatment, yet they are required to pay for the treatment. Sex offenders face more obstacles in finding employment, and their treatment is usually more costly. Thus, if sex offenders can't pay for their treatment, they are in violation and may be returned to jail/prison. A similar issue was noted by the ex-offenders in our study regarding fees for UAs (urinanalyses) and background checks that were often numerous and a hindrance to their effectively managing finances in tandem with achieving their other goals. Interviews with CCOs also indicated their frustration with the current state of the economy and the negative impact it has had on the services for ex-offenders and for their ability to succeed. For instance, some CCOs pointed to the lack of quality treatment available to ex-offenders or the reduction in treatment options available to ex-offenders. In sum, for all ex-offenders, regardless of race, social class, or gender, satisfying the basics needs necessary for functioning in society and finding support services that address their needs are factors that promote success.

What Needs to Be Done?

The ex-offenders' and CCOs' perspectives presented here offer rich information regarding what can be done to enhance reentry success. Among their suggestions, we found the development of transition programs that bridge prison and community, centralization of services in the community, public education to reduce the stigma of incarceration, better training and resource support for CCOs, individualized and nuanced supervision and intervention strategies, and changes in policies that hinder reentry success unnecessarily.

Financial Support

For all ex-offenders, several reforms within the criminal justice system may help enhance reentry success. L. L. Martin (2011) recommends that ex-offenders be provided with some financial support and financial literacy training to foster successful reentry. Rather than just simply being pushed toward obtaining employment, offenders need to be given skills to manage their money. If offenders cannot budget their earned income effectively, they will not develop assets that L. L. Martin (2011) views as another critical factor to successful reintegration. The current economy has played a clear role in interrupting ex-offender reentry success. That is, reentry success may be more difficult now than in years past for ex-offenders as the poor economy has resulted in services being cut in all areas of corrections (e.g., jails, prisons, community corrections) (Petersilia, 2005). Further, those agencies that often provide support (e.g., food, housing, treatment) for ex-offenders are facing cuts as well, which has hindered their ability to provide wraparound services for ex-offenders during their transition, thereby inhibiting successful reentry. Thus, one factor that is needed within corrections to foster reentry is the infusion of money and resources (Petersilia, 2005). As reported by several CCOs in our sample, the state of the economy has hit community corrections hard and has resulted in many CCO positions being cut with the outcome being fewer CCOs left to manage ever-larger caseloads. In one CCO office in Washington State, CCO staff had been cut from nineteen CCOs to four. These reductions can contribute to breaking down the abilities of CCOs to effectively supervise their clients and provide them with the much-needed support during reentry. For an infusion of dollars to occur within state and federal correctional budgets, the public needs to support such action. Petersilia (2005) states that, oftentimes, public opinion has supported the reduction or elimination of programming for ex-offenders. This trend may be due to fears associated with ex-offenders reoffending in the community, or rather it may be due to the opinion that in harsh economic times, monies should be funneled to the public school system rather than to ex-offenders. Therefore, community support is needed, and a partnership needs to be developed between corrections and the public.

Recall that this theme of enhancing the community role in offender reentry was also echoed from our interviews of CCOs. Many CCOs identified community support as a key factor in promoting reentry success. The gap between the community and ex-offenders is often difficult to bridge due to the stigma surrounding anyone having a criminal record. US society often places a strong emphasis on shaming those who violate the law but less focus on forgiving these individuals and welcoming them back into their communities. Thus, building community support will require a transformation in how citizens think about ex-offenders and a shift to a community/restorative justice orientation that recognizes that the traditional formal correctional controls of offender management, risk assessment, treatment, surveillance/control, and punishment must be supplemented and in some cases supplanted by community justice informal social controls such as neighborhoods and communities, community partnerships, recognition of the needs and interests of victims, a problem-solving approach, and restoration (Clear, Hamilton, and Cadora, 2002). That is, the approach to reentry needs to be restorative rather than retributive, and individuals convicted of crimes are only initially shamed for their behavior but then forgiven and finally meaningfully supported in the reintegration process (Braithwaite, 1989; Swanson, 2009; Van Ness and Strong, 2010; Zehr, 2002). Such an approach would go a long way toward improving the opportunities for successful reentry. Beyond the infusion of funds and development of community support for ex-offenders, other reforms may also be useful in promoting reentry success.

Strengthening Programming

Petersilia (2003) suggests several reforms to improve ex-offender reentry success. These reforms provide a framework not only for the discussion of prisoner reintegration but also for the aid of those ex-offenders who are reentering society but who did not serve any time in jail or prison. One such reform calls for the altering of "the in-prison experience" (p. 171). Specifically, Petersilia suggests that programming experiences (e.g., employment, education, and rehabilitation) should be enhanced for those who are incarcerated. We would add first, that such programming enhancement should also involve mentorship that straddles prison and community and, second, that programming is also needed for ex-offenders serving sentences in their communities, such as in day-reporting centers.

A multitude of research has been published on the effectiveness of rehabilitative programs, specifically those that target criminogenic needs and risk factors, in reducing recidivism (see Andrews and Bonta, 2010; Andrews et al., 1990; Gendreau and Ross, 1979; Listwan, Cullen, and Latessa, 2006; Van Voorhis, Braswell, and Lester, 1997). Cognitive behavioral therapy, for example, has been identified as one effective treatment at reducing recidivism for offenders—including sex offenders (see Bahr, Masters, and Taylor, 2012; Landenberger and Lipsey, 2005; Moster, Winuk, and Jeglic, 2008). Petersilia (2003) urges that, within prison, cognitive-behavioral programs for sex offenders continue to be utilized in an effort to reduce their recidivism rates.

As reported in earlier chapters, both male and female offenders can suffer from drug and alcohol addictions. Thus, addiction is a risk factor for these offenders to experience recidivism and stymies successful reentry. C. Visher, J. Yahner, and N. La Vigne (2010) note that the few months following postrelease from prison is the critical time period that ex-offenders are most at risk for relapse and recidivism. Therefore, another form of programming Petersilia (2005) recommends is therapeutic communities for drug addicts. This treatment modality is one of the more widely used treatment styles for helping drug offenders both within and outside of prison (Zhang, Roberts, and McCollister, 2011). Numerous researchers have found support for therapeutic programming to assist drug offenders even for offenders who suffer from co-occurring problems such as mental illness (Inciardi, Martin, and Butzin, 2004; Martin, Butzin, and Inciardi, 1995; McKendrick et al., 2006; Pearson and Lipton, 1999; Van Stelle and Moberg, 2004). In particular, those therapeutic community programs that assist offenders both within prison and in the community upon release have been linked to lower rates of drug relapse and criminal recidivism (Martin, Butzin, and Inciardi, 1995; McCollister et al., 2003).

For female ex-offenders, B. A. Herrschaft and colleagues (2009) state that reentry programs need to be designed with them specifically in mind, not just modeled after reentry programs that have been designed for men. Thus, programming that addresses the needs for women, such as coming to terms with prior sexual abuse, is critical both within prison and in the community for all races and ethnicities (Belknap, 2007; Chesney-Lind, 1989). Fostering the ability of female offenders to set realistic expectations when reentering their communities (rural or urban) is also needed (Kellett and Willging, 2011).

Additionally, treatment programs must be sensitive to cultural differences. Thus, a one-size-fits-all approach to reforming ex-offenders is not likely providing the opportunity for all ex-offenders to succeed but rather just a select few (Vigesaa, 2013). Since CCOs noted that some treatment programs being offered to ex-offenders in the community are lacking in rigor and quality, periodic evaluations of treatment programs being offered to ex-offenders in the community would appear to be necessary.

In sum, those treatment programs that are designed to target criminogenic needs and risk factors will assist ex-offenders in successful reentry. As Petersilia puts it, "there is, therefore, ample scientific evidence to suggest that treatment programs—*if* well designed and implemented—can reduce both recidivism and costs" (2003, p. 179). Clearly, treatment programs must also be tailored to ex-offenders' specific needs in terms of racial/ethnic and gender differences.

One issue that should be considered regarding prison treatment programs is the timing, placement, and individualization of programs in both the prison and community settings. The ex-offenders in the current study were particularly frustrated with the requirement of certain programs either too early or too late in their incarceration. For example, one ex-offender who entered prison at age fifteen and was released at age forty-five noted that when he was required to complete the state-mandated anger management program at the end of his thirty-year incarceration, the experience held little meaning for him given that he felt he no longer had the same anger issues he had when he committed his crime. This is just one of many examples that highlight the need for more individualized programmatic options that closely attend to the principles of risk-need-responsivity, but that also take into account the changes an individual experiences during long-term imprisonment (Flanagan, 1995) and the nuanced and complex nature of reentry and the desistance process over the life course (Geiger and Timor, 2001;

Kurlycheck, Bushway, and Brame, 2012; Serin and Lloyd, 2009; Visher and Travis, 2003).

Beyond the above-mentioned treatment programs, Petersilia (2005) recommends vocational education. Offenders provided with employment training while incarcerated will have marketable job skills that should assist them in obtaining legal employment when they reintegrate back into their communities. Previous research on the impact of various types of vocational educational programs on successfully reducing recidivism has been somewhat mixed (Bloom et al., 1994; Harer, 1995; Saylor and Gaes, 1992; Schumaker, Anderson, and Anderson, 1990; Van Steele, Lidbury, and Moberg, 1995). That is, some researchers have found recidivism rates to actually increase for offenders participating in vocational education programs rather than decrease (see Bloom, Chesney-Lind, and Owen, 1994; Van Steele, Lidbury, and Moberg, 1995). Despite such research findings, the use of vocational training should continue to be utilized both within prison and in the communities to assist other types of offenders besides prisoners such as those sentenced to work release and day-reporting centers.

As mentioned earlier in this book, education is lacking in ex-offender populations. A recent publication in Washington State has identified that 75 percent of all incarcerated offenders within the state are high school dropouts ("PAO Recognizes," 2012). Thus, enhancing the education levels of ex-offenders is critical, and education has also been recognized to have an impact on recidivism rates within the criminal justice literature. As an example, D. J. Stevens and C. S. Ward (1997), in a comparison of sixty male and female inmates who had earned their associate or baccalaureate degrees while incarcerated to those male and female inmates who did not participate in such an educational program in North Carolina, found that those offenders who earned an advanced degree had lower recidivism rates. Further, the researchers found that those offenders who had earned degrees also reported higher incomes. Providing a college education to offenders is often an unpopular idea with the general public, but the benefit to the offenders and society cannot be ignored. At a minimum, the continued implementation of basic high school education within prison and as part of other community corrections programs such as day-reporting centers should continue. Additionally, a subset of offenders in prison and ex-offenders in the community have obtained a GED or high school degree, an associate's degree, or, in some cases, a college degree and desire continuing education. Programs such as the Post-Prison Education Project and University Beyond Bars[2] have been described by the ex-offenders in this study as life changing. Recognition of this subpopulation of prisoners and ex-offenders who seek college higher education is important in that this subgroup of ex-offenders are the most likely to succeed in the reentry process. The findings here show how much prisoners and ex-offenders value education and the opportunity to earn a degree, and that this opportunity brings with it motivation to engage in a prosocial lifestyle, personal dignity, self-efficacy, and a positive social network, all of which are factors associated with desistance and reentry success (Serin and Lloyd, 2009; Visher and Travis, 2003).

For those offenders that are incarcerated or are in the community serving sentences, access to meaningful programming opportunities can assist them in desisting from previous criminal offending patterns and provide them with the necessary skills and tools to succeed on their own in their communities. Thus, the money invested in these programs to assist ex-offenders now can pay off in the future in regard to lower recidivism rates and the costs associated with recidivism (e.g., police, courts, corrections costs). Perhaps as the public is made aware of the possible long-term cost savings with an investment in services today, then maybe public opinion can be swayed to support the infusion of money into the correctional system, and community members will understand *why* the funding is needed and *how* it is a win-win situation for ex-offenders and the public whose taxes will support such programs.

Revisions to Policy

A second area of reform that Petersilia (2003) calls for is prison release policies. Petersilia advocates for the use of comprehensive prerelease planning that she describes as currently "too little, too late" (p. 185) and operating haphazardly. That is, a lot of prerelease programming involves a discussion of the nuts and bolts of the actual release such as requirements on parole and development of various life skills (i.e., how to fill out a job application), when ex-offenders need planning on how to get critical needs, such as treatment for substance abuse or mental health, met while in the community. Ex-offenders are also at high risk of contracting Hepatitis C, AIDS, and tuberculosis. Thus, preventative health care efforts should be part of these planning conversations (Woods et al., 2013). Again, while Petersilia's focus is on prison release, we would also argue that comprehensive prerelease planning is needed for all ex-offenders (e.g., those serving probation, day-reporting, and work release sentences). Those ex-offenders serving day-reporting sentences, for instance, should be funneled into programs that are going to target their needs, and instructors of these programs in conjunction with CCOs should work with the offenders to further assist them in designing their specific reentry plan. Specifically, for any ex-offender, many critical services need to be provided during the first six months of release especially since approximately 30 percent of all ex-offender prisoners recidivate within the first six months (Petersilia, 2005).

Petersilia (2003) also recommends reinstituting discretionary parole release. Approximately sixteen states, including Washington State, have abolished parole (Bureau of Justice Statistics, 2012). This has resulted in many institutional problems such as overcrowding but also has left offenders with little incentive to participate in any rehabilitative programming within the prison (Latessa and Smith, 2011; Seiter and Kadela, 2003). After all, offenders in these states only need to serve their time, and once that is over, they are free to walk back into the community. Thus, some offenders opt to forgo any treatment or programming while incarcerated and walk out of the prison walls following their sentences with no useful tools to assist them during the reentry process. Moreover, having no parole system also means that the normal support structure (e.g., parole officer, treatment services, and wraparound services) that would be in place for ex-offenders is absent (Travis, 2005). As Petersilia states, "in the long run, no one is more dangerous than a criminal who has no incentive to straighten himself out while in prison, and who returns to society without a structured and supervised release plan" (2005, p. 189). In the context of all ex-offenders reentering society besides those just releasing from prison, we would suggest that incentives be put in place to help all ex-offenders that are serving a wide range of sentences to facilitate these ex-offenders' taking advantage of the programming available to them.

Altering Postprison Services

Petersilia (2003) proposes that parole field services should be changed—that "the new parole model should commit to a community-centered approach to parole supervision and should utilize technological advances to monitor high-risk and sex offenders, deliver intensive treatment to substance abusers, and establish intermediate sanctions for parole violators" (p. 193). With advances in technology, these advancements should work their way into the tool bags of CCOs. In today's economy, CCOs are required to supervise a greater number of offenders, and their caseloads are more likely to be filled with higher risk offenders. Thus, technology can assist them in their jobs to effectively monitor their clients while also ensuring public safety. Several CCOs in our study expressed concerns for their safety and admitted that entering the homes of their clients is a dangerous task to do solo. Therefore, better technology can assist CCOs not only in monitoring high-risk offenders but also in carrying out home inspections in a safe manner. In regard to Petersilia's point about intensive treatment for substance abusers, access to programming in the community may be limited, or the length of postprison programming may be inadequate for ex-offenders. For instance, several CCOs in our study stated that programming for substance-abusing ex-offenders can sometimes be difficult to procure, or the length of the programming is not sufficient. Additionally, some CCOs questioned the effectiveness of select treatment providers. This lag or gap in services can undermine successful reentry. S. Haimowitz (2004) stresses that for mentally ill ex-offenders, strong intersystem collaborations must be in place between those in corrections who supervise these offenders in the community (e.g., parole officers) and service providers. Without such effective collaborations, Haimowitz warns that mentally ill ex-offenders will not properly adjust in the community, resulting in their being funneled back into the correctional system. A. J. Lurigio, J. A. Rollins, and J. Fallon (2004) also stress that untreated mentally ill offenders are more likely to return to prison. The notion of strong intersystem collaborations cannot be understated as such collaborations have been identified as a key strategy in promoting successful reentry (Burke, 2001).

The community-centered approach to correctional interventions and offender reentry, one that Petersilia (2003) proposes, is consistent with research in recent years that has called for a reintegrative community justice (Braithwaite, 1989; Clear, Hamilton, and Cadora, 2002) and restorative justice frameworks (Bazemore and Schiff, 2001; Braithwaite, 2002; Braswell, Fuller, and Lozoff, 2000; Helfgott et al., 2000; Swanson, 2009; Van Ness and Strong, 2010; Zehr, 1990, 1995, 2002). This restorative/community approach to ex-offender reintegration recognizes that both victims and offenders share at least one common problem—they are stigmatized and treated like outcasts by the community.

A Restorative Approach

Restorative justice, an alternative way of "doing justice," centers around recognizing crime as harm and repairing the damage caused by that harm through nonadversarial processes that acknowledge the needs, interests, and responsibilities of offenders, victims, community members, and governmental agencies. A growing body of empirical research has emerged over the past thirty years, and in recent years restorative justice has achieved the status of an "evidence-based" practice that offers promising findings that have the potential to greatly enhance reentry initiatives (Bazemore and Maruna, 2009). Many authors have noted the practical ways in which restorative principles can be incorporated into the existing adversarial framework to strengthen reentry policy and practice (Bazemore and Boba, 2007; Bazemore and Stinchcomb, 2004; Clear, 2007; Clear, Hamilton, and Cadora, 2002; Settles, 2009; Swanson, 2009; Travis, 2001, 2005; Van Ness and Strong, 2010).

Restorative justice is a way of thinking about and responding to crime loosely rooted in ancient practices of many cultures and religions. The restorative justice perspective views crime as harm that creates an obligation for offenders to make things right. This perspective provides an alternative framework for dealing with crime in which victim needs are central, offenders are held accountable, and the government is a secondary player in the process of restoring victims, offenders, and communities to a state of wholeness. Emerging in its contemporary form in the 1970s, restorative justice gained widespread recognition in the 1980s, and by the 1990s became a focus of correctional policy and practice in the United States and countries around the world. Today, restorative justice has converged with the notion of community justice[3] to become an alternative paradigm to the adversarial-retributive justice model.

Community justice is an "alternative that promises a new set of values that might lead us to new ways of justice" (Clear, 2007, p. 176). It is a broad strategy that includes focus on high-impact locations where criminal and criminal justice activity are concentrated, utilizing informal social controls such as families, neighborhoods, and social supports as a proactive strategy to increase public safety, and partnerships that strengthen community capacity to coordinate the way in which public safety problems are addressed (see Clear, Hamilton, and Cadora, 2002; Clear, 2007). Community justice ideals change the traditional way of responding to ex-offenders by recognizing the importance of informal social controls such as the neighborhoods and interpersonal networks, partnerships between criminal justice and noncriminal justice agencies and groups, victim needs and interest, a problem-solving orientation, and a focus on restoration and reparation. These informal controls are utilized and integrated with traditional formal controls of offender management, treatment, risk assessment, and surveillance (Clear, Hamilton, and Cadora, 2002).

A restorative/community approach to corrections identifies the community as a key player in dealing with the aftermath of crime, enhancing public safety, and furthering the goals of social and criminal justice. In institutional and community corrections contexts, restorative-justice-oriented practices involve victims and citizens at different points along the correctional continuum. On an individual level, the restorative/community justice approach to offender reentry suggests that ex-offenders need to feel safe, they need affirmations that they are worthy so that they no longer feel like outsiders, they need practical assistance in dealing with their immediate challenges and needs, and they need moral and spiritual guidance and care that provide hope for the future (Van Ness and Strong, 2010). Although disagreement can be found about what practices can be considered truly restorative, victim-offender mediation and reconciliation, family group conferencing, peacemaking and sentencing circles, and surrogate encounter programs are generally considered restorative (Van Ness and Strong, 2010). Restorative/community justice is concerned with deeper issues at the root of offending behavior such as personal meaning and sense of belonging, and a holistic approach to offender reentry that recognizes that crime is harm—to offenders, victims, and communities—and that this harm needs to be acknowledged and addressed with some attempt to repair the damage (Swanson, 2009).

Restorative justice provides a framework for a balanced and holistic approach to corrections that acknowledges the needs and interests of victims, offenders, and citizens. Restorative justice has been formally included in the mission and vision statements of a number of state departments of corrections (e.g., Minnesota, Washington, Oregon, Vermont), and correctional agencies throughout the United States, Canada, New Zealand, Australia, Great Britain, and other countries have implemented the restorative justice model through a broad range of programs, policies, and practices. The application of restorative justice principles to correctional practice entails identifying the community as a key player in dealing with the consequences of crime (including victim and offender needs), enhancing public safety, and furthering the goals of social and criminal justice (Helfgott, 2005).

Restorative correctional programs, practices, and policies provide opportunities for victim and community participation in surveillance, treatment/rehabilitation, and reentry/reintegration of offenders, along with opportunities for offenders to take steps to make amends and repair harms resulting from their crimes. Correctional practices embodying the principles of restorative justice exist across the correctional continuum in community and custodial contexts. Zehr (2002) suggests that restorative justice models can be viewed along a continuum from fully restorative to pseudo- or nonrestorative and proposes six questions to assess the extent to which a program, policy, or practice is fully, mostly, partially, potentially, or pseudo-restorative:

1. Does the model address harms, needs, and causes?
2. Is it adequately victim oriented?

3. Are offenders encouraged to take responsibility?
4. Are all relevant stakeholders involved?
5. Is there an opportunity for dialogue and participatory decision-making?
6. Is the model respectful to all parties?

From this perspective, conferencing, circles, surrogate encounter programs, and reparative boards can be considered fully restorative while victim impact panels in a correctional setting (generally involving a one-way presentation of information) can be considered partially restorative. Community service, work crews, and offender reintegration programs can be considered potentially restorative, but unless such programs are consistent with the fundamental principles of restorative justice—involving all stakeholders, collectively identifying and addressing needs, harms, and obligations in an attempt to make things as right as possible—then such programs could in fact be pseudorestorative. For example, Washington State has implemented the "victim wraparound process," whereby a committee of victim advocates, victims of crime, community members, and state correctional officials develop a supervision plan for offenders released into the community. However, for the protection of victims, offenders are not part of the process. While the victim is seen as central to the process, the exclusion of the offender may place the practice on the pseudo- or nonrestorative end of the continuum.

Variations of victim-offender mediation, victim-offender reconciliation programs, and victim-offender conferencing have emerged that extend the concept of encounter and mediation to meetings between surrogate victims and incarcerated offenders in institutional corrections contexts. For example, a program developed by Howard Zehr in Graterford prison in Pennsylvania in the early 1990s involved encounters between lifers and family members of homicide victims interested in engaging in dialogue and asking questions of offenders. The program provided a forum for victims who could not meet with the offenders in their particular cases to ask questions of surrogate offenders for the purpose of healing and understanding. Other programs involve bringing together unrelated victims, offenders, and citizens in prison settings to read educational material on restorative justice and engage in "storytelling" and seminar-style discussions about the impact of crime, offender accountability, the needs of participants, and concrete ways to engage in the restorative process (Helfgott et al., 2000; Helfgott, Lovell, and Lawrence, 2002). Restorative justice is increasingly being applied to correctional settings involving adult violent offenders.

More restorative-justice-oriented correctional options are available today than ever before. While victim-offender mediation (specifically with juvenile property offenders), victim impact in sentencing and parole decisions, and the use of restitution and community service as a sanction have existed for many years, newer programs and practices such as surrogate encounter programs in custodial settings, victim-offender reconciliation involving violent offenders, community reparative boards, peacemaking circles, and conferencing offer creative and hopeful alternatives to the traditional correctional options of the retributive model. These restorative correctional options enable the principles of the restorative justice model to be applied, in whole or in part, across the continuum of correctional contexts with different types of offenders (Helfgott, 2005).

Fostering Collaborations

Petersilia (2003) and others (Bazemore and Boba, 2007; Bazemore and Maruna, 2009; Bazemore and Stinchcomb, 2004; Clear, 2007; Clear, Hamilton, and Cadora, 2002; Settles, 2009; Travis, 2001, 2005) have encouraged community partners to foster collaborations with one another and work together. That is, police, CCOs, and nonprofit partners should work in tandem to assist in successful reentry. Community corrections needs the support of community partners to help ex-offenders secure basic necessities, such as food and clothing, housing, employment, and substance abuse treatment. These agencies are invaluable to community corrections. In the city of Seattle, for example, the Seattle Work Release Advisory Group (SWAG), in a partnership with the Community Partnership for Transition Services (CPTS) and the Washington State Department of Corrections, first established a transition resource fair in 2010. This fair bridges together CCOs and community partners (i.e., sources of food, clothing, and shelter, along with employers) in an effort to promote successful reentry for not only ex-offenders serving work release sentences but all ex-offenders in the community. At the fair, ex-offenders are given the opportunity to participate in mock job interviews, get assistance with their resumes, and learn basic computer skills. Currently, the fair is held only annually, but there are discussions to expand this resource assistance on a quarterly basis to better serve the needs of ex-offenders throughout the year and include more workshops on topics such as health care, budgeting, and legal guidance. Another example of linking resources to ex-offenders involving community partners are efforts put forth by SWAG. Recently, several work release facilities were identified as in critical need of clothing donations for both male and female residents. Thus, SWAG has rolled out a new program to have clothing donation drives to benefit ex-offenders twice per year and has established a partnership with two student clubs affiliated with the Seattle University Criminal Justice Department to organize and run the donation drives and Goodwill to assist in providing clothing voucher coupons to residents of work release facilities. Seattle, however, is not alone in organizing community partners to assist ex-offenders. For instance, several cities such as San Francisco, Cleveland, Des Moines, and Indianapolis hold job fairs for ex-offenders. In fact, the Northern California Service League (NCSL) has been hosting an annual job fair for ex-offenders in San Francisco since 1996. These job fairs directly link ex-offenders with employers willing to hire them. The NCSL has served approximately 400 ex-offenders at each of these annual fairs and has had great success at helping these ex-offenders secure employment. The National HIRE Network, a national advocacy group, strives to increase employment opportunities for those with criminal records through improving employment practices and educating the public. Other organizations such as Fair Shake, an online reentry resource center, aims to connect employers, property managers, families of ex-offenders, and community members together to enhance opportunities for ex-offenders. This organization has a stated mission of "belief in success" for ex-offenders.

Another form of collaboration mentioned by Petersilia (2003) is the strengthening of informal social control mechanisms. As mentioned by CCOs in Chapter 7, some CCOs reached out to family members or other loved ones of the client in an effort to promote change and cultivate successful reentry. This theme emerged from our CCO interviews. Many of the CCOs discussed how they view informal social control to be extremely important in fostering reentry success. In some cases, the CCOs reported that a threat to call the client's mother was a better way to get the client to conform to conditions as opposed to the threat of arrest. Drawing from research in life-course criminology, individuals who establish quality bonds through social institutions such as marriage are more likely to desist from previous criminal offending patterns (Horney, Osgood, and Marshall, 1995; Sampson and Laub, 1993). Developing family support and establishing bonds and custody of children can insulate the offender and thwart temptations to reoffend.

Legal Reforms

T. R. Clear (2007) suggests several legal reforms that could divert individuals from the prison system entirely or reduce the length of time individuals are incarcerated or under supervision: the elimination of mandatory sentencing, reductions in sentence length, and elimination of technical violations. In regard to the elimination of mandatory sentencing, Clear explains, "Eliminating mandatory prison terms across the board would have a substantial impact on the prison population. Much of this impact would involve having fewer people serving time for drug-related crime" (p. 187). More individuals being diverted from serving prison sentences would result in greater ex-offender reentry success as these ex-offenders would avoid more of the consequences of incarceration altogether (e.g., loss of job, disruption in family). As for eliminating technical violations for probationers and parolees, Clear explains, "One-third of all prison admissions are parolees or probationers who have not been accused of a new crime, but instead have failed to abide by the conditions of their supervision" (p. 189). He further mentions that such elimination would not harm public safety. Thus, perhaps the threat of being reincarcerated due to technical violations is not facilitating reentry success but rather is undermining the chances for ex-offenders to be successful. What may be needed is greater support for the ex-offender during reentry by CCOs as opposed to CCOs' searching for reasons, apart from arrest, to send the offender back to prison.

Yet another reform suggested by Petersilia (2005) is the establishment of a "U.S. Rehabilitation of Offenders Act" (p. 190). This act, as proposed by Petersilia, would seek to establish procedures that would allow ex-offenders to move past their criminal record in the future through expunging their records. That is, ex-offenders would not have to suffer the consequences of having criminal records for the rest of their lives, but rather they could eventually have their record cleared after a period of time of no further criminal involvement. The National HIRE Network strives to implement legal reforms to help those with criminal records have a better chance at securing employment. As noted in previous chapters, the presence of a criminal record hinders ex-offenders' opportunities to obtain employment and housing. Further, a criminal record interferes with the ability of ex-offenders to have many of the rights the rest of the population takes for granted, like access to public assistance and custody of their children. Without having their records expunged, ex-offenders are plagued with these difficulties for the remainder of their lives. Recall from Chapter 3, that ex-offenders are prohibited from working in the health care or education fields for life (Heinrich, 2000; Petersilia, 2003, 2005). The long-term collateral consequences of having a criminal record are pervasive for ex-offenders. Those unsure of their state's laws regarding the total, or partial, vacating of criminal records can consult the National Reentry Resource

Center (established in 2008 by the Second Chance Act legislation) website, which provides this information.

Other legal reforms that would also be useful for ex-offenders are those that allow the reestablishment of various rights that they lost due to their conviction, including the right to vote, the right to serve on a jury, the right to hold a political office, and the right to serve in the military (Ewald, 2002; Pinard and Thompson, 2006). Additionally, legal reforms that would allow ex-offenders to more easily secure housing, employment, health care, public assistance, and custody of their children are also needed (Freudenberg et al., 2005; Henry and Jacobs, 2007; Pogorzelski et al., 2005). One such reform to assist with employment is the "ban the box" campaign, which has been adopted in several cities and are currently under consideration in cities such as Seattle. J. S. Henry and J. B. Jacobs (2007) discuss several cities such as Boston, Chicago, and San Francisco that have adopted "ban the box" campaigns in the last several years to end ex-offender employment discrimination. The "ban the box" movement allows job applicants to no longer be forced to check a box on a job application and reveal their previous conviction history. Other reforms in the area of child custody would be beneficial. With one provision of the Adoption and Safe Families Act of 1996 requiring termination of parental rights for children who have been in foster care for at least fifteen months, many ex-offenders are blocked from regaining custody of and reuniting with their children (Petersilia, 2003). For female ex-offenders, the difficulties in regaining custody of their children can contribute to their inability to succeed during reentry. As discussed in Chapter 4, the difficulties in regaining custody create a source of strain for female ex-offenders and may result in their relapsing to previous drug and alcohol use to cope with the strain and psychological pain. Given that some research has found that ex-offenders who spend time with their children postrelease have lower rates of recidivism, eliminating barriers for ex-offenders to reunite with their children would appear to benefit ex-offenders and society as a whole (Waller, 1974). Further, as noted by Alise in Chapter 6, her brief interaction with her newborn daughter was the catalyst for her breaking away from her criminal pattern.

Celebrating Success

Quite a bit of attention has been devoted, by correctional authorities, the public, and the media, to finding ways for ex-offenders to avoid failing during reentry. However, celebrating the success of ex-offenders is a relatively recent phenomenon that has been popping up around the nation and may serve as yet another useful strategy in fostering successful reentry. For instance, in Alexandria, Virginia, in 2012, Harley-Davidson was a cosponsor of the "Faces of Freedom Rally," an event designed to celebrate ex-offender success stories through a motorcycle ride and a community fair (e.g., food and craft vendors and live music; "Rally in Alexandria," 2012). In 2011, the Restorative Justice Ministry Network of Texas hosted a faith-based ex-offender celebration. In Washington State, the Everett Community Justice Center, for the past eight years, has hosted a twice annual "Celebrate Success" dinner gathering (open to those who have just recently begun community supervision to those who successfully completed their supervision years ago), the Post-Prison Education Program holds regular celebrations and events to recognize the accomplishments of ex-offenders who complete college and graduate degrees, and the If Project engages women and men coming out of prison with youth in schools and juvenile detention facilities to help break the cycle of offending.[4] These programs and events serve as opportunities to remind ex-offenders that despite their struggles, they have made it. These events also give others in the ex-offenders' lives a chance to reinforce the ex-offenders' positive choices. Additionally, such events may help those who may be hitting a bump in their journey by reminding them that many individuals are out there who are willing to help them get back on the path to successful reentry. Thus, building such events to celebrate success by bringing together the community, corrections agencies, and ex-offenders can also contribute to the sustained success of ex-offenders who have reintegrated.

Conclusion

While H. I. McDunnough, played by Nicolas Cage, in the 1987 movie *Raising Arizona* is an ex-offender caught in the revolving door of the criminal justice system, the film does not accurately portray the experience of all ex-offenders. Despite such portrayals, ex-offenders are not far beyond any help that can be provided to them. Wilkinson describes offender reentry as a storm that is overdue and cautions that no "reentry utopia" exists (2001, p. 50). Although reentry is complex, success can be enhanced by several factors.

First, if ex-offenders have their basic needs met (food, housing, employment), the foundation for success has been laid. Clearly, if ex-offenders are to have a fighting chance at being successful in society, they need to have their basic needs met and not have strings attached to getting these needs met. Ex-offenders are under immense pressure to find housing and obtain employment upon release from prison, and this stress is exacerbated by their struggles to reacquaint themselves with society and reunite with family members willing to accept them back into their family—if there even is a family to return to. If ex-offenders can't find employment, which is a difficult task for this group in general and even more so with the state of the economy, then they can't pay their restitution orders or even pay for court-ordered treatment. Obviously, if they can't pay for their treatment, they aren't obtaining treatment, which means they are in violation of the conditions of their release, and they could be arrested for failing to comply with their conditions. Thus, successful reentry for this group is difficult given the many barriers this group faces.

Second, ex-offenders must receive quality treatment that addresses their core problems (e.g., substance abuse, mental illness, prior sexual abuse). Treatment providers should recognize the intersection of gender, race, ethnicity, and social class in how they go about assisting their clients. That is, one model of treatment certainly does not fit all.

Third, if ex-offenders establish trust and build rapport with their CCOs, this connection may assist them in reintegrating successfully. Fourth, community support and collaborations are needed to assist ex-offenders during all phases of their transition into the community. Finally, current laws can be modified to alleviate problems in gaining employment, by not having ex-offenders answer questions about a criminal record, by not restricting employment or aid, and by removing bans on those with records. New laws can also be codified to make reentry easier. Through these changes, ex-offenders may have more success in reintegrating.

Ultimately, successful offender reentry comes down to application of a single basic idea: when ex-offenders reenter the community, they need to be welcomed as whole, contributing, productive citizens, not rejected as distrusted, stigmatized, and excluded outsiders. They need gestures of support, help in making connections, assistance in meeting their needs and challenges, and opportunities in their communities to live hopeful and meaningful lives. Adopting optimistic attitudes about success during reentry has been linked to desistance from crime for females and males (Burnett, 2004; Cobbina and Bender, 2012; Maruna, 2001). Thus, family members, CCOs, treatment providers, and members of the public need to work together to help ex-offenders develop a positive outlook on their success. Ex-offenders need to be given the benefit of the doubt, through second chances and opportunities to show they can be trusted, until they demonstrate otherwise. They should be recognized for their successes while held accountable for their failures. Additionally, they need understanding and gestures from the community that invite them in rather than keep them out. In truth, the issue of offender reentry presents an extremely difficult paradox. Ex-offenders have committed crimes that have violated public safety and public and private confidences. In some cases their crimes are violent, heinous, and severe, and they may have a history of revolving door interactions with the criminal justice system. In other cases, their crimes may be less serious but involve persistent lifestyle patterns influenced by mental health issues, substance abuse, or social disadvantage. Welcoming, trusting, and giving the benefit of the doubt to these individuals fly in the face of the contemporary culture of control that revolves around risk assessment, actuarial prediction, and surveillance activities designed to enhance public safety (Garland, 2001a). However, as many scholars have noted (e.g., Bazemore and Maruna, 2009; Braithwaite, 1989, 2002; Clear, 2007; Clear, Hamilton, and Cadora, 2002; Fox, 2013; Garland, 2001a, 2001b; Harcourt, 2006; Helfgott, 1997; Petersilia, 2003; Swanson, 2009; Van Ness and Strong, 2010), punitive, control-oriented, and actuarial approaches to enhancing public safety have the potential to backfire when they are not coupled with complementary interventions oriented toward inclusion rather than exclusion. The fixation on risk associated with the actuarial age paints a bleak and hopeless picture of a world filled with perpetrators and potential victims. This tension between accountability, risk assessment, and community need for public safety on the one hand, and opportunity for ex-offenders to abandon the outsider identity and start a new civic engagement through true community support and acceptance on the other, is the crux of the reentry dilemma (Fox, 2013). Restorative- and community justice–oriented approaches to reentry that emphasize humanity over risk in ways that stress accountability without imposing a negative label offer hope in resolving this dilemma.

In 2001, J. Travis stated that innovative approaches to responding to crime such as those used in the pretrial stage of the criminal justice process for offenders who have been incarcerated for a short period in jail and then released (e.g., victim notification, developing safety plans, release to a drug treatment facility), new ways of thinking about justice such as restorative justice, and programs such as the Neighborhood Based Supervision (NBS) program in Washington State that place CCOs in neighborhoods working with community police officers are all initiatives that are under way and characterize today's correctional climate. These programs offer a community oriented approach to doing justice (Clear, 2001). Over a decade later, we have accumulated even more examples of alternative initiatives, restorative/community justice principles and practices have been widely implemented and have empirical support, and we have a more nuanced understanding of the ways in which alternative methods of "dispensing" justice can be integrated into the traditional adversarial framework to promote public safety. Reentry programs "must traverse a line gracefully between enforcing accountability and seeming to do surveillance or social control" (Fox, 2013, p. 112) by shifting the paradigm to success rather than failure and meaningfully engaging the community in the reentry process. The time has come to abandon the age-old "us versus them" approach to offender reentry, recognize the damage that has come from politically driven pendulum shifts that have dictated correctional policy, and utilize evidence to reform reentry practices in meaningful ways that recognize and repair the harms resulting from crime and ultimately enhance public safety.

Notes

1. See F. T. Cullen, A. J. Meyer, and E. J. Latessa's (2009) eight lessons that corrections can learn from the approach described in the book *Moneyball* about the statistical and scientific "evidence-based baseball" approach used by Billy Beane, general manager of the Oakland Athletics, to achieve winning seasons amidst severe budget constraints.

2. The Post-Prison Education Program (http://postprisonedu.org/) and University Beyond Bars (http://www.universitybeyondbars.org/) are programs founded in Washington State that many of the ex-offenders who participated in this study were involved in and that they cited as instrumental to their success.

3. See T. R. Clear, J. R. Hamilton, and E. Cadora (2002) and T. R. Clear (2007).

4. See the Post-Prison Education Program (http://postprisonedu.org/) and the If Project (http://www.theifproject.com/).

APPENDIX

Notes on Methods and Data

Method: Ex-Offender Data

The data presented in Chapter 6 is gleaned from twenty-one interviews with ex-offenders who have spent time in correctional facilities in Washington State and were subsequently released. Prior to the interviews being conducted, approval was sought and granted by the Institutional Review Board (IRB) at Seattle University and the Research Review Committee at the Washington State Department of Corrections (WA DOC).

Procedure

Interview subjects were solicited through announcements that were sent out through various channels (e.g., Facebook, WA DOC Listserv, Criminal Justice Advisory Committee Listserv; Seattle Work Release Advisory Board Listserv), through local ex-offender support/referral agencies and community programs that involve ex-offenders, or through previous professional interactions.[1] Those individuals who were interested in being interviewed contacted the researchers, and an interview date and time were selected and arranged by a graduate research assistant. All interviews were conducted by the second author (J. Helfgott) at Seattle University in a faculty office. The interviews ranged in length from forty-five minutes to over one hour. The interviews were audio recorded with the permission of the subject. During the interview, the interviewer took notes via a computer. Following the interview, the notes were given to a graduate research assistant who transcribed the entire interview verbatim. Subjects were given a consent form describing the study and were asked to sign regarding their preference for having their name used or to have a fictitious name assigned to them for the reporting of results. Thus, names reported within this book may or may not be the real interviewees' first names.

Interview Subjects

Interview subjects were male (67 percent, $n = 14$) and female (33 percent, $n = 7$) ex-offenders who had spent time in Washington State correctional facilities and had been released. The majority of the interviewees were white (71.4 percent, $n = 15$), followed by black (14 percent, $n = 3$), Hispanic (10 percent, $n = 2$), and Asian/Pacific Islander (5 percent, $n = 1$). The crimes for which the interview subjects had been convicted most recently and for which they served their sentences were murder (33 percent, $n = 7$), vehicular homicide (10 percent, $n = 2$), assault/robbery (19 percent, $n = 4$), drugs/theft/forgery (33 percent, $n = 7$), and child molestation (5 percent, $n = 1$). The number of years spent in jail/prison ranged from two to thirty ($M = 11$, $Sd = 8.7$), and the time since release ranged from one month to twenty-seven years ($M = 4$, $Sd = 6.1$). All but two interview subjects served their last period of incarceration in a prison setting. Two of the interview subjects served one year in county jail followed by a period in in-patient treatment or work release but had a history of short-term periods of jail incarcerations.[2] The age at which the interview subjects reported they had first engaged in delinquent or criminal behavior ranged from thirteen to forty-two ($M = 19$, $Sd = 6.2$).[3]

Interview Schedule

All interviews of ex-offenders utilized an interview schedule consisting of eight questions including two questions regarding background and six questions regarding experiences in the reentry process. The first set of two questions asked interview subjects about their background regarding delinquent and criminal behavior and their history of incarceration and reentry. Specifically, ex-offenders were asked:

- How long of a prison sentence did you serve and for what offense(s)?
- How long has it been since you have reentered your community?

The second set of six questions asked about experiences during reentry. Ex-offenders were asked:

- What were your initial experiences during reentry?
- Were any of these challenges/needs unexpected?
- What have your experiences been in regard to reentry? Does it differ at different points in reentry (i.e., initial versus several years later)?
- What do you attribute your success since release to?
- Did your CCO (community corrections officer) contribute to your success in any way?
- What things can be done both in prison and in the community to further enhance reentry success?
- Is there anything else you would like to add regarding your success or on the topic of successful ex-offender reentry?

Additional questions were asked depending on the nature of the interviewee response. Subjects were probed based on their responses and encouraged to deviate from the schedule and add their own commentary and opinions about ex-offender reentry success or to share any additional information they thought relevant to explain their own desistance and reentry process.

Method: Practitioner Data

The data presented in Chapter 7 were gleaned from nineteen interviews of state CCOs in Washington State in 2012. Prior to the interviews being conducted, approval was sought and granted by the IRB at Seattle University and the Research Review Committee at the WA DOC. In order to solicit volunteers for the study, e-mail announcements about the research were sent out to various channels (e.g., WA DOC Listserv, Criminal Justice Advisory Committee Listserv; Seattle Work Release Advisory Board Listserv) to secure subjects. Those CCOs that were interested in being interviewed contacted the researchers, and an interview date and time were selected. All interviews took place at Seattle University in a faculty office. All interviews were conducted by faculty researchers, and the interviews ranged in length from thirty-five minutes to over one hour. The interviews were audio recorded with the permission of the subject. During the interview, the interviewer took notes via a computer. Following the interview, the notes were given to a research assistant who transcribed the entire interview verbatim. Subjects either agreed to have their first name used or to have a fictitious name assigned to them for the reporting of results. Thus, first names reported within this book may or may not be the real interviewees' first names.

Interview Subjects

The majority of our sample was male (57 percent) and overwhelmingly Caucasian. Our sample included one African American, one Hispanic American, and two Asian American CCOs. Participants ranged in age from twenty-nine to fifty-four years with an average age of forty years. Our sample participants served from one to twenty-nine years with an average of 8.5 years.

Interview Schedule

All interviews of CCOs utilized an interview schedule consisting of twelve standard questions. The first set of three questions queried CCOs on their background. Specifically, CCOs were asked:

- Describe your current position. How long have you been employed there?
- What other related criminal justice positions did you hold prior to becoming a CCO?
- What is your educational background?

The second set of five questions asked about CCOs' experiences. Questions for the experience section included the following:

- How do you personally define reentry success?
- What do you think makes for successful reentry?
- What recollections of success stories do you have?
- How do you think you contributed to the success?
- In a previous study of ours, offenders stated that CCOs do not understand their needs. In that study, many CCOs attributed rational choice as the reason for ex-offenders lack of success upon reentry. Given this discrepancy in perceptions, do you think rational choice plays a role in offender success?

The final set of four questions asked CCOs about their opinions regarding obstacles to offender success. Questions for this final section of the interview schedule included the following:

- In your opinion, what are the primary factors obstructing the offender's ability to successfully reenter society?
- In your opinion, what are the primary factors that contribute to an offender's ability to successfully reenter society?

- Now that you have identified these primary obstacles and factors that divert from or enhance success, how do you help offenders address these issues in your work with them?
- What would help you assist ex-offenders in getting these met?

While an interview schedule was utilized to guide the interview sessions, interviewees were permitted to deviate from the schedule and add their own commentary and opinions about ex-offender reentry success anytime.

Notes

1. The authors have worked in a range of correctional contexts conducting research and coordinating prison programs in institutional and community settings. A number of the interviewees were recruited as a result of this previous interaction.

2. A number of interview subjects had been in and out of prison multiple times including one individual with thirty bookings in a several-year time frame, several with long juvenile and county jail histories prior to a long prison sentence, one with a thirty-year history of several years in and several years out, and two with histories of jail time followed by in-patient treatment or work release. For data summary purposes, the time in prison reflects the length of the most recent conviction. However, the actual number of years spent incarcerated for the sample including all time spent incarcerated is much higher.

3. Most of the interview subjects described many years of delinquent activity in their juvenile years but gave the year at which they first formally entered the juvenile justice system. Thus some reported delinquent activity began before age thirteen.

References

Ackerman, A. R., M. Sacks, and L. N. Osier. (2013). The experiences of registered sex offenders with internet offender registries in three states. *Journal
of Offender Rehabilitation* 52(1): 29–45.

Acoca, L. (1998). Outside/inside: The violation of American girls at home, on
the streets, and in the juvenile justice system. *Crime and Delinquency*
44(4): 561–589.

Aday, R. H., and J. J. Krabill (2011). *Women aging in prison: A neglected population in the correctional system.* Boulder, CO: Lynne Rienner.

Agnew, R. (1991). The interactive effects of peer variables on delinquency.
Criminology 29: 47–72.

———. (1992). Foundations for a general theory of crime and delinquency.
Criminology 30(1): 47–87.

Ajzenstadt, M. (2009). The relative autonomy of women offenders' decision
making. *Theoretical Criminology* 13(2): 201–225.

Akers, R. L. (1990). Rational choice, deterrence, and social learning theory:
The path not taken. *Journal of Criminal Law and Criminology* 81(3): 653–
676.

Akers, R. L., M. Krohn, L. Lanza-Kaduce, and M. Radosevich (1979). Social
learning and deviant behavior: A specific test of a general theory. *American
Sociological Review* 44: 636–655.

Akers, R. L., and C. S. Sellers (2008). *Criminological theories: Introduction,
evaluation, and application,* 5th ed. New York: Oxford University Press.

Alarid, L. F., V. S. Burton, and F. T. Cullen (2000). Gender and crime among
felony offenders: Assessing the generality of social control and differential
association theories. *Journal of Research in Crime and Delinquency* 37:
171–199.

Alarid, L. F., J. W. Marquart, V. S. Burton, F. T. Cullen, and S. J. Cuvelier
(1996). Women's roles in serious offenses: A study of adult felons. *Justice
Quarterly* 13: 431–454.

Albanese, J. S. (1984). Concern about variation in criminal sentences: A cycli-
cal history of reform. *Journal of Criminal Law and Criminology* 75(1):
260–271.

Alemagno, S. A. (2001). Women in jail: Is substance abuse treatment enough?
American Journal of Public Health 91: 798–800.

Allard, P. (2002). *Life sentences: Denying welfare benefits to women convicted of drug offenses*. Washington, D.C.: Sentencing Project.

Allender, D. M. (2004). Offender reentry: A returning or reformed criminal. *FBI Law Enforcement Bulletin* 73: 1–10.

Alvarez, L. (2011). Florida mother is found not guilty of murder. *New York Times,* July 6. http://www.nytimes.com.

Anderson, D. C. (1995). *Crime and the politics of hysteria: How the Willie Horton story changed American justice*. New York: Random House.

Anderson, M. (2008). *Sociology: Understanding a diverse society*. Belmont, CA: Wadsworth.

Andrews, B. (1995). Bodily shame as a mediator between abusive experiences and depression. *Journal of Abnormal Psychology* 104: 277–285.

Andrews, D. A., and J. Bonta (2010). *The psychology of criminal conduct*. Cincinnati, OH: Anderson.

Andrews, D. A., I. Zinger, R. D. Hoge, J. Bonta, P. Gendreau, and F. T. Cullen (1990). Does correctional treatment work? A clinically relevant and psychologically informed meta-analysis. *Criminology* 28(3): 369–404.

Angell, B. G., and M. G. Jones (2003). Recidivism, risk, and resiliency among North American Indian parolees and former prisoners: An examination of the Lumbee First Nation. *Journal of Ethnic and Cultural Diversity in Social Work* 12(2): 61–77.

Anglin, M. D., and B. Perrochet (1998). Drug use and crime: A historical review of research conducted by the UCLA Drug Abuse Research Center. *Substance Use and Misuse* 33: 1871–1914.

Anglin, M., M. Prendergast, D. Farabee, and J. Cartier (2002). *Final report on the substance abuse program at the California substance abuse treatment facility (SATF-SAP) and state prison at Corcoran*. Sacramento: California Department of Corrections, Office of Substance Abuse Programs.

Apel, R. (2011). Transitional jobs program: Putting employment-based reentry into context. *Criminology and Public Policy* 10(4): 939–942.

Arditti, J. A., and A. L. Few (2006). Mothers' reentry into family life following incarceration. *Criminal Justice Policy Review* 17: 103–123.

Aresti, A., V. Eatough, and B. Brooks-Gordon (2010). Doing time after time: An interpretative phenomenological analysis of reformed ex-prisoners' experiences of self-change, identity, and career opportunities. *Psychology, Crime, and Law* 16(3): 169–190.

Armstrong, K., and J. Martin (2010). *The other side of mercy: A killer's journey across the American divide*. Indianapolis, IN: Dog Ear.

Arya, N., F. Villarruel, C. Villaneuva, and I. Augarten (2009). *America's invisible children: Latino youth and the failure of justice*. Washington, DC: Campaign for Youth Justice.

Atkin, C. A., and G. S. Armstrong (2013). Does the concentration of parolees in a community impact employer attitudes towards the hiring of ex-offenders? *Criminal Justice Policy Review* 24: 71–93.

Bagley, C., and L. Young (1987). Juvenile prostitution and child sexual abuse: A controlled study. *Canadian Journal of Community Mental Health* 6: 5–26.

Bahn, C. (1977). *Sentence disparity and civil rights*. New York: John Jay College of Criminal Justice.

Bahn, C., and L. Davis (1991). Social-psychological effects of the status of probationer. *Federal Probation* 55: 17–25.

Bahr, S. J., A. H. Armstrong, B. G. Gibbs, P. E. Harris, and J. K. Fisher (2005). The reentry process: How parolees adjust to release from prison. *Fathering* 3(3): 243–265.

Bahr, S. J., A. L. Masters, and B. M. Taylor (2012). What works in substance abuse treatment programs for offenders? *Prison Journal* 92(2): 155–174.

Bailey, J. A., and L. A. McCloskey (2005). Pathways to adolescent substance use among sexually abused girls. *Journal of Abnormal Child Psychology* 33: 39–53.

Baker, P. L., and A. Carson (1999). "I take care of my kids": Mothering practices of substance abusing women. *Gender and Society* 13: 347–363.

Barak, G., J. M. Flavin, and P. S. Leighton (2001). *Class, race, gender, and crime.* Los Angeles: Roxbury.

Barnes, J. C., and K. M. Beaver (2012). Marriage and desistance from crime: A consideration of gene-environment correlation. *Journal of Marriage and Family* 74: 19–33.

Barnes, J. C., T. Dukes, R. Tewksbury, and T. M. De Troye (2009). Analyzing the impact of a statewide residence restriction law on South Carolina sex offenders. *Criminal Justice Policy Review* 20: 21–43.

Baskin, D. R., and I. Sommers (1998). *Casualties of community disorder: Women's careers in violent crime.* Boulder, CO: Westview.

Bazemore, G., and R. Boba (2007). "Doing good" to "make good": Community theory for practice in a restorative justice civic engagement reentry model. *Journal of Offender Rehabilitation* 46(1/2): 25–56.

Bazemore, G., and S. Maruna (2009). Restorative justice in the reentry context: Building new theory and expanding the evidence base. *Victims and Offenders* 4: 375–384.

Bazemore, G., and M. Schiff (2001). *Restorative community justice.* Cincinnati, OH: Anderson.

Bazemore, G., and J. Stinchcomb (2004). A civic engagement model of reentry: Involving community through service and restorative justice. *Federal Probation* 68(2): 14–24.

Beauchamp, T. L., and N. E. Bowie (1993). *Ethical theory and business,* 4th ed. Englewood Cliffs, NJ: Prentice-Hall.

Beauvais, F. (1996). Trends in drug use among American Indian students and dropouts, 1975 to 1994. *American Journal of Public Health* 8: 1594–1598.

Beck, A., and B. Shipley (1989). *Recidivism of prisoners released in 1983.* Washington, DC: US Department of Justice, Bureau of Justice Statistics.

Becker, H. (1963). *Outsiders: Studies in the sociology of deviance.* New York: Free Press.

Belknap, J. (2007). *The invisible woman: Gender, crime, and justice.* Belmont, CA: Thomson, Wadsworth.

Belknap, J., K. Holsinger, and M. Dunn (1997). Understanding incarcerated girls: The results of a focus group study. *Prison Journal* 77(4): 381–404.

Bellair, P. E., and B. R. Kowalski (2011). Low-skill employment opportunity and African American–White difference in recidivism. *Journal of Research in Crime and Delinquency* 48: 176–208.

Benda, B. B., N. J. Toombs, and R. F. Corwyn (2005). Self-control, gender and age: A survival analysis of recidivism among boot camp graduates in a 5-year follow-up. *Journal of Offender Rehabilitation* 40(3/4): 115–132.

Bennett, J. (2006). The good, the bad, and the ugly: The media in prison films. *Howard Journal* 45(2): 97–115.

Beran, S. (2005). Native Americans in prison: The struggle for religious freedom. *Nebraska Anthropologist,* no. 2: 46–55.

Berg, M. T., and B. M. Huebner (2011). Reentry and the ties that bind: An examination of social ties, employment, and recidivism. *Justice Quarterly* 28(2): 382–410.

Bergseth, K. J., K. R. Jens, L. Bergeron-Vigesaa, and T. D. McDonald (2011). Assessing the needs of women recently released from prison. *Women and Criminal Justice* 21: 100–122.

Berry, P. E., and H. M. Eigenberg (2003). Role strain and incarcerated mothers: Understanding the process of mothering. *Women and Criminal Justice* 15: 101–119.

Biles, D., R. Harding, and J. Walker (1999). The deaths of offenders serving community corrections orders. *Trends and Issues in Crime and Criminal Justice,* no. 107: 1–6.

Binswanger, I. A., M. F. Stern, R. A. Devo, P. J. Heagerty, A. Cheadle, J. G. Elmore, and T. D. Koepsell (2007). Release from prison—A high risk of death for former inmates. *New England Journal of Medicine* 356: 157–165.

Bloom, B., M. Chesney-Lind, and B. Owen (1994). *Women in California prisons: Hidden victims of the war on drugs.* San Francisco, CA: Center on Juvenile and Criminal Justice.

Bloom, B., B. Owen, and S. Covington (2003). *Gender-responsive strategies: Research, practice, and guiding principles for women offenders.* Washington, DC: National Institute of Corrections, US Department of Justice.

Bloom, B., B. Owen, J. Rosenbaum, and E. P. Deschenes (2003). Focusing on girls and young women: A gendered perspective on female delinquency. *Women and Criminal Justice* 14: 117–136.

Bloom, H., L. L. Orr, G. Cave, S. H. Bell, F. Doolittle, and W. Lin (1994). *The national JTPA study: Overview of impacts, benefits, and costs of Title IIA.* Cambridge, MA: ABT Associates.

Blumstein, A., J. Cohen, J. A. Roth, and C. A. Visher (1986). *Criminal careers and "career criminals."* Washington, DC: National Research Council.

Bonczar, T. P. (2008). *Characteristics of state parole supervising agencies, 2006.* Washington, DC: US Department of Justice, Bureau of Justice Statistics.

Bonczar, T. P., and A. J. Beck (1997). *Lifetime likelihood of going to state or federal prison.* Washington, DC: US Department of Justice, Bureau of Justice Statistics.

Bouffard, J. A., and L. Bergeron (2007). Reentry works: The implementation and effectiveness of a serious and violent offender reentry initiative. *Journal of Offender Rehabilitation* 44(3): 1–29.

Boyd, C. J. (1993). The antecedents of women's crack cocaine abuse: Family substance abuse, sexual abuse, depression and illicit drug use. *Journal of Substance Abuse Treatment* 10: 433–438.

Boyer, D., L. Chapman, and B. K. Marshall (1993). *Survival sex in King County: Helping women out.* Seattle, WA: King County Women's Advisory Board, Northwest Resource Associates.

Bradley, D. E. (1995). Religious involvement and social resources: Evidence from the Americans' changing lives data. *Journal for the Scientific Study of Religion* 34: 259–267.

Bradley, K. H., B. M. Oliver, N. C. Richardson, and E. M. Slayter (2001). *No place like home: Housing and the ex-prisoner.* Boston, MA: Community Resources for Justice.

Braithwaite, J. (1989). *Crime, shame and reintegration.* Cambridge, UK: Cambridge University Press.

———. (2002). *Restorative justice and responsive regulation.* Oxford, UK: Oxford University Press.

Braswell, M., J. R. Fuller, and B. Lozoff (2000). *Corrections, peacemaking, and restorative justice: Transforming individuals and institutions.* Cincinnati, OH: Anderson.

Brazzell, D., and N. G. La Vigne (2009). *Prisoner reentry in Houston: Community perspectives.* Washington, DC: Urban Institute Justice Policy Center.

Breese, J. R., K. Ra'el, and G. K. Grant (2000). No place like home: A qualitative investigation of social support and its effects on recidivism. *Sociological Practice: A Journal of Clinical and Applied Research* 2(1): 1–21.

Brodsky, S., and F. Scogin. (1988). Inmates in protective custody: First data on emotional effects. *Forensic Reports* 1: 267–280.

Brookman, F., C. Mullins, T. Bennett, and R. Wright (2007). Gender, motivation and the accomplishment of street robbery in the United Kingdom. *British Journal of Criminology* 47(6): 861–884.

Brown, G. (2010). *The intersectionality of race, gender, and reentry: Challenges for African-American women.* Washington, DC: American Constitution Society for Law and Policy.

Brown, J. (2004a). Challenges facing Canadian federal offenders newly released to the community. *Journal of Offender Rehabilitation* 39: 19–35.

———. (2004b). Managing the transition from jail to community: A Canadian parole officer perspective on the needs of newly released federal offenders. *Western Criminology Review* 5(2): 97–107.

Brown, M., and B. Bloom. (2009). Reentry and renegotiating motherhood: Maternal identity and success on parole. *Crime and Delinquency* 55(2): 313–336.

Browne, A., and K. R. Williams (1989). Exploring the effect of resource availability and the likelihood of female-perpetrated homicides. *Law and Society Review* 23: 63–73.

Buikhuisen, W., and F. P. H. Dijksterhuis (1971). Delinquency and stigmatization. *British Journal of Criminology* 11: 185–217.

Bureau of Justice Assistance. (2011). *Second Chance Act of 2007.* Washington, DC: US Department of Justice.

Bureau of Justice Statistics. (1977). *National prisoner statistics.* Washington, DC: US Department of Justice.

———. (1997). *National prisoner statistics.* Washington, DC: US Department of Justice.

———. (2012). *Reentry trends in the US.* Washington, DC: US Department of Justice.

Bureau of Labor Statistics (2013). *The employment situation.* Washington, DC: US Department of Labor.

Burkart, K. (1973). *Women in prison.* Garden City, NY: Doubleday.

Burke, P. B. (2001). Collaboration for successful prisoner reentry: The role of parole and the courts. *Corrections Management Quarterly* 5(3): 11–22.

Burnett, R. (2004). To reoffend or not to reoffend? The ambivalence of convicted property offenders. In S. Maruna and R. Immarigeon (eds.), *After crime and punishment: Pathways to offender reintegration.* Cullompton, UK: Willan, pp. 152–180.

Burton, V. S., F. T. Cullen, T. D. Evans, L. F. Alarid, and R. G. Dunaway (1998). Gender, self-control, and crime. *Journal of Research in Crime and Delinquency* 35: 123–147.

Bush-Baskette, S. R. (2000). The war on drugs and the incarceration of mothers. *Journal of Drug Issues* 30(4): 919–928.

Bushway, S., and G. Sweeten (2007). Abolish lifetime bans for ex-felons. *Criminology and Public Policy* 6(4): 697–706.

Caldwell, M. (1951). Preview of a new type of probation study made in Alabama. *Federal Probation* 15(2): 3–11.

Calhoun, T. C., and G. Weaver (1996). Rational decision-making among male street prostitutes. *Deviant Behavior: An Interdisciplinary Journal* 17: 209–227.

Camp, C. G., and G. M. Camp (2000). *The corrections yearbook 2000—Adult corrections.* Middletown, CT: Criminal Justice Institute.

Canter, R. J. (1982). Family correlates of male and female delinquency. *Criminology* 20: 149–167.

Carothers, C. (2010). Important role of advocacy. In H. A. Dlugacz (ed.), *Reentry planning for offenders with mental disorders.* Kingston, NJ: Civic Research Institute, pp. 5-1–5-14.

Cartagena, J. (2008). Lost votes, body counts and joblessness: The effects of felon disfranchisement on Latino civic engagement. *Latino Studies* 6: 192–200.

Centers for Disease Control and Prevention. (2007). *Fighting HIV among African Americans: A heightened national response.* Atlanta, GA: US Department of Health and Human Services.

Cernkovich, S. A., and P. C. Giordano (1987). Family relationships and delinquency. *Criminology* 25: 295–321.

Chajewski, M., and C. C. Mercado (2009). An evaluation of sex offender residency restriction functioning in town, county, and city-wide jurisdiction. *Criminal Justice Policy Review* 20: 44–61.

Chambliss, W. J., and R. H. Nagasawa (1969). On the validity of official statistics: A comparative study of white, black and Japanese high-school boys. *Journal of Research in Crime and Delinquency* 6: 71–77.

Chapple, C. L., J. A. McQuillian, and T. A. Berdahl (2005). Gender, social bonds, and delinquency: A comparison of boys' and girls' models. *Social Science Research* 34(2): 357–383.

Chen, X., K. A. Tyler, L. B. Whitbeck, and D. R. Hoyt (2004). Early sexual abuse, street adversity, and drug use among female homeless and runaway adolescents in the Midwest. *Journal of Drug Issues* 34(1): 1–21.

Chesney-Lind, M. (1989). Girl's crime and woman's place: Toward a feminist model of female delinquency. *Crime and Delinquency* 35(1): 8–10.

Chesney-Lind, M., and L. Pasko (2004). *The female offender: Girls, women, and crime.* Thousand Oaks, CA: Sage.

Chesney-Lind, M., and R. Shelden (2004). *Girls, delinquency, and juvenile justice.* Belmont, CA: Thompson Wadsworth.

Chiricos, T., P. Jackson, and G. Waldo (1972). Inequality in the imposition of a criminal label. *Social Problems* 19: 553–572.

Chu, D. C. (2007). Religiosity and desistance from drug use. *Criminal Justice and Behavior* 34(5): 661–679.

Clark, L. M. (2007). Landlord attitudes toward renting to released offenders. *Federal Probation* 71(1): 20–30.

Clear, T. R. (2007). *Imprisoning communities: How mass incarceration makes disadvantaged neighborhoods worse.* New York: Oxford University Press.

Clear, T. R., and G. Cole (1997). *American corrections.* Belmont, CA: Wadsworth.

Clear, T. R., J. R. Hamilton, and E. Cadora (2002). *Community justice.* Cincinnati, OH: Anderson.

Cobbina, J. E. (2009). *From prison to home: Women's pathways in and out of crime.* Washington, DC: US Department of Justice.

———. (2010). Reintegration success and failure: Factors impacting reintegration among incarcerated and formerly incarcerated women. *Journal of Offender Rehabilitation* 49: 210–232.

Cobbina, J. E., and K. A. Bender (2012). Predicting the future: Incarcerated women's views of reentry success. *Journal of Offender Rehabilitation* 51(5): 275–294.

Coll, C., J. Surrey, P. Buccio-Notaro, and B. Molla (1998). Incarcerated mothers: Crimes and punishments. In C. Coll, J. Surrey, and K. Weingarten (eds.), *Mothering against the odds: Diverse voices of contemporary mothers.* New York: Guilford, pp. 255–274.

Collins, R. E. (2004). Onset and desistance in criminal careers: Neurobiology and the age-crime relationship. *Journal of Offender Rehabilitation* 39(3): 1–19.

Comack, E. (2005). Coping, resisting, and surviving: Connecting women's law violations to their histories of abuse. In L. Alarid and P. Cromwell (eds.), *In her own words: Women offenders' views on crime and victimization.* Los Angeles: Roxbury, pp. 33–43.

Connett, A. V. (1972). The perspective of an ex-offender. *University of San Francisco Law Review* 6: 7–26.

Corden, J., J. Kuipers, and K. Wilson (1978). *After prison: A study of the post-release experiences of discharged prisoners.* Papers in community studies, 21. New York: University of York.

Cornish, D. B., and R. V. Clarke (1986). *The reasoning criminal: Rational choice perspectives on offending.* New York: Springer-Verlag.

Covington, S. (2002). *A woman's journey home: Challenges for female offenders and their children.* Washington, DC: US Department of Health and Human Services, Urban Institute.

Covington, S., and J. Kohen (1984). Women, alcohol, and sexuality. *Advances in Alcohol and Substance Abuse* 4(1): 41–56.

Cowan, D. S., and J. Fionda (1994). Meeting the need: The response of local authorities' housing departments to the housing of ex-offenders. *British Journal of Criminology* 34: 444–458.

Crayton, A., L. Ressler, D. A. Mukamal, J. Jannetta, and K. Warwick (2010). *Partnering with jails to improve reentry: A guidebook for community-based organizations.* Washington, DC: Urban Institute.

Culhane, D. P., S. Metraux, and T. Hadley (2002). Public service reductions associated with placement of homeless persons with severe mental illness in supportive housing. *Housing Policy Debate* 13(1): 107–163.

Cullen, F. T. (1994). Social support as an organizing concept for criminology: Presidential address to the Academy of Criminal Justice Sciences. *Justice Quarterly* 11: 527–559.

Cullen, F. T., and K. E. Gilbert (1982). *Reaffirming rehabilitation.* Cincinnati, OH: Anderson.

Cullen, F. T., A. J. Meyer, and E. J. Latessa (2009). Eight lessons from *Moneyball*: The high cost of ignoring evidence-based corrections. *Victims and Offenders* 4: 197–213.

Cusson, M., and P. Pinsonneault (1986). The decision to give up crime. In D. B. Cornish and R. V. Clarke (eds.), *The reasoning criminal: Rational choice perspectives of offending.* New York: Springer-Verlag, pp. 72–82.

D'Alessio, S. J., and L. Stolzenberg (1993). Socioeconomic status and the sentencing of the traditional offender. *Journal of Criminal Justice* 21(1): 61–77.

Daly, K., and M. Chesney-Lind (1988). Feminism and criminology. *Justice Quarterly* 5(4): 497–538.

Davis, L., and S. Pacchiana (2004). Health profile of the state prison population and returning offenders: Public health challenges. *Journal of Correctional Health Care* 10: 303–331.

Dekovic, M. (1999). Risk and protective factors in the development of problem behavior during adolescence. *Journal of Youth and Adolescence* 28: 667–685.

Delgado, M. (2012). *Prisoner reentry at work: Adding business to the mix.* Boulder, CO: Lynne Rienner.

Deutsch, L. (2002). Ryder gets three years probation, community service for theft. *Seattle Times,* December 6. http://www.seattletimes.nwsource.com.

DiZerega, M. (2011). *Why ask about family?* New York: Vera Institute of Justice.

Dodge, M., and M. R. Pogrebin (2001). Collateral costs of imprisonment for women: Complications of reintegration. *Prison Journal* 81: 42–54.

Doherty, E. E., and M. E. Ensminger (2013). Marriage and offending among a cohort of disadvantaged African-Americans. *Journal of Research in Crime and Delinquency* 50(1): 104–131.

Dressler, D. (1962). *Practice and theory of probation and parole.* New York: Columbia University Press.

Duhigg, C. (2012). *The power of habit: Why we do what we do in life and business.* New York: Random House.

Durant, R. H., J. Knight, and E. Goodman (1997). Factors associated with aggressive and delinquent behaviors among patients attending an adolescent medicine clinic. *Journal of Adolescent Health* 21: 303–308.

Earle, K. A., B. Bradigan, and L. I. Morgenbesser (2001). Mental health care for American Indians in prison. *Journal of Ethnic and Cultural Diversity in Social Work* 9(3/4): 111–132.

Earls, C. M., and H. David (1990). Early family and sexual experiences of male and female prostitutes. *Canada's Mental Health* 11: 7–11.

Ekland-Olson, S., M. Supanic, J. Campbell, and K. J. Lenihan (1983). Postrelease depression and the importance of familial support. *Criminology* 21(2): 253–275.

Elliott, D. S. (1994). Serious violent offenders: Onset, developmental course and termination. *Criminology* 32: 1–22.

Elmer, J. P., and S. H. Cohen (1978). Prediction of work release success with youthful, nonviolent, male offenders. *Criminal Justice and Behavior* 5(2): 181–192.

England, R. (1955). A study of postprobation recidivism among five hundred federal offenders. *Federal Probation* 19: 10–16.

Enos, S. (2001). *Mothering from the inside: Parenting in a women's prison.* Albany: State University of New York Press.

Erisman, W., and J. B. Conardo (2005). *Learning to reduce recidivism: A 50-state analysis of postsecondary correctional educational policy.* Washington, DC: Institute for Higher Education Policy.

Ewald, A. C. (2002). Civil death: The ideological paradox of criminal disenfranchisement law in the United States. *Wisconsin Law Review* 5: 1045–1135.

Fagan, A. A. (2005). The relationship between adolescent physical abuse and criminal offending: Support for an enduring and generalized cycle of violence. *Journal of Family Violence* 20: 279–290.

Fahey, J., C. Roberts, and L. Engel (2006). *Employment of ex-offenders: Employer perspectives.* Boston, MA: Crime and Justice Institute.

Fair Shake Reentry Resource Center. (2012). *About Fair Shake.* http://fair shake.net.

Farrall, S., G. Sharpe, B. Hunter, and A. Calverley (2011). Theorizing structural and individual-level processes in desistance and persistence: Outlining an integrated perspective. *Australian and New Zealand Journal of Criminology* 44(2): 218–234.

Farrell, G. (2004). Martha Stewart convicted of four felonies. *USA Today,* March 5.

Farrington, D. P. (1986). Age and crime. *Crime and Justice* 7: 189–250.

Federal Bureau of Investigation (FBI) (2011). *Uniform Crime Report.* Washington, DC: Federal Bureau of Investigation.

Fei, M. T., and G. P. Lopez (2005). Learning how regularly to improve our capacity to meet the challenges of Asian and Pacific Islander re-entry. *Amerasia Journal* 31(3): 61–74.

Felson, M. (2002). *Crime and everyday life.* Thousand Oaks, CA: Sage.

———. (2006). *Crime and nature.* Thousand Oaks, CA: Sage.

Ferns, R. (2008). Habits of thinking: Working within correctional environments to introduce and sustain personal change. *Journal of Community Corrections* 17(2): 9–11.

Ferraro, K. J., and A. M. Moe (2003). Mothering, crime, and incarceration. *Journal of Contemporary Ethnography* 32(1): 9–40.

Flanagan, T. J. (1995). *Long-term imprisonment: Policy, science, and correctional practice.* Thousand Oaks, CA: Sage.

Fontaine, J., and J. Biess (2012). *Housing as a platform for formerly incarcerated persons.* Washington, DC: Urban Institute.

Fontaine, J., C. G. Roman, and M. R. Burt (2010). *System change accomplishments of the Corporation for Supportive Housing's Returning Home Initiative.* Washington, DC: Urban Institute.

Forrest, W., and C. Hay (2011). Life-course transitions, self-control, and desistance from crime. *Criminology and Criminal Justice* 11(5): 487–513.

Fox, K. J. (2013). Redeeming communities: Restorative offender reentry in a risk-centric society. *Victims and Offenders: An International Journal of Evidence-based Research, Policy, and Practice* 7(1): 97–120.

Frease, D. (1964). *Factors related to probation outcome.* Olympia, WA: Department of Institutions, Board of Prison Terms and Parole.

Freeman, R. B. (2003). *Can we close the revolving door? Recidivism vs. employment of ex-offenders in the US.* Paper presented at the Urban Institute Reentry Roundtable, New York University School of Law, May 19.

French, L. A. (2000). *Addictions and Native Americans.* Westport, CT: Praeger.

French, M. T., G. A. Zarkin, R. L. Hubbard, and J. V. Rachal (1993). The effects of time in drug abuse treatment and employment on posttreatment drug use and criminal activity. *American Journal on Drug and Alcohol Abuse* 19: 19–33.

Freud, S. (1933). *New introductory lectures on psychoanalysis.* Trans. W. J. H. Sprott. New York: W.W. Norton.

Freudenberg, N., J. Daniels, M. Crum, T. Perkins, and B. E. Richie (2005). Coming home from jail: The social and health consequences of community reentry for women, male adolescents, and their families and communities. *American Journal of Public Health* 95(10): 1725–1736.

Friedman, J., and D. P. Rosenbaum (1988). Social control theory: The salience of components by age, gender, and type of crime. *Journal of Quantitative Criminology* 4: 363–381.

Frisman, L. K., J. Swanson, M. C. Marin, and E. Leavitt-Smith (2010). Estimating costs of reentry programs for prisoners with severe mental illnesses. In H. A. Dlugacz (ed.), *Reentry planning for offenders with mental disorders: Policy and practice.* Kingston, NJ: Civic Research Institute, pp. 4-1–4-11.

Funk, P. (2004). On the effective use of stigma as a crime deterrent. *European Economic Review* 48(4): 715–728.

Gaarder, E., and J. Belknap (2002). Tenuous borders: Girls transferred to adult court. *Criminology* 40(3): 481–518.

Garland, D. (1990). *Punishment and modern society: A study in social theory.* Chicago: University of Chicago Press.

———. (2001a). *The culture of control: Crime and social order in contemporary society.* Chicago: University of Chicago Press.

———. (ed.) (2001b). *Mass imprisonment: Social causes and consequences.* Thousand Oaks, CA: Sage.

Garland, B., E. Wodahl, and R. Schuhmann (2013). Value conflict and public opinion toward prisoner reentry initiatives. *Criminal Justice Policy Review* 24: 27–48.

Garland, B., E. J. Wodahl, and J. Mayfield (2011). Prisoner reentry in a small metropolitan community: Obstacles and policy recommendations. *Criminal Justice Policy Review* 22: 90–110.

Gauthier, D. K., and W. B. Bankston (1997). Gender equality and the sex ratio of intimate killing. *Criminology* 35: 577–600.

Gauthier, D. K., N. K. Chaudoir, and C. J. Forsyth (2003). A sociological analysis of maternal infanticide in the United States, 1984–1996. *Deviant Behavior* 24(4): 393–404.

Geiger, B., and U. Timor (2001). An inside look at Israeli prisoners' world of values. *Journal of Offender Rehabilitation* 34(2): 63–83.

Geller, A., and M. A. Curtis (2011). A sort of homecoming: Incarceration and the housing security of urban men. *Social Science Research* 40: 1196–1213.

Gendreau, P., and R. R. Ross (1979). Effective correctional treatment: Bibliotherapy for cynics. *Crime and Delinquency* 25: 463–489.

Gendreau, P., T. Little, and C. Goggin (1996). A meta-analysis of the predictors of adult offender recidivism: What works! *Criminology* 34(4): 575–608.

Gerber, J., and E. J. Fritsch (1995). Adult academic and vocational correctional education programs: A review of recent research. *Journal of Offender Rehabilitation* 22(1/2): 119–142.

Gilfus, M. E. (1992). From victims to survivors to offenders: Women's routes of entry and immersion into street crime. *Women and Criminal Justice* 4: 63–89.

Giordano, P. C., S. A. Cernkovich, and M. D. Pugh (1986). Friendships and delinquency. *American Journal of Sociology* 91: 1170–1202.

Giordano, P. C., S. A. Cernkovich, and J. L. Rudolph (2002). Gender, crime, and desistance: Toward a theory of cognitive transformation. *American Journal of Sociology* 107(4): 990–1064.

Glaze, L. E., and T. P. Bonczar. (2011). *Probation and parole in the United States, 2010*. Washington, DC: Bureau of Justice Statistics, US Department of Justice.

Glaze, L. E., and L. M. Maruschak (2008). *Parents in prison and their minor children*. Washington, DC: Bureau of Justice Statistics, US Department of Justice.

Glaze, L. E., and E. Parks (2012). *Correctional populations in the United States, 2011*. Washington, DC: Bureau of Justice Statistics, US Department of Justice.

Goffman, E. (1963). *Stigma: Notes on the management of spoiled identity*. New York: Simon and Schuster.

Gomes, M. T. (2012). Considerations for immigrant ex-offenders facing deportation. *Corrections Today* 74(2): 90–91.

Goodkind, S., I. Ng, and R. C. Sarri (2006). The impact of sexual abuse in the lives of young women involved or at risk of involvement with the juvenile justice system. *Violence Against Women* 12: 456–477.

Gottfredson, M. R., and T. Hirschi (1990). *A general theory of crime*. Stanford, CA: Stanford University Press.

Gould, L. C. (1969). Who defines delinquency: A comparison of self-reported and officially reported indices of delinquency for three racial groups. *Social Problems* 16(3): 325–336.

Gove, W. R., and R. D. Crutchfield (1982). The family and juvenile delinquency. *Sociological Quarterly* 23: 301–319.

Gowdey, C. E., and G. C. Turnbull (1978). *Report on employment and training programs for adult offenders in Washington State*, vol. 1 and 2. Olympia, WA, Employment Development Services Council.

Graffam, J., A. Shinkfield, and L. Hardcastle (2008). The perceived employability of ex-prisoners and offenders. *International Journal of Offender Therapy and Comparative Criminology* 52(6): 673–685.

Graffam, J., A. Shinkfield, B. Lavelle, and W. McPherson (2004). Variables affecting successful reintegration as perceived by offenders and professionals. *Journal of Offender Rehabilitation* 40(1/2): 147–171.

Grassian, S. (1983). Psychopathological effects of solitary confinement. *American Journal of Psychiatry* 140: 1450–1454.

Greenhouse, S. (2004). Abercrombie & Fitch: Bias case is settled. *New York Times,* November 17, p. 16.

Grella, C. E., and L. Greenwell (2006). Correlates of parental status and attitudes toward parenting among substance-abusing women offenders. *Prison Journal* 86(1): 89–113.

Grobsmith, E. S. (1989a). The relationship between substance abuse and crime among Native American inmates in the Nebraska Department of Corrections. *Human Organization* 48(4): 285–298.

———— (1989b). The impact of litigation on the religious revitalization of Native American inmates in the Nebraska Department of Corrections. *Plains Anthropologist* 32(1): 135–147.

Grobsmith, E. S., and J. Dam (1990). The revolving door: Substance abuse treatment and criminal sanctions for Native American offenders. *Journal of Substance Abuse* 2(4): 405–425.

Grubesic, T. H., A. T. Murray, and E. A. Mack (2011). Sex offenders, residence restrictions, housing, and urban morphology: A review and synthesis. *Cityscape: A Journal of Policy Development and Research* 13(3): 7–31.

Gunnison, E., and J. B. Helfgott (2007). Community corrections officers' perceptions of ex-offender reentry needs and challenges. *Journal of Police and Criminal Psychology* 22(1): 10–21.

———— (2011). Factors that hinder offender reentry success: A view from community corrections officers. *International Journal of Offender Therapy and Comparative Criminology* 55(2): 287–304.

Gunnison, E., and P. Mazerolle (2007). Desistance from serious and not so serious crime: A comparison of psychosocial risk factors. *Criminal Justice Studies* 20(3): 231–253.

Gunnison, E., and L. M. McCartan (2005). Female persisters in criminal offending: A theoretical examination of predictors. *Women and Criminal Justice* 1: 43–65.

Haigh, Y. (2009). Desistance from crime: Reflections on the transitional experiences of young people with a history of offending. *Journal of Youth Studies* 12(3): 307–322.

Haimowitz, S. (2004). Slowing the revolving door: Community reentry of offenders with mental illness. *Psychiatric Services* 55(4): 373–375.

Hamilton, Z., A. Kigerl, and Z. Hays (2013). Removing release impediments and reducing correctional costs: Evaluation of Washington State's housing voucher program. *Justice Quarterly* 30: 1–33.

Hammet, T. M., C. Roberts, and S. Kennedy (2001). Health-related issues in prisoner re-entry. *Crime and Delinquency* 47(3): 446–461.

Hammonds-White, S. E. (1989). Those who make it: A naturalistic inquiry into the reintegration experience of male and female offenders. PhD diss., Vanderbilt University. University Microfilms International (UMI No. 9006828).

Haney, C. (2003). Mental health issues in long-term solitary and "supermax" confinement. *Crime and Delinquency* 49: 124–156.

Hannon, L., and R. DeFina (2010). The state of the economy and the relationship between prison reentry and crime. *Social Problems* 57(4): 611–629.

Hanrahan, K., J. J. Gibbs, and S. E. Zimmerman (2005). Parole and revocation: Perspectives of young adult offenders. *Prison Journals* 85(3): 251–269.

Harcourt, B. E. (2006). From the asylum to the prison: Rethinking the incarceration revolution. *Texas Law Review* 84(7): 1751–1786.

Harding, A., and J. Harding. (2006). Inclusion and exclusion in the re-housing of former prisoners. *Probation Journal* 53(2): 137–153.

Hare, R. D., L. M. McPherson, and A. D. Forth (1988). Male psychopaths and their criminal careers. *Journal of Consulting and Clinical Psychology* 56(5): 710–714.

Harer, M. D. (1995). *Prison education program participation and recidivism: A test of the normalization hypothesis.* Washington, DC: Office of Research and Evaluation, Federal Bureau of Prisons.

Harlow, C. W. (1999). *Prior abuse reported by inmates and probationers.* Washington, DC: Office of Justice Programs, Bureau of Justice Statistics, US Department of Justice.

———. (2003). *Education and correctional populations.* Washington, DC: US Department of Justice, Bureau of Justice Statistics.

Harm, N. J., and S. D. Phillips (2001). You can't go home again: Women and criminal recidivism. *Journal of Offender Rehabilitation* 32: 3–21.

Harris, O., and R. Miller (2003). *Impacts of incarceration on the African American family.* New Brunswick, NJ: Transaction.

Harris, P. M., and K. S. Keller (2005). Ex-offenders need not apply: The criminal background check in hiring decisions. *Journal of Contemporary Criminal Justice* 21: 6–30.

Hattery, A. J., and E. Smith (2010). *Prisoner reentry and social capital: The long road to reintegration.* Lanham, MD: Lexington.

Heimer, K., and S. DeCoster (1999). The gendering of violent delinquency. *Criminology* 37(2): 277–317.

Heinrich, S. (2000). *Reducing recidivism through work: Barriers and opportunities for employment of ex-offenders.* Chicago: Great Cities Institute.

Helfgott, J. B. (1997). Ex-offender needs versus criminal opportunity in Seattle, Washington. *Federal Probation* 61: 12–24.

———. (2005). Restorative justice. In M. Bosworth (ed.), *Encyclopedia of prisons and correctional facilities.* Thousand Oaks, CA: Sage.

———. (2008). *Criminal behavior: Theories, typologies, and criminal behavior.* Thousand Oaks, CA: Sage.

Helfgott, J. B., and E. Gunnison (2008). The influence of social distance on community corrections officer perceptions of offender reentry needs. *Federal Probation* (June): 2–12.

Helfgott, J. B., M. L. Lovell, and C. F. Lawrence (2002). Citizens, victims, and offenders restoring justice: Accountability, healing, and hope through storytelling and dialogue. *Crime Victims Report* 6: 3–4.

Helfgott, J. B., M. L. Lovell, C. F. Lawrence, and W. H. Parsonage (2000). Results from the pilot study of the citizens, victims, and offenders restoring justice program at the Washington State Reformatory. *Journal of Contemporary Criminal Justice* 16: 5–31.

Helfgott, J. B., and B. M. Strah (2013). Actuarial prediction in determinate-plus sex offender release decisions. In J. B. Helfgott (ed.), *Criminal Psychology,* vol. 3. Santa Barbara, CA: Praeger, pp. 113–135.

Henderson, M., and D. Hanley (2006). Planning for quality: A strategy for reentry initiatives. *Western Criminology Review* 7(2): 62–78.

Henetz, P. (2003). Widow of cleared Smart kidnap suspect sues. *Seattle Times,* August 20. http://www.seattletimes.nwsource.com.

Henry, J. S., and J. B. Jacobs (2007). Ban the box to promote ex-offender employment. *Criminology and Public Policy* 6(4): 755–762.

Herivel, T., and P. Wright (2003). *Prison nation: The warehousing of America's poor.* New York: Routledge.

Herrschaft, B. A., B. M. Veysey, H. R. Tubman-Carbone, and C. Christian (2009). Gender differences in the transformation narrative: Implications for revised reentry strategies for female offenders. *Journal of Offender Rehabilitation* 48(6): 463–482.

Hightower, K. (2011). Anthony trial: Attorneys paint 2 sides of mother. *Seattle Times,* May 25. http://www.seattletimes.nwsource.com.

Hill, G. D., and E. M. Crawford (1990). Women, race, and crime. *Criminology* 28(4): 601–626.

Hindelang, M. J. (1973). Causes of delinquency: A partial replication and extension. *Social Problems* 20: 471–487.

Hing, B. O. (2005). Deporting our souls and defending our immigrants. *Amerasia Journal* 31(3): 11–32.

Hirsch, A. E., S. M. Dietrich, R. Landau, P. D. Schneider, I. Ackelsberg, J. Bernstein-Baker, and J. Hohenstein (2002). *Every door closed: Barriers facing parents with criminal records.* Washington, DC: Center for Law and Social Policy.

Hirschfield, P. J., and A. R. Piquero (2010). Normalization and legitimation: Modeling stigmatizing attitudes toward ex-offenders. *Criminology* 48: 27–55.

Hirschi, T. (1969). *Causes of delinquency.* Berkeley: University of California Press.

Hirschi, T., and M. Gottfredson (1983). Age and the explanation of crime. *American Journal of Sociology* 89: 552–584.

Hoffman, P. B. (2011). *History of the federal parole system.* Washington, DC: US Department of Justice.

Hollin, C. R. (2000). To treat or not to treat? A historical perspective. In C. R. Hollin (ed.), *Handbook of offender assessment and treatment.* Chichester, UK: Wiley, pp. 3–15.

Holzer, H. J. (1996). *What employers want: Job prospects for less-educated workers.* New York: Russell Sage Foundation.

Holzer, H. J., S. Raphael, and M. A. Stoll (2003). *Employer demand for ex-offenders: Recent evidence from Los Angeles.* Washington, DC: Urban Insititute.

Horney, J. (2006). An alternative psychology of criminal behavior. *Criminology* 44(1): 1–16.

Horney, J., D. W. Osgood, and I. H. Marshall (1995). Criminal careers in the short-term: Intra-individual variability in crime and its relation to local life circumstances. *American Sociological Review* 60: 655–673.

Huebner, A. J., and S. C. Betts (2002). Exploring the utility of social control theory for youth development: Issues of attachment, involvement and gender. *Youth and Society* 34(2): 123–145.

Hughes, T., and D. J. Wilson (2004). *Reentry trends in the United States.* Washington, DC: US Department of Justice, Bureau of Justice Statistics.

Hunt, J. W., J. E. Bowers, and N. Miller (1973). *Laws, licenses, and the offender's right to work: A study of state laws restricting the occupational licensing of former offenders.* Washington, DC: National Clearinghouse on Offender Employment Restrictions.

Inciardi, J. A. (1992). *The war on drugs II: The continuing epic of heroin, cocaine, crack, crime, AIDS, and the public policy.* Mountain View, CA: Mayfield.

Inciardi, J. A., S. S. Martin, and C. A. Butzin (2004). Five-year outcomes of therapeutic community treatment of drug-involved offenders after release from prison. *Crime and Delinquency* 50(1): 88–107.

Inciardi, J. A., S. S. Martin, C. A. Butzin, R. M. Hooper, and L. D. Harrison (1996). An effective model of prison-based treatment for drug-involved offenders. *Journal of Drug Issues* 27(2): 261–278.

Indeterminate Sentencing Review Board (2008). Access Washington. http://www.srb.wa.gov/index.shtml.

Irwin, J. (1970). *The felon*. Englewood Cliffs, NJ: Prentice-Hall.

James, D. J., and L. E. Glaze (2006). *Mental health problems of prison and jail inmates*. Washington, DC: US Department of Justice, Bureau of Justice Statistics.

Jancic, M. (1998). Does correctional education have an effect on recidivism? *Journal of Offender Rehabilitaion* 49(4): 152–161.

Jannetta, J., H. Dodd, and B. Elderbroom (2011). *The elected official's toolkit for jail reentry*. Washington, DC: Urban Institute.

Jensen, E. L., and G. E. Reed (2007). Adult correctional education programs: An update on the current status based on recent studies. *Journal of Offender Rehabilitation* 44(1): 81–98.

Johnson, G. (2009). Family of Amanda Knox vows to continue the fight. *Seattle Times,* December 4. http://www.seattletimes.nwsource.com.

Kaifi, B. A., W. Aslami, S. A. Noori, and D. Korhummel (2011). A decade after the 9/11 attacks: The demand for leaders with emotional intelligence and counseling skills. *Journal of Business Studies Quarterly* 2(2): 54–67.

Kaplan, M. S., and A. Green (1995). Incarcerated female sexual offenders: A comparison of sexual histories with eleven female nonsexual offenders. *Sexual Abuse: A Journal of Research and Treatment* 7(4): 287–300.

Karstedt, S. (2000). Emancipation, crime and problem behavior of women: A perspective from Germany. *Gender Issues* 18(3): 21–58.

Kellett, N. C., and C. E. Willging (2011). Pedagogy of individual choice and female inmate reentry in the US Southwest. *International Journal of Law and Psychiatry* 34(4): 256–263.

Kelly, C. E., and J. J. Fader (2012). Computer-based employment applications: Implications for offenders and supervising officers. *Federal Probation* 76(1): 14–18.

Kenemore, T. K., and I. Roldan (2006). Staying straight: Lessons from ex-offenders. *Clinical Social Work Journal* 34(1): 5–21.

Kilpatrick, D. G., R. Acierno, B. E. Saunders, H. S. Resnick, C. L. Best, and P. Schnurr (2000). Risk factors for adolescent substance abuse and dependence: Data from a national sample. *Journal of Consulting and Clinical Psychology* 68: 19–30.

Kirk, D. S. (2009). A natural experiment on residential change and recidivism: Lessons from Hurricane Katrina. *American Sociological Review* 74(3): 484–505.

———. (2012). Residential change as a turning point in the life course of crime: Desistance or temporary cessation. *Criminology* 50(2): 329–358.

Koban, L. A. (1983). Parents in prison: A comparative analysis of the effects of incarceration on the families of men and women. *Research in Law, Deviance, and Social Control* 5: 171–183.

Kondo, L. L. (2000). Therapeutic jurisprudence. Issues, analysis and applications: Advocacy of the establishment of mental health specialty courts in the provision of therapeutic justice for mentally ill offenders. *Seattle University Law Review* 24: 373–464.

Koons, B. A., J. D. Burrow, M. Morash, and T. Bynum (1997). Expert and offender perceptions of program elements linked to successful outcomes for incarcerated women. *Crime and Delinquency* 43: 512–532.

Koons-Witt, B. A., and P. J. Schram (2003). The prevalence and nature of violent offending by females. *Journal of Criminal Justice* 31(4): 361–371.

Koss, M. P., N. P. Yuan, D. Dightman, R. J. Prince, M. Polacca, B. Sanderson, and D. Goldman (2003). Adverse childhood exposures and alcohol dependence among seven Native American tribes. *American Journal of Preventative Medicine* 25(3): 238–244.

Krajick, K. (1983). Abolishing parole: An idea whose time has passed. *Corrections Magazine* 9(3): 33–40.

Kubrin, C. E., and E. A. Stewart (2006). Predicting who reoffends: The neglected role of neighborhood context in recidivism studies. *Criminology* 44: 165–197.

Kurlycheck, M. C., S. D. Bushway, and S. Brame (2012). Long-term crime desistance and recidivism patterns—Evidence from the Essex County Convicted Felon Study. *Criminology* 50(1): 71–103.

Kusuda, P. (1976). *1974 probation and parole terminations.* Madison: Wisconsin Corrections Division.

La Ganga, M. L., and S. Goldmacher (2010). Jaycee Lee Dugard's family will receive $20 million from California. *Los Angeles Times,* July 2. http://articles.latimes.com.

LaGrange, T. C., and R. A. Silverman (1999). Low self-control and opportunity: Testing the general theory of crime as an explanation for gender differences in delinquency. *Criminology* 37: 41–72.

Lamarine, R. J. (1988). Alcohol abuse among Native Americans. *Journal of Community Health* 13(3): 143–155.

Landenberger, N., and M. Lipsey (2005). The positive effectives of cognitive-behavioral programs for offenders: A meta-analysis of factors associated with effective treatment. *Journal of Experimental Criminology* 1(4): 451–476.

Landis, J. R., J. D. Mercer, and C. E. Wolff (1969). Success and failure of adult probationers in California. *Journal of Research in Crime and Delinquency* 6: 34–40.

Langan, P., and M. A. Cunniff (1992). *Recidivism of felons on probation, 1986–1989.* Washington, DC: US Department of Justice, Bureau of Justice Statistics.

Langan, P. A., and D. J. Levin (2002). *Recidivism of prisoners released in 1994.* Washington, DC: US Department of Justice, Bureau of Justice Statistics.

Lansford, J. E., K. A. Dodge, G. S. Pettit, J. E. Bates, J. Crozier, and J. Kaplow (2002). A 12-year prospective study of the long-term effects of early child physical maltreatment on psychological, behavioral, and academic problems in adolescence. *Archives of Pediatrics and Adolescent Medicine* 156: 824–830.

Lansford, J. E., S. Miller-Johnson, L. J. Berlin, K. A. Dodge, J. E. Bates, and G. S. Pettit (2007). Early physical abuse and later violent delinquency: A prospective longitudinal study. *Child Maltreatment* 12 (3): 233–245.

Latessa, E. J. (2012). Why work is important and how to improve the effectiveness of correctional reentry programs that target employment. *Criminology and Public Policy* 11(1): 87–91.

Latessa, E. J., and P. Smith (2011). *Corrections in the community,* 4th ed. Cincinnati, OH: Anderson.

Lattimore, P. K. (2008). *SVORI programs: Positive impacts in housing, employment, and substance abuse.* Washington, DC: White House Faith-Based and Community Initiative National Conference on Research and Evaluation.

Lattimore, P. K., S. Brumbaugh, C. Visher, C. H. Lindquist, L. Winterfield, M. Salas, and J. Zweig (2004). *National portrait of the serious and violent offender reentry initiative.* Research Triangle Park, NC: Research Triangle Institute.

Lattimore, P. K., and C. Visher (2009). *The multi-site evaluation of SVORI: Summary and synthesis.* Research Triangle Park, NC: Research Triangle Institute.

Lattimore, P. K., C. A. Visher, L. Winterfield, C. H. Lindquist, and S. Brumbaugh (2005). Implementation of prisoner reentry programs: Findings from the serious and violent offender reentry initiative multi-site evaluation. *Justice Research and Policy* 7: 87–109.

Laub, J. H., and R. J. Sampson (1993). Turning points in the life course: Why change matters in the study of crime. *Criminology* 31(3): 301–325.

———. (2001). Understanding desistance from crime. *Crime and Justice* 28: 1–70.

———. (2003). *Shared beginnings, divergent lives: Delinquent boys to age 70.* Cambridge, MA: Harvard University Press.

La Vigne, N. (2010). Female D.C. code felons: Unique challenges in prison and at home. Testimony to the House of Representatives Oversight and Government Reform Subcommittee on Federal Workforce, Postal Service, and the District of Columbia, July 27.

La Vigne, N., C. Visher, and J. Castro (2004). *Chicago prisoners' experiences returning home.* Washington, DC: Urban Institute.

LeBel, T. P. (2012). "If one doesn't get you another one will": Formerly incarcerated persons' perceptions of discrimination. *Prison Journal* 92(1): 63–87.

Leff, L. (2011). Sentencing set for couple that held woman 18 years. *Seattle Times,* June 2. http://www.seattletimes.nwsource.com.

Leung, R. (2009). The look of Abercrombie and Fitch. CBS News, February 11. http://www.cbsnews.com.

Levenson, J. S., and A. L. Hern (2007). Sex offender residence restrictions: Unintended consequences and community reentry. *Justice Research and Policy* 9(1): 59–73.

Levenson, J. S., and R. Tewksbury (2009). Collateral damage: Family members of registered sex offenders. *American Journal of Criminal Justice* 34: 54–68.

Leverentz, A. M. (2006a). *People, places, and things: The social process.* Washington, DC: US Department of Justice.

———. (2006b). The love of a good man? Romantic relationships as a source of support or hindrance for female ex-offenders. *Journal of Research in Crime and Delinquency* 43(4): 459–488.

———. (2010). People, places, and things: How female ex-prisoners negotiate their neighborhood context. *Journal of Contemporary Ethnography* 39(6) 646–681.

Lewis, B. F., and R. Ross (1994). Retention in therapeutic communities: Challenges for the nineties. In F. M. Tims, G. De Leon, and N. Jainchill (eds.), *Therapeutic community: Advances in research and application.* Washington, DC: US Government Printing Office, pp. 99–116.

Lin, N. (2000). Inequality in social capital. *Contemporary Sociology* 29(6): 785–795.

Listwan, S. J., F. T. Cullen, and E. J. Latessa (2006). How to prevent prisoner reentry programs from failing: Insights from evidence-based corrections. *Federal Probation* 70(3): 19–25.

LoBianco, T., and T. Coyne (2011). Mother of slain girl worried about neighbors in trailer park. *Chicago Tribune,* December 28. http://www.chicagotribune.com.

Lockwood, S., J. M. Nally, T. Ho, and K. Knutson (2012). The effect of correctional education on postrelease employment and recidivism: A 5-year follow-up study in the state of Indiana. *Crime and Delinquency* 58(3): 380–396.

Lombroso, C. (1876). l'Homme criminel (*The criminal man*). Milan: Hoepli.

———. (1911). *Criminal man.* New York: Knickerbocker.

Lombroso, C., and W. Ferrero (1895). *The female offender.* New York: D. Appleton.

Lopez, M. H., and M. T. Light (2009). *A rising share: Hispanics and federal crime.* Washington, DC: Pew Hispanic Center.

Lucken, K., and L. M. Ponte (2008). A just measure of forgiveness: Reforming occupational licensing regulations for ex-offenders using BFOQ analysis. *Law and Policy* 30(1): 46–72.

Lui, M., B. Robles, B. Leondar-Wright, R. Brewer, R. Adamson (2006). *The color of wealth: The story behind the US racial wealth divide.* New York: New Press.

Lurigio, A. J. (1996). Responding to the mentally ill on probation and parole: Recommendations and action plans. In A. J. Lurigio (ed.), *Community corrections in America: New directions and sounder investments for persons with mental illness and codisorders.* Seattle, WA: National Coalition for Mental and Substance Abuse Health Care in the Justice System, pp. 166–171.

Lurigio, A. J., A. Rollins, and J. Fallon (2004). The effects of serious mental illness on offender reentry. *Federal Probation* 68(2): 45–52.

Lurigio, A. J., and J. A. Swartz (2000). *Changing contours of the criminal justice system to meet the needs of persons with serious mental illness.* Washington, DC: National Institute of Justice.

Luster, T., and S. A. Small (1997). Sexual abuse history and problems in adolescence: Exploring effects of moderating variables. *Journal of Marriage and the Family* 59: 131–142.

MacCoun, R. J., and P. Reuter (2001). *Drug war heresies: Learning from other vices, times, and places.* New York: Cambridge University Press.

Maher, L. (1997). *Sexed work: Gender, race and resistance in a Brooklyn drug market.* Oxford, UK: Clarendon.

Maher, L., and R. Curtis (1992). Women on the edge of crime: Crack cocaine and the changing context of street-level sex work in New York City. *Crime, Law, and Social Change* 18: 221–258.

Mail, P. D., S. Heurtin-Roberts, S. E. Martin, and J. Howard (2002). *Alcohol use among American Indians: Multiple perspectives on a complex problem.*

Bethesda, MD: National Institute on Alcohol Abuse and Alcoholism, National Institutes of Health.

Mallik-Kane, K., and C. A. Visher (2008). *Health and prisoner reentry: How physical, mental, and substance abuse conditions shape the process of reintegration.* Washington, DC: Urban Institute.

Maltz, M. D., and J. M. Mullany (2000). Visualizing lives: New pathways for analyzing life course trajectories. *Journal of Quantitative Criminology* 16(2): 255–281.

Mapson, A. (2013). From prison to parenting. *Journal of Human Behavior in the Social Environment* 23(2): 171–177.

Marcenko, M. O., and M. I. Striepe (1997). A look at family reunification through the eyes of mothers. *Community Alternatives* 9(1): 33–48.

Marsh, B. (2009). *A decade of desistance: An exploratory study in desistance theory.* PhD diss., Dublin Institute of Technology.

Martin, L. L. (2011). Debt to society: Asset poverty and prisoner reentry. *Review of Black Political Economy* 38(2): 131–143.

Martin, S. S., C. A. Butzin, and J. A. Inciardi (1995). Assessment of a multistage therapeutic community for drug-involved offenders. *Journal of Psychoactive Drugs* 27(1): 109–116.

Martin, Y. (2008). ¿Y ahora qué'? New York City Latino/as coping mechanisms: Prison reentry and recidivism. *Latino Studies* 6: 220–228.

Martinez, D. J. (2004). Felony disenfranchisement and voting participation: Considerations in Latino ex-prisoner reentry. *Columbia Human Rights Law Review* 36(1): 217–240.

———. (2007). Informal helping mechanisms: Conceptual issues in family support of reentry of former prisoners. *Journal of Offender Rehabilitation* 44(1): 23–37.

Martinez, D. J., and J. Christian (2009). The familial relationships of former prisoners: Examining the link between residence and informal support mechanisms. *Journal of Contemporary Ethnography* 38(2): 201–224.

Martinson, R. (1974). What works? Questions and answers about prison reform. *The Public Interest* 35: 22–54.

———. (1979) New findings, new views: A note of caution regarding sentencing reform. *Hofstra Law Review* 7(2): 243–258.

Maruna, S. (2001). *Making good: How ex-convicts reform and rebuild their lives.* Washington, DC: American Psychological Association.

Maruschak, L. M., and E. Parks (2012). *Probation and parole in the United States, 2011.* Washington, DC: US Department of Justice, Bureau of Justice Statistics.

Matsuama, K., and L. Prell (2011). Education, employment, and offender reentry. *Corrections Today* (August): 90–91.

Maume, M. O., G. C. Ousey, and K. Beaver (2005). Cutting the grass: A reexamination of the link between marital attachment, delinquent peers and desistance from marijuana use. *Journal of Quantitative Criminology* 21: 27–53.

McCall, N. (1994). *Makes me wanna holler: A young black man in America.* New York: Random House.

McCarthy, B., and R. Langworthy (1987). *Older offenders: Perspectives in criminology and criminal justice.* New York: Praeger.

McCartney, A. (2011). Judge: Lohan needs to speed up community service. *Seattle Times,* July 21. http://www.seattletimes.nwsource.com.

McClam, E. (2004). Martha Stewart ready for prison. *Seattle Times,* September 16. http://www.seattletimes.nwsource.com.

McClanahan, S. F., G. M. McClelland, K. M. Abram, and L. A. Teplin (1999). Pathways into prostitution among female jail detainees and their implications for mental health services. *Psychiatric Services* 50: 1606–1613.

McCollister, K. E., M. T. French, M. Prendergast, H. Wexler, S. Sacks, and E. Hall (2003). Is in-prison treatment enough? A cost-effectiveness analysis of prison-based treatment and aftercare services for substance abusing offenders. *Law and Policy* 25(1): 62–83.

McCormick, C. T., and Y. M. Perret (2010). Assessing public benefits: More advocacy than entitlement. In H. A. Dlugacz (ed.), *Reentry planning for offenders with mental disorders: Policy and practice.* Kingston, NJ: Civic Research Institute, pp. 3-1–3-21.

McGuigan, W. M., and W. Middlemiss (2005). Sexual abuse in childhood and interpersonal violence in adulthood: A cumulative impact on depressive symptoms in women. *Journal of Interpersonal Violence* 20: 1271–1287.

McGuire, J., and R. Hatcher (2001). Offense-focused problem-solving: Preliminary evaluation of a cognitive skills program. *Criminal Justice and Behavior* 28: 564–587.

McKean, L., and J. Raphael (2002). *Drugs, crime, and consequences: Arrests and incarceration in North Lawndale.* Chicago: Center for Impact Research.

McKendrick, K., C. Sullivan, S. Banks, and S. Sacks (2006). Modified therapeutic community treatment for offenders with MICA disorders: Antisocial personality disorder and treatment outcomes. *Journal of Offender Rehabilitation* 44(2/3): 133–159.

McLean, R., and M. D. Thompson (2007). *Repaying debts.* New York: Bureau of Justice Assistance.

McRoberts, O. M. (2002). *Religion, reform, community: Examining the idea of church-based prisoner reentry.* Washington, DC: Urban Institute.

Mele, C., and T. Miller (2005). *Civil penalties, social consequences.* New York: Routledge.

Mercado, C. C., S. Alvarez, and J. Levenson (2008). The impact of specialized sex offender legislation on community reentry. *Sexual Abuse: Journal of Research and Treatment* 20(2): 188–205.

Merton, R. K. (1938). Social structure and anomie. *American Sociological Review* 3(5): 672–682.

Michalsen, V. (2011). Mothering as a life course transition: Do women go straight for their children? *Journal of Offender Rehabilitation* 50: 349–366.

Miller, B. A., and W. R. Downs (1993). The impact of family violence on the use of alcohol by women. *Alcohol Health and Research World* 17: 137–142.

Miller, H., and G. Young (1997). Prison segregation: Administrative detention remedy or mental health problem? *Criminal Behaviour and Mental Health* 7: 85–94.

Miller, H. V., and J. M. Miller (2010). Community in-reach through jail reentry: Findings from a quasi-experimental design. *Justice Quarterly* 27(6): 893–910.

Miller, M., and I. Ngugi (2009). *Impacts of housing supports: Persons with mental illness and ex-offenders.* Olympia: Washington State Institute for Public Policy.

Minton, T. D. (2013). *Jail inmates at mid-year 2012: Statistical tables.* Washington, DC: Bureau of Justice Statistics, US Department of Justice.

———. (2011). *Jails in Indian country, 2009.* Washington, DC: US Department of Justice, Bureau of Justice Statistics.

Mischowitz, R. (1994). Desistance from a delinquent way of life? In E. G. M. Weitekamp and H. J. Kerner (eds.), *Cross-national longitudinal research on human development and criminal behavior.* Dordrecht, Netherlands: Kluwer Academic, pp. 303–327.

Moffitt, T. E. (1993). Adolescence-limited and life-course-persistent antisocial behavior: A developmental taxonomy. *Psychological Review* 100(4): 674–701.

Moran, D. (2012). Prisoner reintegration and the stigma of prison time inscribed on the body. *Punishment and Society* 14: 564–583.

Morani, N. M., N. Wikoff, D. M. Linhorst, and S. Bratton (2011). A description of the self-identified needs, service expenditures, and social outcomes of participants of a prisoner-reentry program. *Prison Journal* 91(3): 347–365.

Morgan, K. (1991). *An analysis of factors influencing probation outcome.* PhD diss. Florida State University.

Morin, J. L. (2005). *Latino/a rights and justice in the United States: Perspectives and approaches.* Durham, NC: Carolina Academic Press.

———. (2008). Latinas/os and US prisons: Trends and challenges. *Latino Studies* 6: 11–34.

Moster, A., D. W. Wnuk, and E. L. Jeglic (2008). Cognitive behavioral therapy interventions with sex offenders. *Journal of Correctional Health Care* 14(2): 109–121.

Motivans, M. (2011). *Federal justice statistics, 2009.* Washington, DC: US Department of Justice, Bureau of Justice Statistics.

Mukamal, D. A. (2000). Confronting the employment barriers of criminal records: Effective legal and practical strategies. *Journal of Poverty Law and Policy* (January–February): 597–606.

Mumola, C. (2000). *Incarcerated parents and their children.* Washington, DC: US Department of Justice.

Myers, J., B. Zack, K. Kramer, M. Gardner, G. Rucobo, and S. Costa-Taylor (2005). Get connected: An HIV prevention case management program for men and women leaving California prisons. *American Journal of Public Health* 95(10): 1682–1684.

Nagin, D., and J. Waldfogel (1998). The effect of conviction on income through the life cycle. *International Review of Law and Economics* 18: 25–40.

Nakhaie, M. R., R. A. Silverman, and T. C. LaGrange (2000). Self-control and social control: An examination of gender, ethnicity, class and delinquency. *Canadian Journal of Sociology* 25(1): 35–59.

Naser, R. L., and N. G. La Vigne (2006). Family support in the prisoner reentry process: Expectations and realities. *Journal of Offender Rehabilitation* 43(1): 93–106.

Naser, R. L., and C. A. Visher (2006). Family members' experiences with incarceration and reentry. *Western Criminology Review* 7(2): 20–31.

National Alliance on Mental Illness (2008). *A guide to mental illness and the criminal justice system.* Arlington, VA: National Alliance on Mental Illness, Department of Policy and Legal Affairs. http://www.nami.org.

National Association of State Mental Health Program Directors Research Institute. (2000). *Closing and reorganizing state psychiatric hospitals: 2000.*

Arlington, VA: National Association of State Mental Health Program Directors Research Institute.

National HIRE Network. (2012) *About us.* http://hirenetwork.org.

National Institute for Literacy. (2001). *Fact sheet: Correctional education.* http://www.nifl.gov/newworld/correct.htm.

National Reentry Resource Center. (2012). *About the National Reentry Resource Center.* http://www.nationalreentryresourcecenter.org.

Nelson, M., P. Deess, and C. Allen (1999). *The first month out: Post-incarceration experiences in New York City.* New York: Vera Institute of Justice.

Northern California Service League (2012). *Job placement and job fairs.* http://www.norcalserviceleague.org.

Ogden, S. (2004). Ex-prisoner Pomo woman speaks out. *Social Justice* 31(4): 63–69.

Oh, A. E., and K. Umemoto (2005). Asian Americans and Pacific Islanders: From incarceration to re-entry. *Amerasia Journal* 31(3): 43–59.

Oliver, W., and C. F. Hairston (2008). Intimate partner violence during the transition from prison to the community: Perspectives of incarcerated African-Americans. *Journal of Aggression, Maltreatment, and Trauma* 16(3): 258–276.

Olson, D. E., M. Alderden, and A. J. Lurigio (2003). Men are from Mars, women are from Venus, but what role does gender play in probation recidivism? *Justice Research and Policy* 5(2): 33–54.

Osher, F., H. J. Steadman, and H. Barr (2003). A best practice approach to community reentry from jails for inmates with co-occurring disorders: The Apic model. *Crime and Delinquency* 49: 79–96.

Owen, B. (1998). *In the mix: Struggle and survival in a women's prison.* Albany: State University of New York Press.

Pager, D. (2007). *Marked: Race, crime, and finding work in an era of mass incarceration.* Chicago: University of Chicago Press.

PAO recognizes academic achievement. (2012). *Prosecutor's Post* 5(4): n.p.

Parsons, M. L., and C. Warner-Robbins (2002). Factors that support women's successful transition to the community following jail/prison. *Health Care for Women International* 23(1): 6–18.

Patterson, G. T. (2013). Prisoner reentry: A public health or public safety issue for social work practice? *Social Work in Public Health* 28: 129–141.

Patterson, G. R., and T. J. Dishion (1985). Contributions of families and peers to delinquency. *Criminology* 23: 63–78.

Paylor, I. (1995). *Housing needs of ex-offenders.* Aldershot, UK: Avebury.

Pearson, F. S., and D. S. Lipton (1999). A meta-analytic review of the effectiveness of corrections-based treatments for drug abuse. *Prison Journal* 79(4): 384–410.

Perez, A., S. Leifman, and A. Estrada (2003). Reversing the criminalization of mental illness. *Crime and Delinquency* 49: 62–78.

Peters, R. H., and H. A. Hills (1993). Inmates with co-occurring substance abuse and mental health disorders. In H. J. Steadman and J. J. Cocozza (eds.), *Providing services for offenders with mental illness and related disorders in prisons.* Washington, DC: National Coalition for the Mentally Ill in the Criminal Justice System, pp. 159–212.

Petersilia, J. (2001a). Prisoner reentry: Public safety and reintegration challenges. *Prison Journal* 81(3): 360–375.

————. (2001b). When prisoners return to communities: Political, economic, and social consequences. *Federal Probation* 65(1): 3–8.

————. (2003). *When prisoners come home: Parole and prisoner reentry.* New York: Oxford University Press.

————. (2005). Meeting the challenges of prisoner reentry. In *What works and why: Effective approaches to reentry.* East Peoria, IL: Versa Press, pp. 175–192.

Petras, H., P. Nieuwbeerta, and A. Piquero (2010). Participation and frequency during criminal careers across the life span. *Criminology* 48: 607–637.

Petrila, J., M. S. Ridgely, and R. Borum (2003). Debating outpatient commitment: Controversy, trends, and empirical data. *Crime and Delinquency* 49: 157–172.

Pettiway, L. (1987). Participation in crime partnerships by female drug users. *Criminology* 25: 741–767.

Phillips, L. A., and M. Lindsay (2011). Prison to society: A mixed methods analysis of coping with reentry. *International Journal of Offender Therapy and Comparative Criminology* 55(1): 136–154.

Pinard, M., and A. C. Thompson (2006). Offender reentry and the collateral consequences of criminal convictions: An introduction. *NYU Review of Law and Social Change* 30: 585–620.

Piquero, A., and P. J. Mazerolle (2001). *Life course criminology: Contemporary and classic readings.* Belmont, CA: Wadsworth.

Pogorzelski, W., N. Wolff, K. Pan, and C. L. Blitz (2005). Behavioral health problems, ex-offender reentry policies, and the "Second Chance Act." *American Journal of Public Health* 95(10): 1718–1724.

Pollak, O. (1950). *The criminality of women.* Philadelphia: University of Pennsylvania Press.

Pollock, J. M. (2002). *Women, prison, and crime.* Belmont, CA: Wadsworth.

Portes, A. (1998). Social capital: Its origins and applications in modern sociology. *Annual Review of Sociology* 24: 1–24.

Prendergast, M., J. Wellisch, and M. Wong (1996). Residential treatment for women parolees following prison drug treatment: Treatment experiences, needs and services, outcomes. *Prison Journal* 76(3): 253–274.

Price, J. H. (2002). Muslims struggle with an image: Focus on Islam after attacks led to mixed perceptions. *Washington Times,* September 10, p. A1.

Queralt, M. (1996). *The social environment and human behavior: A diversity perspective.* Needham Heights, MA: Allyn and Bacon.

Raine, A. (1993). *The psychopathology of crime: Criminal behavior as a clinical disorder.* San Diego, CA: Academic Press.

Rainey, Y. (2001). *Dear lover.* Las Vegas, NV: Beginning II End.

Rally in Alexandria to celebrate ex-offenders' success stories. (February 28, 2012). *The Town Talk.* http://www.thetowntalk.com.

Raynor, P., and M. Vanstone (1996). Reasoning and rehabilitation in Britain: The results of the Straight Thinking on Probation (STOP) programme. *Journal of Offender Therapy and Comparative Criminology* 40: 272–284.

Reckless, W. C. (1961). A new theory of delinquency and crime. *Federal Probation* 25: 42–46.

Reentry Policy Council. (2011). *Second Chance Act.* Lexington, KY: Justice Center, Council of State Governments. http://reentrypolicy.org.

Reinemann, D. H., K. D. Stark, and S. M. Swearer (2003). Family factors that differentiate sexually abused and nonabused adolescent psychiatric inpatients. *Journal of Interpersonal Violence* 18: 471–489.

Reisig, M. D., K. Holtfreter, and M. Morash (2002). Social capital among women offenders: Examining the distribution of social networks and resources. *Journal of Contemporary Criminal Justice* 18(2): 167–187.

Renner, J. (1978). *The adult probationer in Ontario.* Ontario, Canada: Ontario Correctional Services Ministry.

Restorative Justice Ministry Network of Texas (2011). *Faith based ex-offender celebration: Continuing to grow in faith, family, and community.* Huntsville, TX: Restorative Justice Ministry Network. http://rjmntexas.net.

Richie, B. E. (2001). Challenges incarcerated women face as they return to their communities: Findings from life history interviews. *Crime and Delinquency* 47: 368–389.

Robbins, C. A., S. S. Martin, and H. L. Surratt (2007). Substance abuse treatment, anticipated maternal roles and reentry success of drug-involved women prisoners. *Crime and Delinquency* 55: 388–411.

Roberts, R. L., and R. Harper (1997). The effects of the fresh start program on Native American parolees' job placement. *Journal of Employment Counseling* 34: 115–123.

Robin, R. W., B. Chester, J. K. Rasmussen, J. M. Jaranson, and D. Goldman (1997). Prevalence, characteristics, and impact of childhood sexual abuse in a southwestern American Indian tribe. *Child Abuse and Neglect* 21: 769–787.

Rodriguez, N., and B. Brown (2003). *Preventing homelessness among people leaving prison.* New York: Vera Institute of Justice.

Roman, C. G., and J. Travis (2006). Where will I sleep tomorrow? Housing, homelessness, and the returning prisoner. *Housing Policy Debate* 17(3): 389–418.

Romano, E., and R. V. De Luca (2000). Male sexual abuse: A review of effects, abuse characteristics, and links with later psychological functioning. *Aggression and Violent Behavior* 6: 55–78.

Rothenberg, P. S. (2010). *Race, class, and gender in the United States.* New York: Worth.

Rounsaville, B. J., M. M. Weissman, H. Kleber, and C. H. Wilber (1982). Heterogeneity of psychiatric diagnosis in untreated opiate addicts. *Archives of General Psychiatry* 39: 161–168.

Salaam, Y. (2006). Muslim leaders discuss effective re-entry initiatives for formerly incarcerated. *Amsterdam News,* August 31, https://nycma.fcny .org.

Sampson, R. J., and J. H. Laub (1992). Crime and deviance in the life course. *Annual Review of Sociology* 18: 63–84.

———. (1993). *Crime in the making: Pathways and turning points through life.* Cambridge, MA: Harvard University Press.

Sampson, R. J., and W. J. Wilson (1995). Toward a theory of race, crime, and urban inequality. In J. Hagan and R. D. Peterson (eds.), *Crime and inequality.* Stanford, CA: Stanford University Press, pp. 37–54.

Saunders, B. E., D. G. Kilpatrick, R. F. Hanson, H. S. Resnick, and M. E. Walker. (1999). Prevalence, case characteristics, and long-term psychological correlates of child rape among women: A national survey. *Child Maltreatment* 4: 187–200.

Saylor, W. G., and G. G. Gaes (1992). *PREP study links UNICOR work experience with successful post-release outcome*. Washington, DC: US Federal
Bureau of Prisons.

Schmitt, J., and K. Warner (2010). *Ex-offenders and the labor market*. Washington, DC: Center for Economic and Policy Research.

Schroeder, R. D., and J. F. Frana (2009). Spirituality and religion, emotional
coping, and criminal desistance: A qualitative study of men undergoing
change. *Sociological Spectrum* 29: 718–741.

Schumacker, R. E., D. B. Anderson, and S. L. Anderson (1990). Vocational and
academic indicators of parole success. *Journal of Correctional Education*
41(1): 8–12.

Scott-Hayward, C. S. (2009). *The fiscal crisis in corrections: Rethinking policies and practices*. New York: Vera Institute of Justice.

Scroggins, J. R., and S. Malley (2010). Reentry and the (unmet) needs of
women. *Journal of Offender Rehabilitation* 49: 146–163.

Seeman, T. E., and B. McEwen (1996). Impact of social environment characteristics on neuroendocrine regulation. *Psychosomatic Medicine* 59: 459–471.

Seiter, R., and K. Kadela (2003). Prisoner reentry: What works, what does not,
and what is promising. *Crime and Delinquency* 49(3): 360–388.

Serin, R. C., and C. D. Lloyd (2009). Examining the process of offender
change: The transition to crime desistance. *Psychology, Crime, and Law*
15(4): 347–364.

Settles, T. (2009). Restorative reentry: A strategy to improve reentry outcomes
by enhancing social capital. *Victims and Offenders* 4: 285–302.

Shapiro, C., and M. Schwartz (2001). Coming home: Building on family connections. *Corrections Management Quarterly* 5(3): 52–61.

Shaw, C. R., and H. McKay (1938). *Juvenile delinquency and urban areas*.
Chicago: University of Chicago Press.

———. (1972). *Juvenile delinquency and urban areas: A study of rates of
delinquency in relation to differential characteristics of local communities
in American cities*. Chicago: University of Chicago Press.

Shekarkhar, Z., and C. L. Gibson (2011). Gender, self-control, and offending
behaviors among Latino youth. *Journal of Contemporary Criminal Justice*
27: 63–80.

Shepherd, J. (2002). Police, prosecutors, criminals, and determinate sentencing:
The truth about truth-in-sentencing laws. *Journal of Law and Economics*
45: 509–534.

Shivy, V. A., J. J. Wu, A. E. Moon, S. C. Mann, J. G. Holland, and C. Eacho
(2007). Ex-offenders reentering the workforce. *Journal of Counseling Psychology* 54(4): 466–473.

Shover, N. (1996). *Great pretenders: Pursuits and careers of persistent thieves*.
Boulder, CO: Westview.

Siegel, J. A., and L. M. Williams (2003). The relationship between childhood
sexual abuse and female delinquency and crime: A prospective study. *Journal of Research in Crime and Delinquency* 40(1): 71–94.

Silbert, M. H., and A. M. Pines (1981). Sexual abuse as an antecedent to prostitution. *Child Abuse and Neglect* 5: 407–411.

Silva, C. (2010). DA: Paris Hilton to avoid felony in Vegas arrest. *Seattle
Times,* September 17. http://www.seattletimes.nwsource.com.

Silverman, J. R., and R. M. Caldwell (2008). Peer relationships and violence
among female juvenile offenders: An exploration of differences among

four racial/ethnic populations. *Criminal Justice and Behavior* 35(3): 333–343.

Simons, R. L., and L. B. Whitbeck (1991). Sexual abuse as a precursor to prostitution and victimization among adolescent and homeless women. *Journal of Family Issues* 12: 361–379.

Simpson, D. D., G. W. Joe, and B. S. Brown. (1997). Treatment retention and follow-up outcomes in the Drug Abuse Treatment Outcome Study (DATOS). *Psychology of Addictive Behaviors* 11: 294–307.

Simpson, D. D., G. W. Joe, B. W. Fletcher, R. L. Hubbard, and M. D. Anglin (1999). A national evaluation of treatment outcomes for cocaine dependence. *Archives of General Psychiatry* 56: 507–514.

Smart, C. (1977). *Women, crime and criminology.* London: Routledge and Kegan Paul.

Smith, D. A., and R. Paternoster (1987). The gender gap in theories of deviance: Issues and evidence. *Journal of Research in Crime and Delinquency* 24: 140–172.

Smith, E., and A. Hattery (2011). Can social capital networks assist re-entry felons to overcome barriers to re-entry and reduce recidivism? *Sociation Today* 9(1). http://www.ncsociology.org.

Solomon, A. L., C. Gouvis, and M. Waul (2001). *Summary of focus group with ex-prisoners in the district: Ingredients for successful reintegration.* Washington, DC: Urban Institute.

Solomon, A. L., J. W. L. Osborne, S. F. LoBuglio, J. Mellow, and D. A. Mukamal (2008). *Life after lockup: Improving reentry from jail to the community.* Washington, DC: Urban Institute.

Sommers, I., and D. R. Baskin (1993). The situational context of violent female offending. *Journal of Research in Crime and Delinquency* 30(2): 136–162.

Sommers, I., D. R. Baskin, and F. Fagan (1994). Getting out of the life: Desistance by female street offenders. *Deviant Behavior* 15(2): 125–149.

Spjeldnes, S., and S. Goodkind (2009). Gender differences and offender reentry: A review of the literature. *Journal of Offender Rehabilitation* 48: 314–335.

Starr, R. (2002). A successful reintegration into the community: One NGRI acquittee's story. *Federal Probation* 66: 59–63.

Staton, M., C. Leukefeld, and J. M. Webster (2003). Substance use, health, and mental health: Problems and service utilization among incarcerated women. *International Journal of Offender Therapy and Comparative Criminology* 47: 224–239.

Steffensmeier, D. J., and E. Haynie (2000). Gender, structural disadvantage, and urban crime. *Criminology* 38: 403–438.

Steffensmeier, D. J., and J. H. Kramer (1980). The differential impact of criminal stigmatization on male and female felons. *Sex Roles* 6: 1–8.

Steketee, M., M. Junger, and J. Junger-Tas (2013). Sex differences in the predictors of juvenile delinquency: Females are more susceptible to poor environments; males are influenced more by low self-control. *Journal of Contemporary Criminal Justice* 29(1): 88–105.

Stelter, B. (2011). Camps are cleared, but "99 percent" still occupies the lexicon. *New York Times,* December 1, p. A1.

Steuer, S., and L. Smith (2003*). Education reduces crime: Three-state recidivism study.* Lanham, MD: Correctional Education Association.

Stevens, A. (2012). "I am the person now I was always meant to be": Identity reconstruction and narrative reframing in therapeutic community prisons. *Criminology and Criminal Justice* 12(5): 527–547.

Stevens, D. J., and C. S. Ward (1997). College education and recidivism: Educating criminals is meritorious. *Journal of Correctional Education* 48(3): 106–111.

Stromberg, M. (2007). Locked up, then locked out. *Planning* 73(1): 20–25.

Sullivan, E., M. Mino, K. Nelson, and J. Pope (2002). *Families as a resource in recovery from drug abuse: An evaluation of La Bodega de la Familia.* New York: Vera Institute of Justice.

Sullivan, M. (1989). *Getting paid: Youth crime and work in the inner city.* Ithaca, NY: Cornell University Press.

Sutherland, E. H. (1947a). *The professional thief.* Chicago: University of Chicago Press.

———. (1947b). *Principles of criminology,* 4th ed. Chicago: J.B. Lippincott.

Swanson, C. (2009). *Restorative justice in a prison community: Or everything I didn't learn in kindergarten I learned in prison.* Lanham, MD: Lexington.

Taxman, F. S., D. Young, and J. Byrne (2002). *Targeting for reentry: Matching needs and services to maximize public safety.* Washington, DC: National Institute of Justice.

Teague, R., P. Mazerolle, and M. Legosz (2008). Linking childhood exposure to physical abuse and adult offending: Examining mediating factors and gendered relationships. *Justice Quarterly* 25(2): 313–348.

Teplin, L. A., K. M. Abram, and G. M. McClelland (1996). Prevalence of psychiatric disorders among incarcerated women. *Archives of General Psychiatry* 53: 505–512.

Tewksbury, R. (2005). Collateral consequences of sex offender registration. *Journal of Contemporary Criminal Justice* 21(1): 67–81.

Tewksbury, R., and H. Copes (2013). Incarcerated sex offenders' expectations for successful reentry. *Prison Journal* 93(1): 101–122.

Thomas, W. I. (1923). *The unadjusted girl.* Boston: Little, Brown.

Thompson, A. C. (2004). Navigating the hidden obstacles to ex-offender reentry. *Boston College Law Review* 45(2): 255–306.

Thornberry, T. P. (1973). Race, socioeconomic status and sentencing in the juvenile justice system. *Journal of Criminal Law and Criminology* 64(1): 90–98.

Tiburcio, N. J. (2008). Long-term recovery from heroin use among female ex-offenders: Marisol's story. *Substance Use and Misuse* 43: 1950–1970.

Tittle, C. R., D. A. Ward, and H. G. Grasmick (2003). Gender, age, and crime/deviance: A challenge to self-control theory. *Journal of Research in Crime and Delinquency* 40: 426–453.

Toth, R. C., G. A. Crews, and C. E. Burton (2008). *In the margins: Special populations and American justice.* Upper Saddle River, NJ: Prentice Hall.

Tracy, P. E. (1987). Race and class differences in official and self-reported delinquency. In M. E. Wolfgang, T. Thornberry, and R. Figilio (eds.), *From boy to man, from delinquency to crime.* Chicago: University of Chicago Press, pp. 87–121.

Travis, J. (2001). But they all come back: Rethinking prisoner reentry. *Corrections Management Quarterly* 5(3): 23–33.

———. (2005). *But they all come back: Facing the challenges of prisoner reentry.* Washington, DC: Urban Institute.

Travis, J., A. Solomon, and M. Waul (2001). *From prison to home: The dimensions and consequences of prisoner reentry.* Washington, DC: Urban Institute.

Tripodi, S. J. (2010). The influence of social bonds on recidivism: A study of Texas male prisoners. *Violence and Victims* 5: 354–370.

Tripp, B. (2003). Incarcerated African American fathers: Exploring changes in family relationships. In O. Harris and R. Miller (eds.), *Impacts of incarceration on the African American family.* New Brunswick, NJ: Transaction, pp. 17–31.

Turner, M. A., M. Fix, and R. J. Struyk (1991). Hiring discrimination against black men. *Urban Institute Policy and Research Report* (Summer): 4–5.

Turner, S., P. W. Greenwood, T. Fain, and J. R. Chiesa (2006). An evaluation of the federal government's violent offender incarceration and truth-in-sentencing incentive grants. *Prison Journal* 86(3): 364–385.

Turner, S., and J. Petersilia (1996). Work release in Washington: Effects on recidivism and corrections costs. *Prison Journal* 76(2): 138–164.

Uggen, C., and C. Kruttschnitt (1998). Crime in the breaking: Gender differences in desistance. *Law and Society Review* 32(2): 336–366.

Uggen, C., and J. Staff (2001). Work as a turning point for criminal offenders. *Corrections Management Quarterly* 5(4): 1–16.

US Census Bureau (2010). *People QuickFacts.* Washington, DC: US Census Bureau.

US Department of Justice. (1990). *Survey of intermediate sanctions.* Washington, DC: US Government Printing Office.

———. (2011). *Tribal Law and Order Act (TLOA). Long term plan to build and enhance tribal justice systems.* Washington, DC: US Department of Justice.

US Government Accountability Office. (2005). *Drug offenders: Various factors may limit the impacts of federal laws that provide for denial of selected benefits.* Washington, DC: US Government Accountability Office.

Van Ness, D., and K. H. Strong (2010). *Restoring justice,* 4th ed. Cincinnati, OH: Anderson.

Van Stelle, K. R., J. R. Lidbury, and D. P. Moberg (1995). *Final evaluation report, Specialized Training and Employment Project (STEP).* Center for Health Policy and Program Evaluation, Wisconsin Department of Corrections.

Van Stelle, K. R., and D. P. Moberg (2004). Outcome data for MICA clients after participation in an institutional therapeutic community. *Journal of Offender Rehabilitation* 39(1): 37–62.

Van Voorhis, M. Braswell, and D. Lester (1997) *Correctional counseling and rehabilitation.* Cincinnati, OH: Anderson.

Ventura, L. A., C. A. Cassel, J. E. Jacoby, and B. Huang (1998). Case management and recidivism of mentally ill persons released from jail. *Psychiatric Services* 49(10): 1330–1337.

Vezzola, M. A. (2007). Harmony behind bars. *Prison Journal* 87(2): 195–210.

Vigesaa, L. E. (2013). Abuse as a form of strain among Native American and white female prisoners: Predictors of substance-related offenses and recidivism. *Journal of Ethnicity in Criminal Justice* 11: 1–21.

Villarruel, F. A., N. E. Walker, P. Minifree, O. Rivera-Vázquez, S. Peterson, and K. Perry (2002). *¿Dónde está la justicia? A call to action on behalf of Latino and Latina youth in the US justice system.* Washington, DC: Michigan State University/Building Blocks for Youth.

Visher, C. (2013). Incarcerated fathers: Pathways from prison to home. *Criminal Justice Policy Review* 24: 9–26.

Visher, C., D. Baer, and R. Naser (2006). *Ohio prisoner's reflections on returning home*. Washington, DC: Urban Institute.

Visher, C., and S. M. E. Courtney (2007). *One year out: Experiences of prisoners returning to Cleveland*. Washington, DC: Urban Institute.

Visher, C., and J. Travis (2003). Transitions from prison to community: Understanding individual pathways. *Annual Review of Sociology* 29: 89–113.

Visher, C., L. Winterfield, and M. B. Coggeshall (2005). Ex-offender employment programs and recidivism: A meta-analysis. *Journal of Experimental Criminology* 1: 295–315.

Visher, C., N. G. La Vigne, and J. Travis (2004). Returning home: Understanding the challenges of prisoner reentry. *Maryland pilot study: Findings from Baltimore*. Washington, DC: Urban Institute.

Visher, C., J. Yahner, and N. G. La Vigne (2010). *Life after prison: Tracking the experiences of male prisoners returning to Chicago, Cleveland, and Houston*. Washington, DC: Urban Institute.

Walker, N. E., J. M. Senger, F. A. Villarruel, and A. M. Arboleda (2004). *Lost opportunities: The reality of Latinos in the US criminal justice system*. Washington, DC: National Council of La Raza.

Walker, S., C. Spohn, and M. DeLone (2007). *The color of justice: Race, ethnicity, and crime in America*. Belmont, CA: Wadsworth.

Waller, I. (1974). *Men released from prison*. Toronto: University of Toronto Press.

Warr, M. (1998). Life-course transitions and desistance from crime. *Criminology* 36(2): 183–216.

Washington State Department of Corrections (2011). *Strategic plan, 2011–2017*. Olympia: Washington State Department of Corrections.

Weatherspoon, F. D. (1996). Remedying employment discrimination against African-American males: Stereotypical biases engender a case of race plus sex discrimination. *Washburn Law Journal* 36(1): 23–87.

Weinsten, I. (2003). Fifteen years after the federal sentencing evolution: How mandatory minimums have undermined effective and just narcotics sentencing. *American Criminal Law Review* 40(1): 87–132.

Weinstein, J. B., and C. Wimmer (2010). Sentencing in the United States. In H. A. Dlugacz (ed.), *Reentry planning for offenders with mental disorders*. Kingston, NJ: Civic Research Institute, pp. 1-1–1-49.

West, D. J., and D. P. Farrington (1977). *The delinquent way of life*. London: Hienemann.

Wexler, H., G. DeLeon, G. Thomas, D. Kressel, and J. Peters. (1999). The Amity Prison TC Evaluation: Reincarceration outcomes. *Criminal Justice and Behavior* 26: 147–167.

Whelan, C. (1973). *Civil disabilities: The punishment does not fit the crime*. New York: Community Society of New York.

White, M. D., J. S. Goldkamp, and S. P. Campbell (2006). Co-occurring mental illness and substance abuse in the criminal justice system: Some implications for local jurisdictions. *Prison Journal* 86(3): 1–26.

Widom, C. S. (1995). *Victims of childhood sexual abuse—Later criminal consequences*. Washington, DC: National Institute of Justice, US Department of Justice.

Widom, C. S., and M. A. Ames (1994). Criminal consequences of childhood sexual victimization. *Child Abuse and Neglect* 18(4): 303–318.

Wiederanders, M. R. (1983). *Success on parole: Final report.* Sacramento: California Department of Youth Authority.

Wilkinson, R. A. (2001). Offender reentry: A storm overdue. *Corrections Management Quarterly* 5(3): 46–51.

Wilkinson, R. A. (2005). Engaging communities: An essential ingredient to offender reentry. *Corrections Today* (April): 86–89.

Wilson, K. J. (2007). *State policies and procedures regarding "gate money."* Davis: Center for Public Policy Research, University of California.

Winterfield, L., P. K. Lattimore, D. M. Steffey, S. Brumbaugh, and C. Lindquist (2006). The serious and violent offender initiative: Measuring the effects on service delivery. *Western Criminology Review* 7(2): 3–19.

Wodahl, E. J. (2006). The challenges of prisoner reentry from a rural perspective. *Western Criminological Review* 7(2): 32–47.

Wolff, N., and J. Draine (2004). Dynamics of social capital of prisoners and community reentry: Ties that bind? *Journal of Correctional Health Care* 10(3): 457–490.

Wood, P. B., and R. G. Dunaway (2003). Consequences of truth-in-sentencing: The Mississippi case. *Punishment and Society* 5(2): 139–154.

Woods, L., S. Lanza, W. Dyson, and D. M. Gordon (2013). The role of prevention in promoting continuity of health care in prisoner reentry initiatives. *American Journal of Public Health* 103(5): 830–838.

Worcel, S. D., S. W. Burrus, M. W. Finigan, M. B. Sanders, and T. L. Allen (2009). *A study of substance-free transitional housing and community corrections in Washington County, Oregon.* Portland, OR: NPC Research.

Wyatt v. Stickney, 324 F. Supp. 781 (M.D. Ala. 1972).

Zahn, M. (1999). Thoughts on the future of criminology: The American society of criminology presidential address. *Criminology* 37: 1–15.

Zamble, E., and V. L. Quinsey (1997). *The criminal recidivism process.* Cambridge, MA: Cambridge University Press.

Zandbergen, P. A., and T. C. Hart (2006). Reducing housing options for convicted sex offenders: Investigating the impact of residency restriction laws using GIS. *Justice Research and Policy* 18(2): 1–24.

Zehr, H. (1990). *Changing lenses: A new focus for crime and justice.* Scottdale, PA: Herald Press.

———. (1995). Justice paradigm shift? Values and visions in the reform process. *Mediation Quarterly* 12: 207–216.

———. (2002). *The little book of restorative justice.* Intercourse, PA: Good Books.

Zgoba, K. M., S. Haugebrook, and K. Jenkins (2008). The influence of GED obtainment on inmate release outcome. *Criminal Justice and Behavior* 35(3): 375–387.

Zhang, S. X., R. E. L. Roberts, and V. J. Callanan (2006). Preventing parolees from returning to prison through community-based reintegration. *Crime and Delinquency* 52(4): 551–571.

Zhang, S. X., R. E. L. Roberts, and K. E. McCollister (2011). Therapeutic community in a California prison: Treatment outcomes after 5 years. *Crime and Delinquency* 57(1): 82–101.

Index

About the Book

IN THIS COMPREHENSIVE EXPLORATION OF THE CORE ISSUES surrounding offender reentry, Elaine Gunnison and Jacqueline Helfgott highlight the constant tension between policies meant to ensure smooth reintegration and the social forces—especially the stigma of a criminal record—that can prevent it from happening.

Gunnison and Helfgott focus on the factors that enhance reentry success as they address challenges related to race, class, and gender. Drawing on accounts from corrections professionals and former inmates to illustrate the real-life consequences of reentry policy, they shed light on one of the key criminal justice issues of our time.

Elaine Gunnison is associate professor of criminal justice at Seattle University. **Jacqueline B. Helfgott** is professor of criminal justice at Seattle University.